# Humanity Dick

## The Eccentric Member for Galway

by

Peter Phillips

Also published by Parapress:

*'Itching After Rhyme', a Life of John Clare,* by Arnold Clay
*Charlotte Brontë and the Mysteries of Love,* by Elizabeth Imlay
*Sea Soldier, an Officer of Marines 1797-1813,* ed. Petrides & Downs



First published in the UK by:

PARAPRESS LTD
The Basement
9 Frant Road
Tunbridge Wells
Kent
TN2 5SD UK

A catalogue record for this book is available
from the British Library



Typeset in Baskerville by Vitaset, Paddock Wood, Kent
Printed in Great Britain by
Biddles Ltd, Guildford & Kings Lynn

# Acknowledgements

Grateful thanks to:

Adrian Martyn
Mary Jo Madden
Des Lally and everyone at Ballynahinch Castle
The staff at Galway Reference and University Libraries
The staff at the British Library and Colindale Newpaper Library
The staff at the RSPCA Archive Department
Richard de Stackpole and everyone in Roundstone
Kevin Joyce
Connemara Community Radio
Lord Altamont and his staff at Westport House
Tom and Desi Kenny
Tim Robinson
Brian Hoban
D'Arcy Martin, Kerry Martin and everyone at the Descendants of Richard Martin
John Byrne
Dr Richard D. Ryder
Dr Padraig Lenihan, University of Limerick
Dr Ruan O'Donnell, University of Limerick
Shevawn Lynam – I wish I could have met her
Harriet Buckley
Lizzie, Christopher, Frieda and Nick at Parapress, and James who had to go to the war

To my father, Bryn, who would have loved researching this book, and to
Charlotte, James, Lewis and Moli, who found Humanity Dick for me

# Contents

# Illustrations

# Introduction

I first became aware of 'Humanity' Dick Martin on holiday in Ireland in the summer of 2000. Our guide book featured the eccentric owner of Ballynahinch Castle in the early 19th century, who used to imprison locals in the now ruined castle in the lake, if he caught them maltreating animals.

Intrigued, I sought to find out more about him and, as I discovered the facts of his remarkable and colourful life, I became surprised that he was not better known. Shevawn Lynam's biography of 1975, to which any researcher must be indebted, is rightly much respected, but requires a detailed knowledge of Irish and British history.

I hope that I have written a book which makes accessible to a wider readership both the facts about Richard Martin's life, and the period of history, Irish, English, French and American, which framed his thoughts and actions –- for the work he began (and his style of doing it) easily transcends time and place.

Peter Phillips

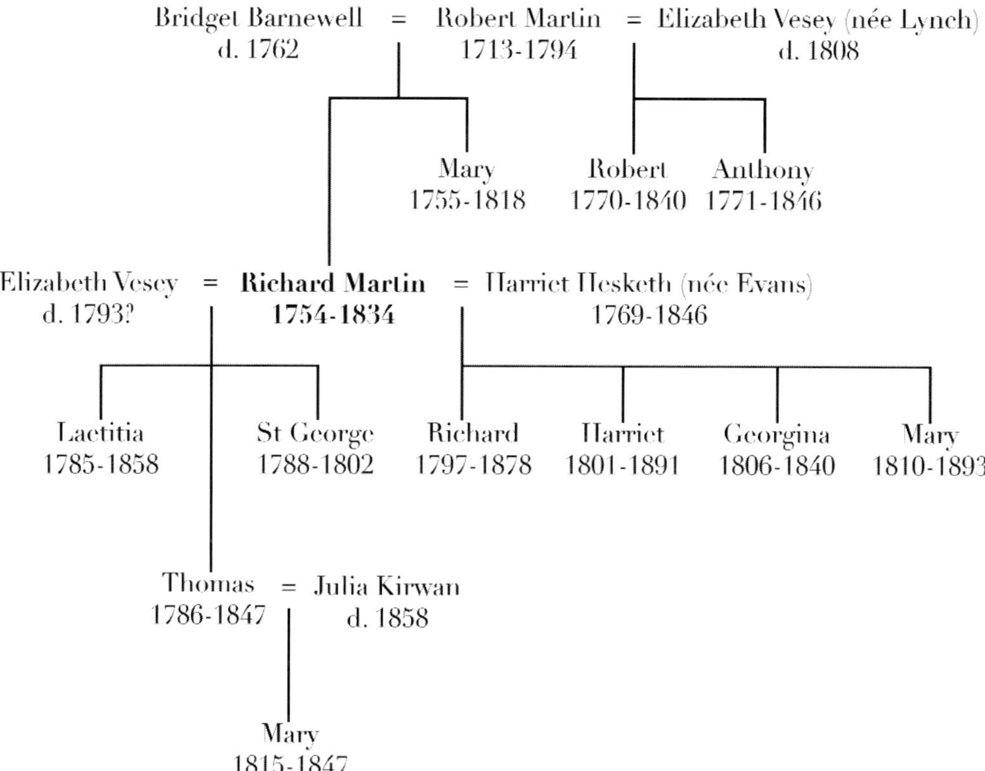

*The Immediate Family of Richard Martin*

*Ireland in the 18th century, showing places mentioned in the text*

# Chapter 1

# The Tribe of Martin

The year was 1691, the place Aughrim Hill, County Galway, and the Jacobite cause in Ireland had met its bloody end. Now, 'Nimble' Dick Martin needed all the resourcefulness that had earned him his name. As a commander in the Irish cavalry, and the largest catholic landowner, he faced at best financial ruin and at worst (and more likely), an ignominious appointment with a protestant executioner.

When the deposed King James II had landed at Kinsale in 1689 with an army, and French support, Irish Catholics such as the Martins had hoped for salvation from years of suppression. James had dispatched Lord Boffin to Galway to raise an army, and Nimble Dick, although in his fifties, readily joined the Jacobites as they moved triumphantly northwards, only to be held at bay outside the city of Derry.

Prevailing here would have ensured catholic domination of the country, but the city famously held firm for three months until, on the verge of starvation, the beleaguered inhabitants were re-supplied by relief ships. On the same day the Jacobites were defeated in battle at nearby Enniskillen. The tide had turned, and now King William of Orange himself arrived in Ireland with new troops to lead the English offensive. On July 12th 1690 both kings led their armies to battle at the Boyne river. William's tactical victory was the turning point not only of the war but also of Irish political history for the next three hundred years.

William had marched to Dublin to take constitutional control. The Jacobites, however, knew that to lose this war would ensure that land settlements by the English would be irrevocable, and that catholic power in Ireland would be stripped for ever, with protestant planters reigning supreme. They had taken advantage of the winter to regroup, and Nimble Dick had retreated west with them. With the arrival of spring 1691, William's Dutch countryman General Ginckel began a fresh offensive, gaining the vital Shannon crossing at Athlone. The stage was set for a final confrontation at Aughrim Hill, 30 miles east of Martin's home.

Although outnumbered and lacking the military fire power of the Williamite army, the Jacobites balanced the odds by taking a superior position on the hill overlooking the roads to Galway and Limerick, and could only be approached by two narrow passes running through a treacherous bog. The English unsuccessfully attacked their weaker centre and right flank, becoming pinned down and suffering terrible losses as the dreaded Irish cavalry came through gaps in the thick hedgerow. It was at this stage that Nimble Dick, perhaps with the doubtful outcome in mind, spared the lives of some English officers of distinction who had fallen in an area known as the Bloody Hollow.

A Jacobite victory looked assured, as the only English hope was to stage a last attack on the seemingly impenetrable left flank, guarded by Colonel Henry Luterell's cavalry, which included Captain Richard Martin. Astonishingly, this regiment put up little resistance, and when past them the English appeared to know the route through the bog. Rallied by this breakthrough, which coincided with the death of the Jacobite general St Ruth, the Williamite infantry followed behind, overran the Irish and bloodily defeated them.

Among the retreating Irish, word soon got round that the causeway through the bog had been betrayed to the English, and Luterell's loyalty, and that of his commanders, became tainted. Nimble Dick, fleeing westwards to his wild Connemara lands, was to be held accountable for their defeat.

The Martins had been established in Ireland nearly four hundred years. They were descended from one of the Norman families who had followed the fortunes of William the Conqueror, extending his conquest across the Irish Sea. Their first home was in Athenry, but they had moved on to settle in Galway by the time Thomas Martyn had bought the mills of the town in 1365. By now, Norman families in remote areas had already begun inter-marrying with the native Irish.

*A Martin-Lynch wedding commemorated on a house in Galway town*

Other families, with closer ties to the English crown, had colonised the region around Dublin, which became known as 'the pale'. Families of Norman blood who were becoming increasingly Irish in their ways, were living 'beyond the pale'. Concerned by such developments, the loyal Anglo-Irish, as they were now becoming, passed the Statutes of Kilkenny in 1366, prohibiting the use of the Irish language, laws and customs.

But the town of Galway had ploughed its own furrow since Richard de Burgo had founded it in 1235. Remote from the influence and control of the Dublin base, but nevertheless a strategic trading town with historic ties to the continental ports, Galway made good use of the merchant skills of its renegade Normans. By the 14th century it was the third most important trading port in the islands of Britain and Ireland, outstripped only by London and Bristol. The town's main problem was not interference by the English, but the threat posed by the wild Gaelic tribes such as the O'Flahertys, living in the mountainous countryside to its north and west.

To combat this threat, the fourteen merchant families who controlled the town, now including the Martins, threw up strong city walls. Thomas Oge Martin constructed the West Bridge, where an inscription read, 'From the Ferocious O'Flahertys Oh Lord Deliver Us.' By the 15th century Galway was virtually a city state, with both civil and ecclesiastical independence. Not even the Lord Lieutenant of Ireland could enter without the express permission of the Mayor.

Fifty years later a die was cast that would divide Ireland even more fundamentally, to this day. Henry VIII, frustrated at not being able to divorce Catherine of Aragon, broke away from allegiance to Rome and appointed himself head of the Church of England, creating an alternative religion to Catholicism. In 1536 the Irish parliament passed an Act making Henry head of the whole church, although the overwhelming majority of the population remained loyal to the Pope. This paradox was to be at the root of Irish troubles for centuries to come.

Henry attempted to repeat the violent protestant Reformation process he had administered throughout England, but his success in Ireland was limited to within the Pale. The Tudor monarchs who followed mostly continued the policy, until the inevitable rebellion in 1594, led by Hugh O'Neill. With the rebels supported by one of England's traditional enemies, Spain, the war dragged on for eight years, but eventually the Irish were worsted, and land-owning Irish Catholics were banished to areas west of the river Shannon.

The effects of the English Civil War were equally disastrous. The Irish uprising and general support of the Stuart cause left Cromwell determined to suppress Ireland once and for all. After his brutal and effective operations, a Protestant ruling class was established throughout the country, save in the far west. The catholic families who still ruled the city of Galway were referred to dismissively by Cromwell as 'the Tribes'.

Amazingly, throughout the turmoil, the 'tribe' of Martin had continued to flourish. Practising mostly as lawyers and moneylenders, their men travelled widely and set up trading links with England, Spain, France and Portugal. One branch of the family developed rich plantations in the West Indies. In all they produced nineteen mayors and nearly thirty bailiffs and sheriffs between 1498 and 1652.

Nimble Dick's father, Robert, had been one of the first citizens among the Tribes to turn his attention beyond Galway town to the lands in Connemara that were occupied by the ferocious O'Flahertys. These he acquired by a variety of methods, some legal and others more dubious. Richard, the youngest but most astute of Robert's sons, continued where his father had left off. On the whole, the other Galway families supported these efforts, which effectively kept the native Irish away from the city; at the same time their opinion of the Martins was expressed in a modification of their ancient motto: 'From Jasper, James and Nimble Dick, good Lord deliver us.'

In 1660 Charles II was invited home to assume the English crown. Irish Catholics who had supported the Stuarts during the Civil War, and of course hated Cromwell and the Parliamentarians, hoped that events

*Blake's Castle in Galway town, ancient home to the tribe of Blake.*

would now turn in their favour. Charles wished to reward their loyalty, but had to come
to a compromise with his parliamentary masters. Catholics, who had owned three-fifths
of the land in Ireland prior to the 1641 uprising, and lost almost all of it under
Cromwell, ended up owning one-fifth by the end of Charles's reign in 1685. But a by-
product of Charles's balancing act was actual peace, and the Irish economy throve
during these years.

Nimble Dick was well positioned to take advantage of the new laws. The Act of
Settlement allowed Catholics to re-acquire land, provided they swore an oath of
allegiance to the Crown. No doubt through gritted teeth, Martin complied, and
proceeded to gain vast swathes of the country, again mostly from the O'Flahertys, by
lending them money and then exploiting the system to foreclose on them.

By the time Charles's openly catholic brother, James, had succeeded to the throne,
Martin owned most of Connemara. It is a mountainous and windswept outpost, and
its agricultural potential was uneven. Nimble Dick moved out of Galway city and built
a fortified manor house at Birchall on the banks of Lough Corrib, the great expanse of
water north of the town, where the country was lush and fertile. His landed estate was
now the largest throughout all James's domain. But that domain was to stay in Stuart
hands no longer. James was ousted, and the English parliament invited his protestant son-
in-law, William of Orange, to take the crown.

Nimble Dick spent the days after the battle of Aughrim considering the rami-
fications of the disaster. Diehard Jacobites who had survived the slaughter were
retreating to Limerick for a final stand. Dick realised its futility. Defeat and brutal
retribution were on the way, and, with an estate of over a quarter of a million acres, he
was an obvious target. He had been a senior Jacobite commander: execution was a
distinct possibility. Moreover, his own countrymen were accusing him of incompetence
and cowardice. Worse still, accusations were being voiced that his regiment had housed
traitors who had betrayed the crucial route through the bog.

In the meantime General Ginckel, though wishing to press on to Limerick, could
not leave Galway to its own devices. On the other hand, if he allowed the Jacobites
another winter to regroup at Limerick, his victory at Aughrim would have been in vain.
Galway, too, was divided over its course of action, but favoured a surrender on the best
possible terms, knowing that Ginckel was anxious to move on. Fourteen thousand of
the General's men were encamped within sight of the city walls, and their supply line
stretched back to the Shannon. A conciliatory message was sent to Ginckel, who
immediately replied that he was willing to negotiate.

Nimble Dick decided to take counsel with his friend, the High Sheriff, who,
anticipating treaty negotiations, had positioned himself as a neutral. Martin, for his
own safety, was taken to Ginckel, and played an important role in the ensuing surrender
talks, the outcome of which was very favourable to the city. The English were to occupy
Galway, and in return safe passage was given to any Jacobites to carry on to Limerick.
The town retained all its liberties and immunities, and the clergy were to be
unmolested. Ginckel, satisfied that he was in physical possession, moved on to Limerick.
There the dispirited Jacobites, abandoned both by their king and by French support,
surrendered in October 1691.

Martin's enemies in Galway now played their hand. They had not arranged for his name to be listed as a Freeman in the Articles of Surrender, and he was still exposed to English retaliation for the rebellion. With speedy initiative, he set out for London, to seek audience with King William.

This was, at the very least, an audacious plan, and on face value it is difficult to understand why the protestant king would even entertain the catholic rebel; but he did, and, although it took him four years, Nimble Dick returned to Ireland with a warrant of his pardon, a confirmed title to his estates, and a reference to the protestant officers whom he had saved at Aughrim. This appears considerable reward for what a gentleman might be expected to do in battle in any case, and credit must be given to his legendary powers of persuasion. It was reported that a 'hat full of sovereigns' had also changed hands, and further it is possible that the accusations of treachery within Martin's regiment were well founded, and Nimble Dick was calling in a more significant marker with the King.

He had achieved a position unimaginable in the days just after Aughrim, but, true to character, he pressed for more. Back in Ireland he wrote to the King stating that, 'with great pain and industry' he had acquired his Connemara acres, but that 'due to the rough nature of the country' he could not obtain tenants without offering them much encouragement. He proposed both to improve the land, and to build a new town, called Clare, where a fair could be held, and he asked the King to elevate his lands to the status of Manor.

At last William responded. All the lands owned by Martin to the West of Galway were promoted into the Manor of Clare. Somehow he had managed to emerge not only with his head and lands intact, but also with a Barony. The powers conferred on him and his heirs virtually made them into petty monarchs in Connemara. They were allowed to hold a Court Baron, with 'full authority to hold pleas', and to levy and use the fines and other moneys arising from the Court.

It was these powers that Nimble Dick's great-grandson, 'Humanity' Richard Martin, would use to such effect on behalf of his fellow creatures, both human and otherwise.

*The Martin crest embellishes an overmantle.*

Chapter 2

# Penal Law

The terms obtained at both Galway and Limerick appeared at first to be generous to the defeated Catholics. However, when Ginckel's treaty arrived in London, certain clauses were missing from it. Worse was to come, when the protestant parliament in Dublin refused to ratify the treaty. William III, satisfied that the Irish threat was over, turned his attention to the more pressing problems which the French were posing in Europe. James Stuart had united with his old ally, Louis XIV, and their immediate response to the defeat in Ireland was to mount an assault on the English navy, in advance of an invasion of the south coast of England. Again the English were victorious, assisted by adverse weather which scattered the French fleet and allowed their enemy to destroy them ship by ship.

By this time war had spread throughout the Continent, with the protestant powers of England, Holland and what was to become Germany fighting a Franco-Spanish coalition. In 1701 the English Parliament passed an Act of Settlement stating that no future monarch could be, or could marry, a Catholic.

Although retribution for the Jacobite uprising was not as violent as that previously inflicted by Cromwell, William of Orange was determined to prevent the Catholics having any future power base. The time was ripe for strict penal measures, and William and his ministers were happy to delegate responsibility for repression to the Dublin parliament which, being protestant dominated, had every incentive to attack both the Catholics' religion, and what remained of their civil rights.

The Banishment Act of 1697 decreed that, 'All popish archbishops, bishops, vicars general, deans, Jesuits, monks, friars and all regular popish clergy and all papists exercising ecclesiastical jurisdiction shall depart out of this kingdom before 1st May 1698.' Failure to comply meant a charge of high treason, and during the next year two hundred priests had taken ship from Galway. In the event, pressure from his ally Prince Leopold of Austria persuaded William to let the others stay if they would swear an oath of abjuration, repudiating the claim of James to the throne of Britain. Not surprisingly, they all refused. Financial measures were then introduced, whose effect was gradually to force the Roman Catholic church underground.

The Irish parliament now turned its attention to stripping the catholic population of their rights. They were banned from entering parliament or holding any form of civic office. What remained of the landholding catholic gentry then came under attack. The Laws of Gavelkind prevented a catholic family from passing its estate wholly to the eldest son. Instead, property had to be divided between all male heirs. Thus the size and power of the estates would diminish down through the generations. Further laws between 1704 and 1709 prevented Catholics from buying new land or holding leases longer than 31 years. Finally, legal inducements were put in place so that, if an heir to an estate converted to Protestantism, he could immediately take over his father's property.

These measures were relatively subtle, certainly compared with Cromwell's brutal approach, but their long-term effect was to reduce catholic land-ownership from 14% when William had grasped power, to less than 5% by 1778.

Although now unable to enter parliament, Catholics still posed a threat by their strong representation in the legal profession, and by holding commissions in the army and navy. The solution was to make them swear an oath abjuring the main tenets of their belief, such as the invocation of the Virgin Mary. Great numbers of catholic barristers converted to Protestantism, some whole-heartedly, others merely paying lip-service. Catholics were prevented from owning or carrying arms, or owning a horse valued at more than £5. Trinity College, Dublin's mighty seat of learning, was open only to the sons of protestant families.

The Penal Laws were brought in gradually, and by and large enforced without resort to violent means. They tended to be more vigorously enforced when outside threats such as French military success against the English, or rumours of a Stuart invasion, were rife. They were, however, effective. By the end of the 18th century the majority population of Catholics were a repressed underclass who could see little prospect of changing their lot.

On the far west coast, neither events in England and Europe, nor the Penal Laws, made much impression on Nimble Dick Martin, protected as he was by the remoteness of his lands and his relationship with King William. As was traditional, he had married into another Galway tribe, the Frenches, who had followed the Martins' lead and moved out of the city, acquiring lands in Sligo and Roscommon. Katherine French bore him two sons, Robert and Anthony, and five daughters. But Dick and Katherine were to pay a terrible price for the sequestration of the O'Flaherty lands.

The O'Flahertys had attempted to kill Nimble Dick on a number of occasions, but were always thwarted by his living in fortified Birchall and only travelling when accompanied by a small army. The Martins' eldest son Robert, who by the time of his youth had acquired the name of 'Robin the Brave', was hotheaded and impetuous. When he heard that O'Flaherty of Lemonhead, head of the clan, had insulted his mother, he mounted his horse and rode away from Birchall to seek satisfaction in a duel. O'Flaherty, though an old man, accepted his challenge, and in the manner of the time the combatants distanced themselves on horseback, ready to ride towards each other at full tilt, sword in hand.

Robin took up his station with his back to a shrubbery. As he waited for the signal to attack, one of the O'Flaherty sons leapt from the bushes and stabbed him deep in the back. Young Martin fell forward onto his horse's neck, and the beast galloped off in the direction of Birchall. Mortally wounded, Robin held on until half way home. The riderless horse continued to Birchall, where a search party, led by Katherine, were heading out to look for the young heir. They found him lying dead, and his mother, frantic with grief, raised an altar upon the spot, part of which remains to this day. The inscription reads:

> *May there be neither luck nor prosperity,*
> *but ever wailing and distraction,*
> *and may there never be a rightful heir in the place*
> *where the murder of young Robert Martin was perpetrated.*

A custom developed of wayfarers casting a stone on the spot where he died, to raise a cairn. In line with the longevity of Irish feuds, the O'Flahertys destroyed it 80 years later. Nimble Dick's revenge was harder-headed than his wife's curse. On 10th October 1707 he obtained a warrant from the Lord Lieutenant which turned his opponents into outlaws. They were never brought to justice, but were forced further into the wilds of Connemara.

On his death, aged ninety, Nimble Dick was succeeded by his younger son, Anthony, who had married Bridget, of the tribe of Kirwen. The couple had four sons and a daughter. Near to where Robin had died, at Killanin, Anthony built a small chapel, where he lies along with other members of the family. Unlike other Martins, Anthony had maintained a low profile. He did, however, judging by his epitaph, appear to have shown a trait of compassion that was to re-surface in his family:

> *Esteemed in life, the Duitious Son, the*
> *Tender Husband, the truly affectionate*
> *Father, Steady in Friendship, Frugal,*
> *Humane, Temperat, Valiant, Beneficent*
> *to the Distressed, only to punish*
> *Ingratitude and Impiety*

But his younger son, Robert, appears to have inherited more unruly genes. He was set to take up arms again for the Jacobite cause.

*Connemara, engraving by William Henry Bartlett, c. 1840*

# Chapter 3

## The Turbulent Robert Martin

By the time Anthony and Bridget gave birth to their second son, Robert, in 1713, the Penal Laws were beginning to bite. Catholics who had provided the nation with leadership and learning had fled the country, or been 'beaten into the clay'. With the absence of education, visual arts were in serious decline. Many of the fine country houses had fallen into ruin, and there was little hope of the catholic aristocracy rebuilding or replacing them. The notable writer, Jonathan Swift, compared the country to 'the carcass of a goose standing up.'

The absentee protestant landlord became the norm, trying to wring every penny out of the land. The vast majority of people lived in abject poverty, housing themselves in small cottages known as 'cabbins', described as 'the most miserable looking hovels that can well be conceived, the furniture consisting mainly of a pot for boiling their potatoes, a bit of a table, and one or two broken stools; beds are not found universally, the family lying on straw.'

Although most catholic churches and abbeys had been destroyed, some had survived and, depending on protestant tolerance, which varied from area to area, continued to operate. Religious festivals were maintained and pilgrims still travelled in great numbers to Lough Derg in the midlands, bringing home wooden 'penal crosses' as souvenirs.

The Martin estate benefited from economic strategies not subject to the troubles of the land, such as smuggling. Nimble Dick's fortune had allowed him to build Anthony and his wife a fine mansion house at Dangan, about eight miles from Birchall in the direction of Galway, and situated on the banks of a narrowing stretch of Lough Corrib. The house faced a fine prospect which may be enjoyed even today, for across the strait stood the Blake family home, Menlo Castle.

*Menlo Castle*

Anxious for young Robert to receive a good catholic education, his parents sent him to Louvain in Belgium. Since its foundation by the Pope in 1425, the school had always attracted students from the most influential families in Europe, and a Galway man, Flaithri O'Mailchonaire, had founded the College of St Anthony there during the 17th century. This college had preserved a sense of Irish identity, through such works as Geoffrey Keating's *Foras Feasa ar Eirinn*, an account of the country since its conquest by Henry II. Needless to say, in the 18th century the school was a hotbed of Jacobite support. It was here that Humanity Dick's father not only learned his country's history, but gained refinement from a number of European cultures.

When Queen Anne died childless in 1714, there was a fleeting hope of a peaceful Stuart succession. The choice was between the Old Pretender, James, son of James II (whom Irish and Scottish Catholics had always recognised as James III), exiled in France, and the line now represented by the Elector of Hanover, George. A section of the Tory party sided with the Stuarts, mostly out of opposition to the idea of a German monarch but, for James to become king, the Act of Succession would have had to be changed. The status quo prevailed, and the Elector became King George I of Britain.

James made a final attempt at seizing the crown, leading the rebellion in Scotland that became known as 'The Fifteen', from the year in which it took place. It was put down, and James, now broken, fled to Rome. Catholic hopes turned to his son Charles Edward, the Young Pretender.

Robert Martin, after undertaking the customary grand gentleman's tour of Europe, returned to Galway well versed in the airs and graces of the European aristocracy, despite being naturally impetuous, of a vicious temper, and a duellist of repute. He had adopted the high fashion of a French dandy, resplendent in broidered waistcoat and outrageously large-brimmed hat, and he affected a French accent.

Galway was still occupied by the English army, and quartered there at the time was the Hon. General Dormer's Royal Regiment of Foot, also known as the Royal Warwickshire Regiment, which had served at the battle of Aughrim. Two officers were playing billiards in a first-floor room of a coffee shop in the Main Guard, near to Galway's west gate, when young Martin came sauntering, beau-like, through the town. Leaning out of the window, the officers called out, 'Macaroni! Macaroni!': an insult of the time somewhat equivalent to 'Fop!' One of the officers went so far as to spit on his head.

Martin ran up the stairs with sword drawn, demanding to know who had spat on him. Captain Edward Southwell, stepping forward, said it was he, but added that he had meant no affront and offered an apology. Martin, in no mood to accept, demanded satisfaction. Southwell and his colleague Lieutenant Henry Jolly were unarmed, and Southwell asked if he could return to barracks to get his sword? He would then give Martin satisfaction. He turned to leave, but Martin lunged at Jolly, and ran his sword several times through the chair the soldier was holding for protection, inflicting severe wounds to his body; fatally wounded, the lieutenant collapsed in a great pool of blood.

Giving himself up for arrest, Robert Martin was charged with murder. In accordance with his status, he was committed for trial at the Court of the King's Bench in Dublin on May 2nd 1735. This was shortly before the death of Nimble Dick, and it may be that one of the last actions of the old patriarch was to exercise his influence on the affair, as, for no obvious reason, the jury all hailed from Galway and contained at least three Burkes and one French, of the original Tribes.

The first witness for the Crown was Lieutenant George Bell, who had arrived on the scene immediately after the quarrel and tried to tend the unfortunate Jolly. He gave evidence that Jolly had received three wounds on his right side, close to the chest, one of which had pierced through to his back. The deceased had also had two wounds to his left side that had penetrated the cavity of his body. In addition there were wounds to Jolly's left hand and arm. Unsurprisingly, Bell had failed to find a pulse.

Captain Southwell next gave evidence. He confirmed that Martin had furiously entered the room, demanding satisfaction of the rascal who had spat at him. With Martin adamant that he would accept no apology, Southwell asked to 'go to my barrack for a sword. I will speedily return and comply with your request.' Crucially, he added: 'there being no sword between him or Jolly'. The prosecuting advocate asked Southwell a final question: 'Was the first attack by the deceased with any instrument before the accused prisoner drew his sword?' Southwell replied, 'No.'

The final witness for the prosecution was Robert Watson, the coffee-boy, who had seen the whole incident. His evidence was that Martin, sword drawn, had approached Jolly, who took up a chair to defend himself, 'through the frame of which the prisoner made several thrusts at the deceased'. The defence called three witnesses, Messrs. Matthews, Bates and Donnelly, none of whom had seen the event, but all testified to Martin's good character.

The judge summed up the evidence and allowed the jury of Galwaymen to adjourn and consider its verdict. After a brief time they returned and delivered one of 'Not guilty'. If this unlikely outcome had not been rigged, there is evidence that further strings would have been pulled in young Robert's favour. Many years later a curious letter was unearthed in the Public Records Office, from the English government to the Lords Justices of Ireland, directing that, in the event of Martin being found guilty as charged, he was to be reprieved until the pleasure of the Crown was known.

The fortunate young Martin returned to Dangan to live with his father and older brother, Richard, where he set about converting the Jacobite fervour which had been nurtured at Louvain into action. Dangan became a centre of plotting for the Stuarts, with Robert channelling his energies into recruiting supporters, and into the traditional smuggling business along the Connemara coastline. It would, however, be ten years before he would have the chance to take up arms in the old cause.

It was in 1745 that Charles Edward Stuart, the Young Pretender, 'Bonnie Prince Charlie', landed with a small army in Scotland. Despite the undying loyalty of the Irish Catholics, the Stuarts had for some years considered those in Scotland to be their best allies in challenging the British monarchy. In Perth, the Highlanders proclaimed Charles king. He quickly conquered the remainder of Scotland, and led his army into England, getting as far south as Derby. News that the Jacobites were within 100 miles of London caused widespread panic. But the Scots were discouraged by the lack of support English Catholics were showing to the cause, and when they started to fall out among themselves Charles retreated to Scotland, now followed by an English army intent on avenging this effrontery.

Meanwhile, in Galway, Robert Martin was keenly disappointed that Charles had not chosen Ireland to mount his challenge. The small army he had been assembling at Dangan would have flown to his aid. Robert decided to travel alone to Scotland to join the fight. He could not take his men, because they would have been cut down en route by loyalist Irish forces. As it was, he would have to travel incognito to avoid arrest, since the authorities, alarmed by events in England, were on full alert.

His journey was trouble-free as far as the northern counties, where any wealthy-looking Catholic would have been very out of place. Robert adopted the guise of a peasant. Attired in rough sacking, he arrived at the port of Larne, to board a ship to Scotland. But he would have to wait: his vessel was not ready to put to sea. Retiring to a nearby tavern, Martin ordered chicken fricassée. This was a dish not usually requested by a peasant. Martin's disguise was demolished: he was arrested and thrown into jail. He managed, probably with the aid of a substantial bribe, to gain his release, and travelled back, disheartened and frustrated, to Dangan.

As events transpired, his choice of supper had probably saved his life. On 15th April 1756 the English army encountered the rebels at Culloden Moor, resulting in the wholesale massacre of Charles's forces. One of the few survivors was the Young Pretender himself, who had fled to the Isle of Skye and thence to France. His people sang, 'Will ye no come back again?', but he never returned.

Still with unfailing loyalty and trust that the Stuarts were to be the salvation of Irish Catholics, Robert stepped up his Jacobite activities at Dangan, and soon began to attract the attention of the new Governor sent to put an end to such threats. Colonel Stratford Eyre, having served in the English army at Culloden, was tasked with cleaning up such unconcealed defiance. His family were Cromwellian plunderers who had settled in Galway, and considered every Catholic a rebel. There was unfinished business between the Eyres and the Martins, the latter believing that a property had been stolen from them by the protestant family two generations earlier.

Eyre quickly focused on the goings-on at Dangan. He was horrified to find out the extent and audacity not only of rebel affairs, but also of the wholesale smuggling. Robert was by now the recognised head of the Jacobites throughout Connaught and had been joined by his cousin Patrick Sarsfield, a descendant of a namesake who had led a rebellion in 1691. They were planning to dispatch a boat, fitted out by Martin, to join the cause of France.

Eyre had an informant called Dennis Macnamara in Galway jail, who confirmed his worst fears. He wrote to his superior in Dublin, 'Within the Liberties lives Robert Martin, a dangerous murdering Jacobite, who can bring in twenty-four hours to the gates of this town 800 desperate villains.' When he received word of the plot to ship men to France, a capital offence, he was desperate to catch his adversary in the act. He failed, and the boat left with the men and 30 cannons, bound for Nantes. It even stopped in nearby County Clare, to pick up a consignment of contraband butter.

Next, Martin found an opportunity further to humiliate Eyre in a totally legal manner. Under Penal Law, Catholics were not allowed to carry arms, an injunction that was blatantly disregarded in Galway. Martin had dispatched a servant with a pistol of his to be repaired in Galway town. A sentry posted on the West Gate stopped the man and confiscated the gun. When the Governor realised whose the weapon was, he returned it to Martin with a curt and somewhat sarcastic note. Martin refused to accept the gun, sending it back to Eyre. He then proceeded to sue Eyre at the next assizes for the sum of £5, being the value of the weapon. The court heard the matter, and found in Martin's favour.

Eyre, outraged at this insult to his authority, not only from the traitorous Martin but also by the entire legal system of the town, set off for London to consult with his superiors. Martin followed him to England, hoping to confront him on ground where Eyre's 'public character would be no bar to demanding the satisfaction usual amongst gentlemen'. Forty years later, Robert Martin's son would go to equal lengths to pursue a foe.

Robert's chance came as Eyre came out of a house in Jermyn Street. Not exactly adhering to the strict rules of duelling, Martin commenced the confrontation by dealing Eyre a couple of blows from behind with a stout stick. He then demanded that the stunned Eyre draw his sword and defend himself. Eyre bravely obliged, and a fierce fight ensued up and down the street. Martin finally gained the upper hand, severely wounding Eyre, who fell to the ground bleeding profusely. He was carried off, but eventually recovered. A friend of Martin's who had witnessed the carnage immediately dispatched news to Galway that he had 'given the Governor the most unmerciful drubbing that ever was heard of in the streets of London.' As irony would have it, this violent event occurred yards from where Robert's son would one day help found the Society for the Prevention of Cruelty to Animals.

But this was the last of Robert's turbulent ways: the last dogged attempt to fight an armed cause for Catholics. On his return to Ireland, now approaching forty, he proposed marriage to the Honourable Bridget Barnewell, third daughter of the 12th Lord Trimlestown, from a noble family who had fought against William III.

For families such as the Martins, the Barnewells, the Fitzwilliams, the Frenches, the realisation was dawning that Stuart liberation was not going to happen. In order to keep their estates they would have to convert, at least in name, to Protestantism. Robert Martin took out a protestant certificate and his brother Richard, who had no heirs, agreed to lease him Dangan for a nominal rent. On 6th April 1753 Robert and Bridget were married. The following February, in Dublin, their first child, Richard, was born.

*The smugglers' inlet on the Martin estate*

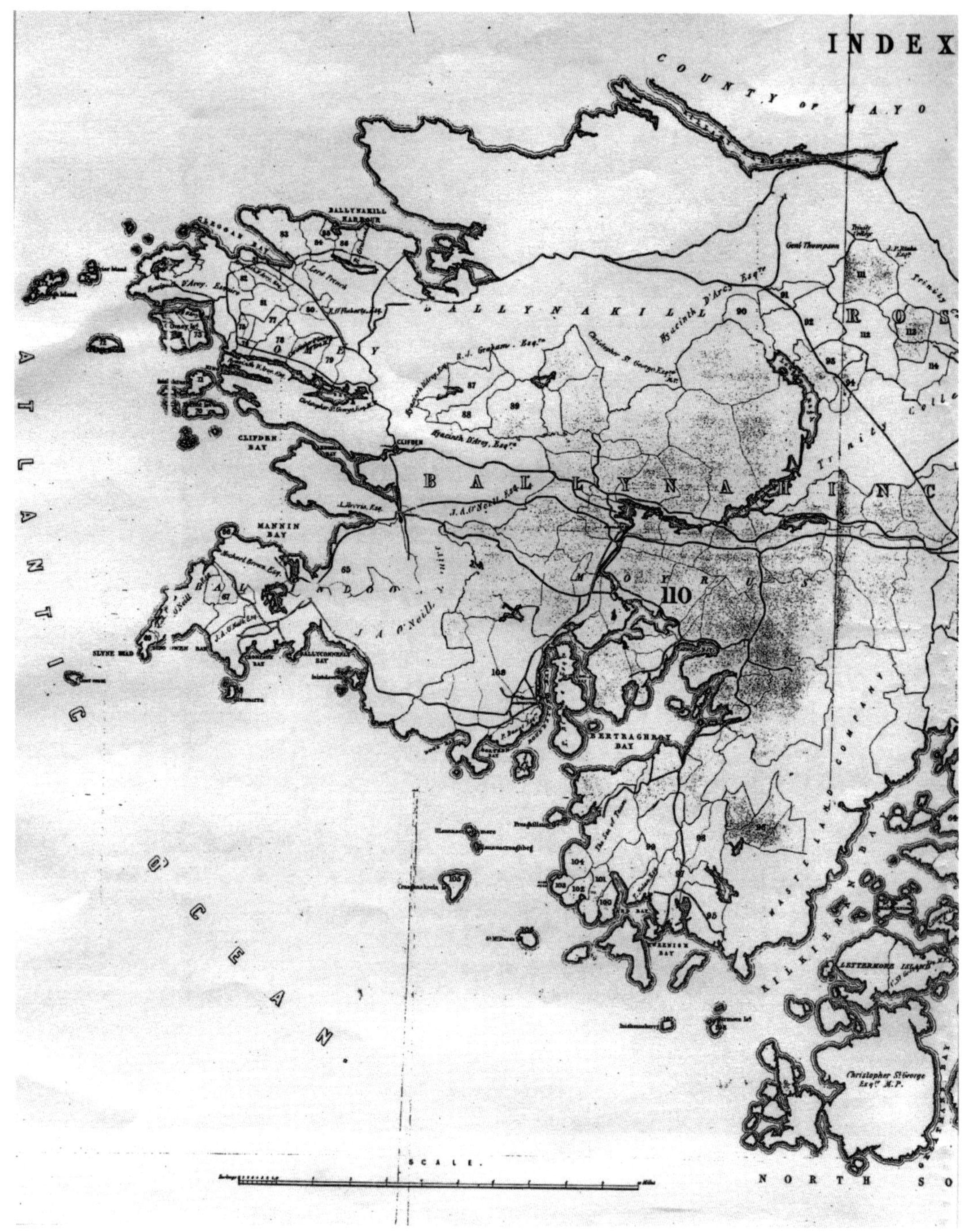


*Map of Connemara drawn up when*

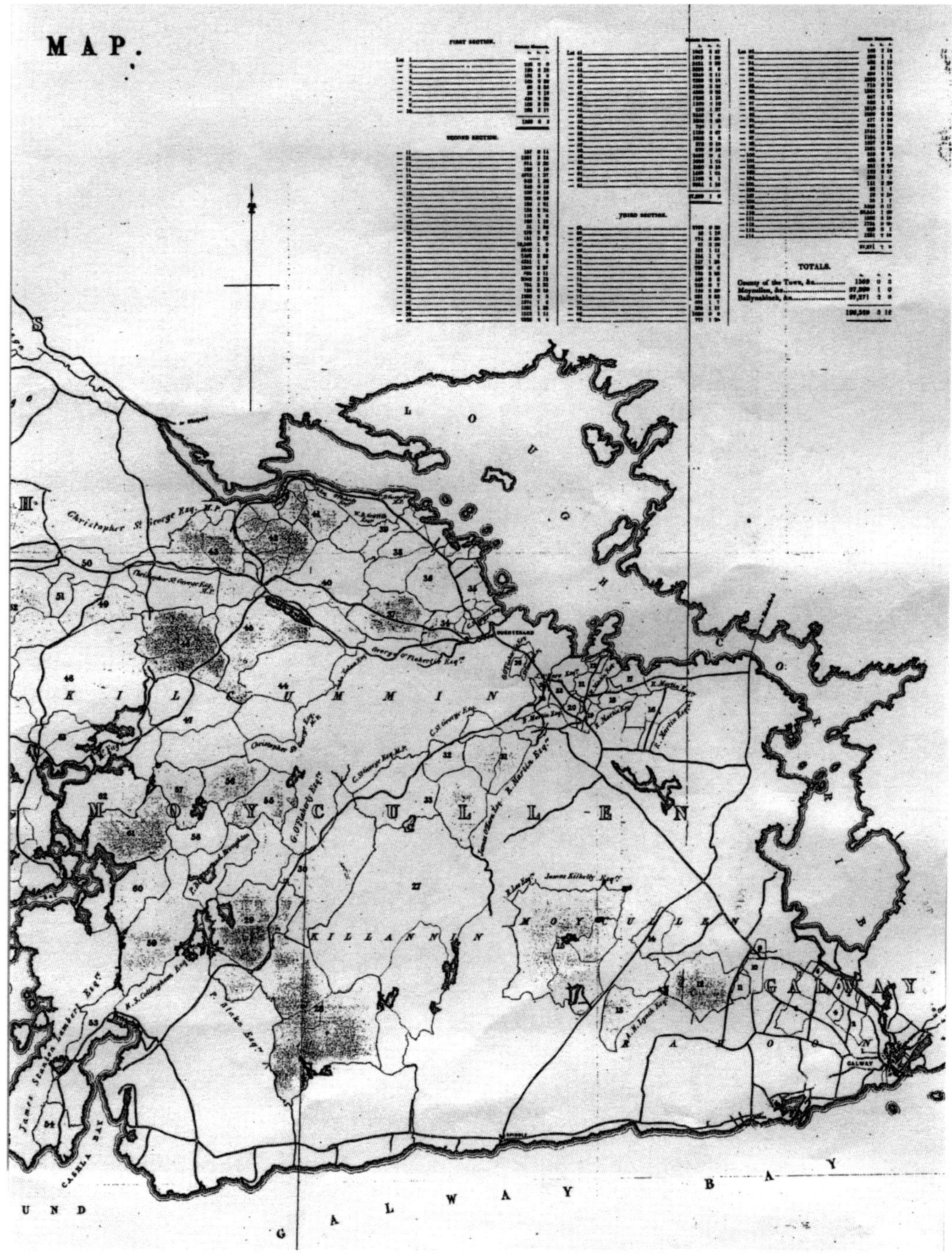


the estate was sold, late 1850s

# Chapter 4

# Childhood Influences

Robert Martin had become what was termed a 'Protestant of Convenience'. Like many catholic aristocrats, he personally maintained his religious beliefs, privately worshipped as a Catholic, and maintained hope that one day equality would be granted: but to the outside protestant world he had converted to that faith and accordingly could take advantage of the law, particularly in respect of land ownership. As a gentleman of the county, now in possession of the much sought-after Protestant Certificate, he was forced to sit at banquets, albeit with a number of fellow clandestine Jacobites, and toast 'the glorious, pious and immortal memory of William the Dutchman'.

Pretending to be a Protestant meant swearing an oath denouncing the Pope and all things papist; to many a Catholic this act of perjury and sacrilege was undoubtedly justified on a needs-must basis. The converts were also expected to attend a protestant church and there take the sacrament in token of their conversion. No inquiry could be realistically made as to the sincerity of the belief involved, especially if the incumbent clergyman had taken a similar route of self-protection.

The Reverend Patrick O'Flynn was typical of a catholic priest who had converted to Protestantism and in return enjoyed an annuity of £40 a year. A tale is told, in a book describing life in County Galway at that time, of two brothers who were paying lip service to the protestant faith. They rode up to Father O'Flynn's church and unceremoniously walked in still wearing their muddy and spurred riding boots. The recusant clergyman resolutely recited the service, including as it did numerous denunciations against the papist faith. At the conclusion, the newly converted brothers spat out the sacramental wine and galloped back to the homes they had saved by the morning's charade.

A year after Culloden, George I died and the British and Irish crown passed to his son George II, who followed his father's lead and ruled through a succession of chief ministers. The politicians played an ongoing game of musical chairs, attempting to gain the monarch's favour, with whomever was left standing when the music stopped being dispatched for a period as Lord Lieutenant of Ireland. It was the era of Hogarth's cartoons and sketches, Doctor Johnson's diary and Handel's *Messiah*. There was also extreme poverty and famine in Ireland.

Britain was again at war in Europe, this time fighting the War of Austrian Succession, basically a Hanoverian cause. This was the start of the growth of the British Empire, with Britain and France finding a new battleground in North America. Both countries had begun to realise the potential of these vast new lands, with France initially concentrating on what is now Canada, Britain preferring to build settlements in New England. Skirmishes were already breaking out.

Full-scale war began in 1756 with Britain and France engaging each other on three fronts: the traditional European hot spots, India and the Americas. Came the hour, came Pitt the Elder who rose Churchill-like to take charge of the war. He galvanised the country and gained the King's ear. Robert Clive took control of India, while Prussia was paid to fight in the European theatre on Britain's behalf, allowing Pitt's attention to turn towards North America.

The French plan was to link their forces controlling Louisiana with the army in Quebec through lands west of the British strongholds on the Eastern seaboard, which they could then assault via the Hudson Valley. Pitt had decided to attack the French by invading Canada. His high-risk plan worked. The British took Quebec and French intentions were thwarted. The French had, however, succeeded in making the colonists in America question the effectiveness of their British masters. At the head of the Hudson valley, a small fort called William Henry had held out for five days against the French and their Native American allies. After the surrender there was a massacre, and ensuing resentment bit into the minds of the New Englanders, that the British could not be trusted to protect them. It was in this campaign that a young Virginian officer named George Washington learned his first military lesson.

When reviewing history from the Irish perspective, from Tudor times up until the start of independence in 1921, a pattern emerges of firm repression, followed by grudging acceptance leading to relaxation of the repression, only for the gradual process to be punctuated by armed rebellion, resulting in more hard-handed repression. A period during Richard Martin's childhood was typical of this cycle.

By 1754, the year of his birth, the Penal Laws were somewhat in abeyance and, by and large, Catholics had learned to live with them, and often find ways of avoiding them. Britain increasingly saw the general catholic population and its representatives as loyal citizens, and considered that their loyalty should therefore be both moderately rewarded and also exploited.

In 1762 when Britain was at war with, ironically, a catholic coalition of France, Austria and Spain, a scheme was under discussion between English and Irish parliaments to recruit Irish catholic regiments to fight in the army of Britain's ally, Portugal. At the same time a bill was before the Irish Parliament that would permit Catholics to take out mortgages to purchase land. But just as the ebb and flow of politics was running in favour of the oppressed, insurrection was about to break forth.

Agrarian workers in Munster were being subjected to enclosure of commonages, forced labour, and ever-increasing rack rents and tithes and, frustrated that their grievances could not be heard in a court of law, created a large, staggered process of protest. They were given the name 'Whiteboys', because they wore coarse white linen overshirts.They took a pragmatic approach to their problems, levelling fences, hedges and walls (hence one of their names, 'the Levellers'), and attempting by coercion to regulate the rural economy along lines it had been run on in the past. The uprising, although easily quashed, gave the more paranoid elements within the protestant Parliament the moral ammunination they needed to resist any repeal of the Penal Laws. Inevitably the mortgage concession was thrown out. In 1766 the first law was passed against the Whiteboys. Ireland was in a state of smothered war. The movement, although unsuccessful and counter-productive to any form of emancipation, had created oathbound secret societies. Particularly in times of distress, people would now obey the local Whiteboy code instead of the law of the land.

But Whiteboy law was unnecesary on the Martin estate, which since Nimble Dick's time been a law unto itself, with tenants largely happy with their treatment. Robert's turbulent days were over and he had settled down to running the estate with his brother Richard, and raising a young family. A year after Dick was born, his mother gave birth to a daughter, Mary. The two children spent their early years together and a strong sibling bond was created that lasted until Mary died.

The family lived mostly at Dangan, which remained a centre for Jacobite supporters. Young Dick would have met a stream of diehard followers of the exiled Stuarts, many of which were fugitives in Ireland, returned from France with tales of imminent salvation. Robert had long decided that armed rebellion was pointless, but he would harbour these men and assist wherever he could.

Dangan was a large Georgian country mansion, more relaxed and rural than most of its English equivalents. The walls of the hall of the 'Great House' were decked with fishing rods, firearms, foxes' brushes, powder flasks, shot pouches, nets and dog collars. There was no strict divide between the masters of the estate and their tenants, whose comings and goings meant the place was always bustling with characters. The Martin family was large and the children had an endless supply of cousins to play with. Like most Irish families, the Martins did not stand on ceremony and the children were encouraged to mix with the adults and join in their conversations at the dinner table.

Young Dick was a sturdy and strong boy, although not tall for his age, with rather obstreperous hair and a large high-bridged nose, a characteristic of the Martin family. He was lively, bright and eager to learn, with the sharp sense of humour that he would put to good use in later years.

Outside Dangan lay 50 miles of magical wilderness enhanced by tales of hidden caves, mythical islands, fairies, mermaids and banshees. By an early age Dick had been taught how to master a horse over the rough terrain of his home. He would travel for days with his father on hunting trips in the remote mountains and boglands, combined with visits to outlying tenants and to the organised groups of smugglers along the 80 miles of coastline who provided the core income for the estate. Illicitly distilled whiskey and poteen went out en-route to England and Europe: French wines and brandies came in.

Yards from the door of Dangan lay the entrance to Lough Corrib with its mists and islands. In addition to being taught horsemanship, Dick had a number of tutors amongst the Martin tenantry who could instruct him in the skills of fishing and of handling a boat. And in years to come the quality of Robert's instruction in fighting and shooting would become evident to all. From boyhood Dick reputedly could handle a sword and accurately aim a pistol.

If there was an influence towards kindness to animals in his early years it apparently would have chiefly come from Bridget, his mother and her two older sisters Thomasine and Margaret, who were to become increasingly close to him. There is no doubt that Bridget and her sisters adored animals, and the abundance of pets they had enjoyed as children on the Barnewell estate was now provided for Dick and Mary.

Their mother would frequently take Dick and his sister to stay at her old childhood home, Trimlestown Castle, another place of legend and excitement. Bridget's brother Robert, who had inherited the title of 12th Baron Trimlestown, was an eccentric but highly respected botanist and zoologist who, sharing the family love of animals, had a large and varied collection of exotic creatures.

Although the Martins were able to enjoy the company of animals as pets, their tenants, like all people living off the land at the time, saw them almost entirely as tools for their survival whose usefulness had to be maximised. A common practice to avoid buying expensive harness was to link a beast to a plough by its tail. Any reluctance to pull the device caused by the ensuing pain would be overcome by beating the animal until it complied. This practice was outlawed on the Martin estate and any culprit caught was subjected to a penalty consistent with the agony that the animal had suffered.

Dick's early education was not, however, limited to the manly arts of riding, hunting and fighting. His mother came from a classically educated and noble family and his father had acquired social skills at the finest European courts. The boy was exposed to classical literature and learned how to appreciate the theatre and other aspects of his culture. The manners he gained, and his familiarity with the complicated etiquette of the day, would allow him as an adult to mix effortlessly with members of the highest society.

His mother had also enjoyed a good standard of education. She had been sent with her sisters, along with the children of the Earls of Tyrconnell and Fingal, to the Dominican nuns at Channel Row in Dublin. This clandestine convent (nearly closed in 1712 when the nuns were forced to appear in court in secular dress, claiming they merely ran a boarding house), provided schooling for aristocratic catholic families. Bridget had retained the airs and graces of her upbringing and insisted on maintaining the trappings of comfort she had been accustomed to despite the wild and rural environment she had chosen to make her home. She insisted on never travelling in anything less than a full coach and horses with liveried footmen. Although generally content to live at Dangan, she and Robert also maintained a house in Dublin where the family would spend the winter, exchanging the unrelenting Connemara weather for the culture of the capital.

Dublin was moving into a renaissance period. George Frederic Handel chose the city for the first ever performance of his *Messiah* in 1742. The previous year, Philip Stanhope, Earl of Chesterfield, out of favour with the King and accordingly shipped off to perform the thankless role of Lord Lieutenant, had galvanised Dublin into laying out Phoenix Park and establishing the Dublin Society, an organisation that would achieve Royal Charter status for the city. Chesterfield was also uncharacteristically sympathetic towards Catholics, writing they 'they were worse used than Negroes by their Lords and Masters.' Not surprisingly, after a brief but spectacular eight-month term of office he was whisked back to London.

When Dick and his family took a second home there, much of Dublin's Georgian splendour was already built. The great Kildare and Tyrone Houses were standing, the massive west front of Trinity College was completed, the Customs House proudly overlooked the Liffey and the Botanic Gardens at Glasnevin had been founded. There was more to come: Stephen's Green was still a rough common.

Commerce was booming, with the traditional trade links augmented by embryonic but flourishing linen manufacture. The north and south walls of the harbour were in place. There was good passenger shipping to Liverpool and Holyhead and regular daily stagecoaches to Athlone, Cork, Kilkenny and Belfast. Printing was endemic, with the streets flooded daily by newspapers, pamphlets, poems and plays. These were mostly protestant publications but an underground polemic catholic press existed around the High Street and Cook Street areas.

The arts centred on theatre and music. Handel had used the magnificent Music-Hall designed by Cassels in Fishamble Street to première his famous oratorio. Thomas Sheridan had opened the Crow Street theatre in 1747, George Faulkner one in Smock Alley and, despite a tendency of audiences to riot during performances, these venues regularly attracted leading actors such as David Garrick from London.

The Martins embarked on the never-ending whirl of theatre visits, routs, masquerades and balls. The fashionable daytime pursuit at establishments such as Lucas's was card playing, four-handed quadrille being the most favoured game. An alternative was taking the air and waters at Templeogue Spa. The Martin children would probably have been given dancing lessons by one of the many French courtiers plying this form of tuition in the city. This regular contrast, between the rough wastes of Connemara and élite city society, set a pattern that Dick was to maintain all his life.

*Dublin Castle, engraving by James Malton*

However, the happy childhood that the boy had enjoyed for his first eight years was about to be tragically interrupted. Despite having a number of doctors in her family, Bridget could not be saved when she fell ill in Dublin, and she died near the time of Dick's birthday, in February 1762. Robert took Dick and Mary back to Dangan, from where they went to stay with Bridget's eldest sister, now Lady Gormanston. The children's other aunt, Margaret, had married Lord Mountgarret and moved to Belgium, but she constantly wrote for news of the welfare of her beloved niece and nephew.

Robert lost no time finding a new wife. On 6th April 1763, just over a year after the death of Bridget, he married Elizabeth Vesey, nee Lynch. Elizabeth was the childless widow of the late John Vesey, grandson of the Lord Archbishop of Tuam and one of the Lord Justices of Ireland. More importantly, by birth she was part of the powerful Lynch family, probably the most dominant of the Galway tribes. Influential banking connections in her arm of the family were often to bale out the Martins in years to come.

The aunts, particularly Lady Mountgarret, were concerned about the effect of this somewhat hasty remarriage on the children. Their concerns were unwarranted as Elizabeth, with no children of her own, quickly assumed the role of a good stepmother to Dick and Mary when they moved back to be with their father at Dangan. Although he must have been terribly distraught at losing the mother he had been so close to, Dick settled into his childhood pursuits in the relative tranquility of the Martin estate.

Four years later an event took place that was to govern the rest of Dick's life. Besides imparting the skills of riding, sailing and shooting, Robert had educated his son in the Jacobite philosophy he had himself learned at Louvain. Dick would have been well schooled in the history of catholic repression in Ireland. Robert told tales of Nimble Dick's support of King James at the battle of the Boyne and at Aughrim, and how he himself had tried to fight at Culloden with Bonnie Prince Charlie. Having since come to the conclusion that the Stuarts, for the most part, had brought nothing but disaster and disillusionment to Ireland, he had taught Dick that armed rebellion was a false route to freedom.

One day, father and son were sailing on Lough Corrib, when they were caught in one of the sudden squalls that often descend on the lake. Robert had put Dick on the tiller and told the boy to keep a course headed toward the hill above Dangan. This was the moment he had chosen to map out the destiny of his son. Richard was to be given a classic English protestant education which would equip him to enter the Irish Parliament, where he would then devote his energy to achieving catholic emancipation.

The boy, not yet in his teens, must leave Dangan for Harrow school in England.

# Chapter 5
# A Protestant Schooling

'Give me a boy until he is seven and I will give you the man,' is the old Jesuit adage. Certainly, by the time he left Ireland for Harrow, Dick had been exposed to the major influences directing his life. His mother and aunts had taught him to respect all living creatures. His father had educated him in the importance of catholic emancipation and how it should be achieved. He had seen compassion shown to dependent people. He had learned to fight with a confidence he would never lose, and to mix with everyone from peasant to aristocrat.

But on 22nd September 1760, while the four-year-old Dick had been blissfully pursuing childhood activities in Connemara, an event had been taking place in London that would frustrate his adult ambitions for the next 60 years: George III was swearing his coronation oath.

George was a somewhat backward and shy young man, but with a degree of obstinacy that grew throughout his long reign. Under the gaze of his subjects, and bedecked with the jewelled Cap of State, he promised to maintain the rights and privileges of the Anglican church. He solemnly undertook to exclude Roman Catholics from any position of authority under the Crown. In years to come he would maintain that if he violated this oath he would 'no longer be legal Sovereign of the country', and that no power on earth could absolve him from 'the due observance of every sentence' of the promise he had made to 'maintain the Protestant reformed religion established by law', unless it suited him on certain occasions to relent if circumstances dictated.

George was in fact a kind-hearted man who certainly never denied Catholics their right to worship, but for 60 years he maintained that the matter was 'beyond the decision of any Cabinet of Ministers'. He was also to claim that the 'catholic question' was the cause of his bouts of madness.

Quite what it must have been like for a twelve-year-old to make the arduous journey from his rural Irish home to the austere and daunting English public school, is difficult to imagine.

Harrow, still a small village, was set in countryside twelve miles from London. The College was approached through a long avenue of trees and scattered over several buildings. Dick, along with the other young pupils in the Lower School, would have resided with one of the 'Dames', stern women who ran the school lodging houses. The older pupils lived with the Masters. Fees were 13 guineas a year, double that if the boy had an 'extraordinary tutor'. Boarding cost 25 guineas, or 30 if the child did not have a 'bedfellow'. Most lessons were charged as extras, so a family probably needed to budget about 70 guineas a year for the privilege of sending one of their offspring there. As is still the case, most of the pupils were there as part of a family tradition, although

*Harrow old school*

Dick would have had schoolmates, especially those from plantation families in the West Indies, who were the first of their line to attend.

Founded in the 16th century, the school had struggled in the first half of the 18th, with numbers falling from 144 in 1721 to 80 in 1739. By the time Dick arrived, they were stood at around 200, and Harrow was about to enter a brilliant period. Percy Thornton, in his definitive Victorian reference work states, 'The standard of knowledge reached by a remarkable band of Harrovians was uncommonly high between 1760 and 1771.'

This high standard was owing to two men: the headmaster, Robert Sumner, and a young master, Samuel Parr. Sumner, in his late thirties when Martin arrived, was good natured, academically brilliant, and eloquent. He had implemented radical reforms, including the introduction of a dancing master, and the foundation of the school library. Parr, a former head boy, was in his early twenties, small of stature and with a lisp, but capable of easily captivating an audience. Beside imparting the classical education that was expected of them, these men had two passions which they shared with their pupils.

From the basic principles of the Whigs, the party that was considered most intellectually alive, they progressed to new dimensions of radical, almost revolutionary politics, focussing on civil rights and freedom for the increasingly restless American colonists. More unusually they, especially Parr, advocated something rarely heard of:

humanity to animals. Abhorring cruelty, Parr coined a phrase that Martin was take up and use to great effect: 'wanton barbarity'.

Parr delivered a famous sermon in which he urged,

> 'He who can look with rapture upon the unoffending and unresisting animal, will soon learn to view the suffering of a fellow creature with indifference; and in time will acquire the power of viewing them with triumph, if that fellow creature should become the victim of his resentment, be it just or unjust.'

He advocated that children, from an early age, should be encouraged to show respect for animals, as, it seems, Dick had already been taught by his mother. He maintained that such respect could not develop if 'the heart has once been familiarised to spectacles of distress, and has been permitted either to behold the pangs of any living creature with cold insensibility, or to inflict them with wanton barbarity.'

It is clear that Harrow at that time did not conform to the stereotyped image of an English public school. Dick was happy there until tragedy, and anarchy, struck.

The academic year was the same as now, with holidays during the late summer, Christmas and Easter periods. Dick settled into a routine of two extended trips home to Ireland. Difficult as it is to comprehend in an era of air travel, the child's journey involved a laborious coach ride of two or three days to the departure ports of Liverpool or Holyhead, and thence onto a sailing boat that, weather permitting, arrived two days, or anything up to a week, later in Dublin. Another even more gruelling two days on a stagecoach took him to Galway, from where he could be taken into the Connemara wilderness.

No doubt, the final leg would have made the demanding journey worth while. Martin's coach would be accompanied the last few miles by trotting 'glossons' and barefoot children. Tenants would perch themselves on vantage points and light beacons to welcome home the young master. Presents, and individual requests for help in various causes, would be thrown into the coach.

Reunited with his father, stepmother and sister, Dick would resume a way of life emphatically different from his experiences in the previous few months. Riding over the treacherous, desolate bogs and mountain terrain to the west of Dangan, and sailing small craft out onto Lough Corrib accompanied by one of his father's ghillies, he would be shown how to turn a turkey feather and some silk into a basket of salmon for the dinner table.

When Dick was fourteen, his uncle Richard died childless. The entire Martin estate, comprising over a quarter of a million acres, passed to his father. The family now alternated between Dangan and Birchall, Nimble Dick's old home a few miles west along the shore of the Lough. This building stood in a setting of almost mystical effect, where the lake horizon plays tricks on the eye that make the shore seem below the water line. Even on otherwise clear days, mists constantly roll off the countless small islands that were once in sight of the house.

With all the estate to manage, Robert now involved his nearly grown son more closely with day-to-day matters. Although Robert had been capable of killing men in cold blood in his youth, in maturity he showed compassion to his tenants, a trait which Dick in turn would pass on to his own son. No Martin tenant was ever evicted for being unable to pay rent. Famine hardly existed before the time of the Great Hunger in 1845. Dick was taught to be fair with the people he controlled and they in turn showed unswerving loyalty. In cold, commercial terms, this method of running an estate was distinctly flawed, and would lead to years of precarious finances.

His stepmother, Elizabeth, had given birth to two sons, Robert and Anthony. In years to come, Dick was to develop more of a fatherly than a brotherly relationship with his half-siblings.

When he returned to Harrow for his penultimate year in 1771, Dick was looking forward to taking further advantage of the teachings of Sumner and Parr, but it was not to be. At the age of forty-one, Sumner suddenly died. Although greatly saddened at losing their well loved headmaster, the pupils took comfort that he would almost certainly be replaced by Parr, his brilliant young protégé, who had joined the school as a thirteen-year-old pupil and, after a brief spell at Cambridge University, returned to take up the post of Head of School, spending five years under Sumner while being groomed for the Headmaster's position. Parr went through what he and the pupils considered was the formality of applying for the post, but the school Governors rejected him and appointed Benjamin Heath, a choice which was by nature contentious, as he had been an assistant master at the arch-rival establishment, Eton College.

The boys, outraged, drew up a petition; it was signed by every pupil in the school. It asked the Governors to take into consideration, 'The unanimous wishes of the whole school that are universally in favour of Mr. Parr. A school cannot be supported when every individual is disaffected.' 'A school of such a reputation as our late Master has made this, ought not to be considered a mere Appendix to Eton: Nor should the plan by which it has been raised to such eminence be subverted by continual innovations from another school.' Towards the end of the document the boys indulged in threatening worse denouncements, should their request fail.

When the Governors refused to co-operate, they embarked on a more pragmatic approach. Governors were assaulted in the street, and the inn where they were meeting was stoned, with every window shattered. Other buildings were attacked, and one of the Governors, a Mr Bucknall, had his carriage completely destroyed on Roxeth Common, now Harrow cricket ground. Retribution was swift, and the school records show that the unnamed ringleaders were immediately removed.

Parr, who had not condoned the insurrection, quietly left Harrow to set up a rival school in nearby Stanmore. Forty pupils and one master followed him, but he was to fail after five years. He went on to become a Prebend in St Paul's, and Dick would retain contact with him, taking advice from his mentor on how barbarity to animals might be prevented by law. Parr died in 1825; in later life he had reflected on the Harrow rebellion, 'One cannot but regret that talents so pre-eminent were thrown away on topics that were only of a temporary nature.'

There is nothing to prove that Dick was involved in the riot, but on the balance of probability his participation appears likely. He was devoted to Parr, and all his life would demonstrate a tendency to take direct and sometimes violent action if he met injustice. With the benefit of knowing Martin's adult style, the wording of the petition appears strongly reminiscent of it, and his youthful nature would have found it hard to restrain the impetuous family genes. The record does show that he left Harrow straight after the notorious incident, a year earlier than intended.

Another pupil who left, and had almost certainly been a ringleader, was Viscount Wellesley, elder brother of Arthur, who was to become the Duke of Wellington. Thereafter the Wellesley family broke with tradition and sent Arthur to Eton, depriving Harrow of ever being able to claim that Waterloo was won on its playing fields.

Dick was too young and ill-prepared to go immediately to Cambridge as his father had planned. Robert decided against enrolling him in Parr's new school, but kept the boy in England, sending him to be personally tutored in the Suffolk village of Sutton by the rector, Joseph Gunning.

The choice of crammer was not random. Little is known of the protestant rector of All Saints church, who had taken the post three years beforehand and would stay until 1806. What is known is that this whole area of Suffolk was a hotbed of catholic activity. Dick lived in the Elizabethan rectory next to the picturesque pebble-built church, and continued his studies.

Eighteen months later he entered Trinity College, Cambridge, again at a period acknowledged as producing a number of outstanding graduates, despite a mediocre standard of teaching. Dick's room-mate was George Ponsonby, whose father was the Speaker of the Irish Parliament and who would himself have a distinguished political career. Other contemporaries included the Marquis of Granby who, as Lord Rutland, was to experience a turbulent political relationship with Martin, and William Pitt, the fourteen-year-old genius son of the British Prime Minister, who would go down in history as one of the country's greatest politicians.

If Dick had enjoyed excellent teaching at Harrow, the reverse was true of his career at Cambridge in the late 18th century. The professors of this era have incurred the indignant scorn of posterity. Samuel Parr reflected that, 'The persons there appointed to professorship have in a few instances disgraced themselves by notorious incapacity or criminal negligence.'

To obtain the degree of Bachelor of Arts, the favoured qualification of the time, a student was encouraged to spend ten terms at the university, perform certain exercises known as 'acts', and finally undergo an informal and invariably inadequate examination before a professor. The student would then be admitted by the Vice Chancellor *'Ad Respondendum Questioni'*. On the first day of the following July, Commencement Day, a degree was awarded. During Martin's time at the university, mathematics was the preferred academic study, but the main point of attending was to provide the opportunity of mixing with and learning from one's peers.

A fellow-student of Dick's called Philip Yorke had an uncle and guardian, Lord Hardwicke, who became concerned that the young man was neglecting his studies, preferring to spend time at nearby Newmarket racecourse. To reassure him, Yorke wrote outlining a typical day at college:

Rise at 7, Chapel from half past 7 til 8: 8-9 breakfast and Demosthenes by myself:
9-10 with Mr Weston: 10-11 classical lecture: 11-12 Euclid: 12-1 walk and dressing
time: 1-2 Dinner and combination room: 2-3 friends' rooms: 3-5 correspondence
or private reading: From half past 5 to 6 Chapel: 6-7 visits: 7-9 Xenophon and
mathematics: 9-11 friends' rooms or company at home.

At this time, in the students' rooms and coffee houses of Cambridge, the only talk
was of the subject preoccupying the country as a whole: the American colonies.

George III, throughout the early period of his reign, was adamant that the colonists
should be taxed. The colonists argued that they were distanced both geographically and constitutionally from Britain, and unlike Scotland, Wales and Ireland, did not
return members to Parliament. 'No taxation without representation' became their
mantra. There was still concern at the lack of British military protection from both
native Indians and the French. George's ear was deaf to complaints and in 1765 a new
Stamp Duty was imposed on all legal documents and even extended to newspapers, a
particularly ill-conceived move, as press opinion now fuelled the fires of dissent.
Rockingham, George's latest First Minister, backed by the aged and infirm Pitt, advised
that this was a tax too far, and it was quickly repealed. The damage, however, was done,
and increased two years later, when duties were levelled on American imports of paper,
glass, lead and, most emotively, tea.

Resentment spilled into violence in March 1770 when the snowballing of British
sentries outside their barracks triggered a riot in which five colonists were killed.
Benjamin Franklin, a Boston scientist and politician who moderates hoped would have
a calming influence, was dispatched to Britain in an attempt to use diplomatic means
to reduce the contentious taxation. He was unsuccessful, but on a visit to Ireland
influenced many people on the subject of the benefits of independence.

Ten years into his reign, George had become wise to the time-honoured tradition
of bribery. Lucrative royal contracts, sinecures and pensions were handed out to
politicians who agreed with what he wanted and sided against what he opposed. A new
political party emerged: the Tories. For some totally inappropriate reason they were
named after the *Toraidhes*, Irish outlaws who had opposed the exclusion of the catholic
Duke of York from becoming King James II. The King appointed Lord North as the
first non-Whig prime minister since the reign of Queen Anne. History would recognise
North as one of its greatest incompetents.

The radical colonists, now calling themselves Patriots, had a leader in John Adams,
who was to become their second president. By now most of the taxes had been quietly
dropped by the British government, and in any event were proving impossible to
collect. One remained: a threepence in the pound levy on tea. The East India
Company, an organisation essentially relied upon by Britain to control India, was in
financial difficulties, and as a result was allowed to import tea into America without
paying duty. Effectively, they had been given a monopoly. The Patriots saw the
opportunity to force a crisis and one night in December 1773, disguised as Red Indians,
they boarded East India Company ships in Boston harbour and threw the cargoes
overboard: the 'Boston Tea Party'. A collision course had been set with the motherland.

# Chapter 6

## Has he Blazed?

The modern phrase 'Men behaving badly' could not be more appropriately applied than to gentlemen of society in the late 18th century. Behaviour as decadent as any was the norm. Excess in all areas of life was commonplace.

The 1770s, when Dick was at Cambridge University, probably saw the peak of debauchery in London circles. Thereafter, as the moral example of King George III came slowly to bear (albeit counteracted by the behaviour of his son Prince George), society began to clean up its act. Etiquette and grace slowly replaced past antics, and acts of hedonism became more discreet.

The godfather of Georgian debauchery was undoubtably Sir Francis Dashwood, the renowned sadist and pervert who founded the infamous Hellfire Club in about 1730. This organisation, dedicated to lavish drinking, black magic and depraved sexual orgies, was efficiently run, with a network of madams scouring the country and supplying young virgins to the membership, which read as a virtual 'Who's Who' of the arts, politics and the Church. At least one serving Prime Minister, a Chancellor of the Exchequer, and a Lord Mayor of London, were all fully paid-up members. Even the historically respected Benjamin Franklin took a passing interest, when he was in England attempting to broker peace.

Little wonder that the second generation of the original membership, who were Dick's contemporaries during his time at Cambridge, aimed to carry the work of their fathers to new depths of depravity. Splinter groups, akin to modern-day inner city street gangs emerged, each with its own brand of viciousness. The Mohawks specialized in 'tipping the lion': crushing the noses of total strangers with a special instrument they had made for the purpose. The Mollies were transvestites who sang to each other 'Tell me, gentle hobble-de-hoy, art thou girl or art thou boy?' The Blasters' pet pastime was exposing themselves to passing women in the street. The Fun Club went in for practical jokes such as setting fire to workmen's cottages. Pure vandalism was the domain of the Hectors, while members of the She-Romps Club preferred violent and orchestrated rape as their pastime. Most ritualistic were the Sweaters, who had invented a game of encircling an innocent passer-by; whomever the unfortunate victim turned his back on was obliged to stab him in the behind.

As these fun-loving young men were from wealthy and influential families, the judiciary, many of whom were original members of the Hellfire Club, took a lenient view. The young Lord Charteris one night was taking part in his club's party piece of 'boxing the watch', a term applied to nailing a night watchman into his sentry box and rolling it down a hill. One victim took umbrage at this game and, drawing his sword, marched the young aristocrat to the local constabulary. In court, the magistrate reprimanded the watchman for interfering with the fun.

Fashion was as extreme as behaviour. This was the period of grossly exaggerated hair and costume. Gentlemen wore high red heels; their faces were a shade of blue as a result of powder continually applied with the aid of an obligatory puff. Hair was carefully coiffed to create the standard 36 curls. Lace adorned all clothing and dressing was not complete without the drawn-out ceremony of tying one's cravat. Women's dress was even more elaborate, often taking the entire morning to arrange. Numerous petticoats and hoops made the skirt eight feet in diameter. Wire frames and artificial hair extended three feet above the head.

London at the time combined a filthy maze of small back alleys awash with raw sewage, with magnificent Wren-inspired architecture. Being less than a day's ride away from Cambridge, the fashionable coffee houses and well-stocked brothels of the capital would have been a magnet for the students. Although there was a pervading air of sexual wickedness and sadistic violence, it was also a time of great culture and art: of luminaries such as Dr Johnson, Oliver Goldsmith, Richard Brinsley Sheridan, William Hogarth and Thomas Gainsborough. Little wonder that in the next century Dickens would describe the period as the best, and worst, of times.

The conduct of young men in Martin's native Ireland was not much better. Probably due to the traditional restraints of Catholicism, sexual deviance was less evident, but the youth of Ireland surpassed their English peers when it came to drinking and gambling. The amount of alcohol consumed by the average Irish 'rake' or 'buck', terms adherent to playboys of the time, was staggering. The traditional drink throughout the day was a strong rum punch, usually kept warm on a stove. Wine, normally claret, was drunk with dinner and continued to be slurped until the early hours of the morning. A moderate drinker would get through four bottles, while the average was nearer six. A man was considered a 'mere nincompoop with his bottle if he could not take his gallon coolly'.

Galway, with its maritime links, had always been a cosmopolitan town and, with its ready supply of French wines and brandies, boasted even higher rates of drinking and the resultant violence. Dublin on the other hand mirrored London even to the extent of having its own Hellfire club, with a sister organisation, the Badgers' Club in Limerick. The Dublin society was based in a tavern called the Eagle and its most famous member was Buck Whaley, who went on to serve as a member of the Irish Parliament alongside Martin.

If there was one thing above all others that united the male culture and psyche throughout England, Ireland and France, it was duelling. It had been part of life since time immemorial and would remain so for another hundred years, but in the late 18th century it was endemic and at its peak. The medieval custom of men settling their disputes by combat had developed into a structured process, complying with strict rules and heavily laced with etiquette. Although it was technically illegal, courts would never convict anybody for assault or murder providing the rules of engagement had been obeyed. In fact, it was part of the basic training for lawyers, so that it was customary to settle any disputes with disgruntled or slow paying clients in this manner. It was impossible for a gentleman at the time to avoid a duel. An officer would be forced to resign his commission if he refused to fight. 'Has he blazed?' was a question often asked about a youth's passage to manhood. 'Gamecocks' and 'fire-eaters' were the terms applied to regular practitioners.

By the 1770s swords had mostly gone out of vogue, being replaced in general by single-shot pistols. Galway remained one of the few places where swords were still commonly used. A gentleman's most prized possession was his duelling pistol, the weapon having been hand crafted to meet his grip and stature, elaborately engraved, and augmented with a notch for every successful encounter. Guns often carried familar names such as 'Sweet Lips' or 'The Darling'.

The terms of engagement were stringent and became even more formalised in 1777 when delegates, including Richard Martin, at the summer Assizes in Clonmel drew up a written code by which affairs of honour must be conducted. This became known as the 'Thirty-Six Commandments', and every Irish gentleman was expected to keep a copy in his pistol case.

Rule One stated, 'The first offence requires the first apology, though the retort may have been more offensive than the insult.' In simple terms, the person first offended could demand his honour and, when that was satisfied, the original aggressor, providing he was still alive and capable of continuing, could then demand reparation for the second insult, effectively offering the contenders the opportunity to fight two duels over the same incident.

The person challenged was given the choice of weapons and venue. If swords were chosen but the opponent swore that he was not a swordsman, then pistols were reverted to. Insults to a lady under a gentleman's care were considered a 'greater offence than if given to the gentleman personally, and to be regulated accordingly'. Rule Fifteen stated the sensible condition that 'Challenges are never to be delivered at night, unless the party challenged intend leaving the place of offence before morning; for it is desirable to avoid all hot-headed proceedings.' Once the combatants were at the scene of the duel there was no going back, according to Rule Seven, which stated, 'No apology can be received in any case after the parties have taken their ground, without the exchange of fires.'

Seconds, the appointed assistants to the combatants, had an important role at the event proper. If pistols were to be used, the person challenged choose his ground, the distance he would stand from his opponent. The Seconds would then decide the firing routine and whether one or two pistols were to be used. The options were: either the combatants were to fire on an agreed signal or command, or alternatively they could walk towards each other and fire at will. The latter method required nerve. You could fire quickly but would be in deep trouble if you missed. Being distinctly more likely to achieve death or wounding, this was the favoured way to settle serious grievances.

The Seconds would decide if honour had been achieved as a result of injuries suffered or, more likely, in the event of both parties missing, a very common outcome directly related to the level of alcohol that had invariably been consumed. Rule Fourteen stated that the Seconds had to be of 'equal rank in society with the principals they attend'. This was essential, as they were frequently drawn into the dispute. In fact if the Seconds fell out themselves they were obliged to fight their duel simultaneously with their principals. Pistol duels were fought with the Seconds standing at right angles to the principals; sword fights started five paces apart.

Given the social climate, with hordes of rich young men having little to do besides drink themselves into belligerence, it is little wonder that duels were commonplace. Most encounters were merely drunken skirmishes with little prospect of either combatant receiving serious injury. Many were a ritual charade to alleviate boredom. But the more serious duels and duellists, including Dick Martin, were to become legendary.

Many duels were fought by notable public figures, a practice that continued into the 19th century. Lords Castlereagh and Canning, both cabinet ministers, fought over the management of a military campaign. Henry Flood and Henry Grattan, the leading Irish politicians of the day, duelled in Dublin. On one occasion a trial at Waterford Assizes was temporarily adjourned by Judge Egan to allow the opposing barristers to settle a legal argument by combat. All major cities had areas more or less designated for duelling. In London, Wimbledon and Putney Commons were frequented. Dubliners settled their differences in Phoenix Park. Galway had its notorious Field of Mars.

Richard Martin would become the most famous duellist of this era, and his meeting with a psychopath called Fighting Fitzgerald was to outshine all others in Irish folklore, but in 1773 he was still a student at Cambridge. It is difficult to imagine that, with a lifetime ahead of him dedicated to humane relief for both people and animals, Martin was drawn into the wilder fringes of behaviour prevailing in his youth. The likelihood of him partaking in acts of random violence against innocent people seems less than remote. Nor in later life was there any evidence of sexual misconduct; in fact, the reverse applied to Martin, who had strict morals in this area. He had, however, been used to a lavish standard of living throughout his childhood and would retain a taste for high life, applied with enormous energy in later years. No doubt as a nineteen-year-old in a society that dedicated itself to enjoyment, he took full advantage of his fortuitous timing.

Now a grown man, Dick was of average height for the day, with a stocky, almost burly build. His hair, with a pronounced reddish quiff, still retained the unkempt tendencies of his boyhood. His natural accent was a rich West-of-Ireland brogue, but, as was common in Georgian society, when in the appropriate company he would affect what is best described as an aristocratic English tone. Over the years he would, to great effect, revert to the Irish brogue to add emphasis to a threatening or humorous point. Harrow and Cambridge would have taught him almost fluent Latin, a smattering of classical Greek and passable French, a language he was soon to become more assured in. All his life he avoided the more obvious physical excesses, drinking in moderation and eschewing the gluttonous intake of rich food so prevalent in those days. He aided the constitution he had been blessed with by sensible living and enjoyed a standard of health extraordinary even by today's standards.

Martin combined his time at Cambridge with socializing in London and visits to his home in Ireland, where there were now two small half-brothers. His cousin Lord Gormanston, the son of his beloved aunt and with whom he spent considerable time as a boy, was by then living in London. A sophisticated beau and dedicated socialite, Gormanston introduced Dick to the uppermost reaches of society. These connections were to result in Dick's eventual close friendship with the Prince of Wales, the future Regent and King. English rakes held their hard-living Irish counterparts in high esteem and the dashing young Martin made a lasting impression on the youthful Prince. Dick's childhood days when, with his parents, he had experienced the social whirl of Dublin, held him in good stead as he plunged into the pleasures of London.

Dick matriculated and was admitted as a Fellow Commoner to Trinity College on 4th March 1773. His father had already secured him a place at the London bar in Lincoln's Inn. The plan was for him to take his training back to Ireland and practise law for a few years before entering politics. However, when he left university his father gave permission for him to take, as Robert himself had done, the customary Grand Tour. This was a journey most sons of upper-class families indulged themselves with, involving extended stays with a network of European counterparts.

As his travelling companion, Dick chose his cousin James Jordon. The Jordons were from Rosleven Castle in County Mayo, the neigbouring county to Galway, reached by a short boat ride across Lough Corrib from Dangan. The boys had spent considerable time playing together as children. James was due to become a lawyer at the Irish bar, a career that would result in tragedy when, a decade after their travels, Dick would be driven to fight his cousin following a fateful argument.

The young men first set out towards Florence, where they stayed two to three months. Little is known of what took place on the tour, but their childhood riding over the rough Connemara terrain would have well prepared them for a favourite practice of young noblemen: racing, for considerable sums of money.

From Italy the cousins travelled, probably via Paris, to the Atlantic port of Bordeaux, thereafter their original plan being to complete the traditional European circuit and return to Britain. They had already been away for nearly a year but, possibly attracted by news of events across the Atlantic, they decided to extend their tour and board a ship to Jamaica.

Their Caribbean destination was quite logical. The Martins had family connections there and a number of Dick's school friends at Harrow were the sons of wealthy plantation owners on the island. The Martins had already made their mark on the colony. In 1679 Thomas Martyn, a member of the Governing Council of Jamaica, had fallen foul of the authorities and was imprisoned after an inspection of his accounts revealed irregularities.

Jamaica was now under British rule and enjoying booming trade with Europe and America, the major export being coffee, now widely regarded as the most prestigious beverage. Over a million tons a year were being exported. Martin and Jordon would have enjoyed an opulent standard of living during their stay, no doubt having time to admire the several Botanical Gardens that had been laid out the year prior to their arrival.

The chief import was African slaves. Dick was to remember seeing at first hand the treatment of negroes as they worked for their white masters in the harsh conditions on the coffee plantations. He witnessed how they were bought and sold in a manner similar to the horse markets he knew so well on the west coast of Ireland. These became prevailing memories for Martin, who in later life formed a close friendship with William Wilberforce and supported the anti-slavery measures eventually passed in the British Parliament.

Dick and James's Grand Tour had one further leg. Martin had been sympathetic to the cause of the American colonists since his days at Harrow. Benjamin Frankin had convinced many in Ireland that they too could hope to achieve independence from Britain. With the objective of catholic emancipation already instilled in him by his father, Dick saw independence for a predominantly catholic Ireland as a quick and effective solution. The young men set sail for New England.

In the broad context of atrocities throughout the ages, the act of dumping a small quantity of tea into a harbour seems fairly innocuous. The behaviour, however, of the American rebels in Boston was to rouse both sides into actions of tremendous historical significance. First came the political bluster. John Adams, who was to become a signatory to the colonists' Declaration of Independence and eventually President of the United States of America, made a famous speech the day after the Boston Tea Party, stating: 'There is a dignity, a majesty and sublimity in this last effort of the Patriots that I greatly admire . . . many persons wish that as many dead carcasses were floating in the harbour as there were chests of tea.'

When news of the Tea Party reached London, there was outrage. Parliament swiftly passed legislation as a precursor to military action. With an eye for an apt title, the House passed the Intolerable Acts, closing Boston Harbour, making it obligatory for colonists to billet British troops in their homes and removing what autonomy the colony of Massachusetts had enjoyed. Edmund Burke, addressing the House of Commons, justified the British Empire as being from 'the throne of heaven . . . guiding and controlling all inferior legislatures'. Pitt the Elder, in his last parliamentary speech, advocated reconciliation.

In September 1774 the colonists held a congress in Philadelphia, where the moderates successfully argued for one last attempt at a peaceful solution. A Declaration of Rights was drawn up asking the British Government to repeal thirteen commercial Acts that had been passed since 1763. The tone was firm but respectful. The British response was a contemptous rejection. War was now inevitable.

The British had been strengthening their troops in Boston, while the Patriots built a garrison in nearby Lexington. On 18th April 1775, 800 British troops left Boston along the Concord road, heading towards their enemy. A young Patriot patrolman, Paul Revere, made his famous ride to warn his countrymen of the forthcoming attack. The first shot of the American War of Independence was fired at Lexington the following morning.

Martin and Jordon were now in New England. Quite what their motives were in travelling there is uncertain. They may have had a notion to join the Patriot cause. They may just have been curious about events and combined this with a youthful sense of adventure. When war broke out, however, they both immediately returned to Ireland.

# Chapter 7

# Into Politics

Martin and his cousin James arrived back in Galway in the summer of 1775, replete with tales of their tour experiences, but the main interest for their fellow countrymen was to hear described their first-hand knowledge of the struggle in America.

The American effort, and ultimate achievement, in gaining independence would have a profound but tragic influence on Ireland. By 1775, the country was experiencing relative calm. It was controlled by a protestant upper class serving in a parliament controlled by the British Government, which at that stage was compliant with King George's wishes. The Stuarts' claim to the throne had been relegated to history and folksong. Penal Laws were still in place, but the more outlandish and petty were not enforced, and blind eyes were turned to families such as the Martins who had the outward appearance of their professed protestant faith.

George III and his government followed the path of minor concessions to appease Irish Catholics when outside threats were looming, for Britain was always vulnerable to her traditional enemies, France and Spain, using Ireland as a base. In 1774, with major trouble brewing across the Atlantic, Britain threw a minor carrot to the Catholics. Those who were prepared to swear an oath of allegiance were allowed to play a greater role in public life, although this did not include becoming a Member of Parliament.

Catholics, however, had built an alternative power base of wealth in the form of hard cash. Robbed of their lands by Cromwell and his successors, middle-class Catholics had turned to traditional trading, at a time of economic boom. This gave them a grievance in common with wealthy protestant traders and landowners, and it was the same that had inflamed American colonists: they resented the taxation system of the British government.

The question for Catholics was whether graciously to accept the latest concession or to push for further emancipation. The American cause was giving the Irish an entirely different focus, which united Protestant and Catholic for the first time in over 200 years, and the country eagerly followed news of events in New England. Why should Ireland have to remain a colony of Britain? America had had the audacity to ask for more: Ireland should follow suit.

Again, this ambition to become independent of the British crown for the first time since the Normans had arrived, gave rise to a fundamental problem as to what route the cause should take: armed uprising or diplomatic pressure? The Americans, having failed with diplomacy, had turned to arms out of frustration, but 3000 miles of sea assisted their home advantage.

Dick was now happily reunited with his father, stepmother, sister and his two half brothers aged four and five. He and Robert turned to addressing the future. Robert remained convinced that the way to catholic emancipation was by political means and he still intended his son to work for this goal. He felt that the immediate priority was for Dick to gain adult credibility by pursuing a career in law, and the young man was dispatched back to London to be called to the Bar at Lincoln's Inn. He was admitted to that venerable legal institution on 1st February 1776 but it would be seven years before he accepted his one and only brief.

Dick took the opportunity of his trip to London via Dublin to renew friendships with his room-mate from Cambridge, George Ponsonby, and another fellow student, the Marquis of Granby. Both men were excited by events in America and impressed that their contemporary had actually met the Patriots. Ponsonby's father was Speaker in the Irish Parliament and Dick listened with interest to the views his friends put forward. Within the political circles of Dublin which supported the American cause and wanted an independent Ireland, the feeling was that their aim could not be achieved by force. America would ultimately win independence, but Ireland did not have the advantages enjoyed by the colonists. Tactics must be based on what the political climate would be as and when Britain lost its hold on the American colonies. The plans which Dick heard so eagerly were aimed at making the Irish Parliament a credible body, that could press for political independence at a time when Britain would prefer not to repeat its experiences with America.

Since 1494, when Henry VII's representative Sir Edward Poyning passed his infamous legislation, the Irish Parliament had been a mere puppet of Britain. Since all major decisions and laws had to be approved in London, Dublin was effectively an administrative arm of the British Government. The Irish Parliament was also used on one hand as a dumping ground for politicians out of favour in London and on the other to reward acts of loyalty to the Crown with lucrative posts in Dublin. The incumbents initially caused resentment, but many stayed on and settled in Ireland. Subsequent generations would consider themselves Irish and, being from influential families, were in a position to fight political causes. A prime example was Jonathan Swift, the famous clergyman and satirical writer of the 18th century, whose English father had been bestowed with high office.

All reform needs strong leadership, and the task of creating a credible political body out of the toothless Irish Parliament fell to Henry Grattan. Grattan was born in Dublin in 1746, making him eight years older than Richard Martin. His father was Recorder of Dublin for many years and his grandfather had been a Chief Justice. After graduating from Trinity College, he was called to the Bar in London by the Middle Temple in 1767. Grattan, who was to become one of the finest speakers of both the Irish and British Parliaments, took advantage of his time in London to hear the oratorical politicians such as Edmund Burke. His landlady complained that he would walk around her garden in the middle of the night addressing an invisible 'Mr. Speaker'.

Returning to Dublin in 1772 he joined the Irish bar and spent the next three years as a practising lawyer until an influential Earl offered him the vacant seat of Charlemont, County Armagh. Grattan entered the Irish Parliament in 1775 just as Henry Flood, who had championed the independence cause in the House, had accepted higher office in the mistaken belief it would make him more influential. Grattan and Flood were to be bitter political opponents, and at one stage would air their differences by duelling.

Grattan immediately made his mark, taking control of Flood's party, openly supporting the American fight for independence and proclaiming in a number of eloquent parliamentary speeches that this should be the aim for Ireland. His strange appearance, small and misshapen with a shrill voice, attracted people's attention, and while he spoke he had a habit of swaying to and fro. Grattan saw the forthcoming general election in the spring of 1776 as the springboard to parliamentary reform. The following 24 years would become known as 'Grattan's Parliament'. This was somewhat misleading, since Grattan never held any senior office.

Ponsonby and Granby were friends and followers of Grattan and presented a strong argument to Martin that the momentum in Dublin, coupled with events unfolding in America, would ensure that the next session of Parliament would be historic. Grattan himself urged the young man to stand for election and join the cause.

A cross the Atlantic, the war had moved into gear. The first major battle was fought in May 1775, on the Bunker and Breed hills, overlooking the port of Boston. The British General Sir William Howe led three lines of redcoats towards the summit. They had got to within 100 metres when 3000 colonial farmers armed with hunting guns opened fire. After 1000 British soldiers had fallen Howe realised the enemy were running short of ammunition and made a successful third rush, driving the rebels from their position and taking the hills. The British had won the battle but the colonial fighters had become heroes. Both sides began to realise that American victory was possible.

Until this stage those fighting for independence were mostly small groups of farmers, loosely coordinated into a rag-tag force. To engage the might of the British army effectively, they needed a leader. The man who came forward to fill that role was the 43-year-old George Washington, who tasked himself immediately with providing the ragged band of patriots at Boston with discipline and munitions. He devoted the winter months, before the inevitable British reinforcements arrived, to preparing for full-scale war.

George III was in no mood to seek conciliation with the American upstarts. He wrote to his First Minister, Lord North,

> The die is now cast. The colonies must either submit or triumph. I do not wish to come to severer measures, but we must not retreat. By coolness and unremitted pursuit of the measures that have been adopted I trust they will come to submit . . . I have no doubt that, if it does not succeed, once vigorous measures appear to be the only means left of bringing the Americans to a due submission to the mother country the colonies will submit . . . I know I am doing my duty and can never wish to retract.

He was later to add that 'with firmness and perseverance America will be brought to submission. If not, old England will . . . perhaps not appear so formidable in the eyes of Europe.'

Historians are united in condemning North as the worst holder of primary office. He was an amiable man, portly in build with flabby cheeks and protruding eyes, which gave him, according to one witness, 'the air of a blind trumpeter'. In his early career he was a competent administrator, but the King, anxious after the resistance to his views he had encountered from Pitt the Elder, wanted a yes-man and promoted North way above his threshold of competence. In fairness to North he was reluctant to take the role and, when in situ, on many occasions went as far as begging the King to release him. North's incompetence pervaded his own financial affairs and he was constantly on the verge of personal bankruptcy, a predicament the King took full advantage of by servicing his Prime Minister's debts, provided he remained in office and executed the royal wishes and policies.

After the battle at Bunker Hill, General Howe took stock and concluded that, despite the perceived strength of the British military, holding on to the American colonies was going to be at best difficult and at worst impossible, should France enter the conflict on the side of the colonists. The British position was not helped by having the bungling Earl of Sandwich (whose place in history relied on his inventing a form of snack that enabled him to remain at the gaming table for days on end) in charge of the British fleet on the eastern seaboard. Howe evacuated Boston, moved his troops north to Halifax in Nova Scotia and sent word of his concerns back to London, urging conciliation as the preferred solution. But the King had already decided to ride roughshod over any argument put forward for diplomacy.

Considered opinion in Ireland sided with General Howe's conclusion: it was only a matter of time before America succeeded and broke free from Britain. With Grattan set to fortify the Irish Parliament, exciting times were on the horizon. Heeding the advice given by his old university friends, young Richard Martin concluded now was not the moment to be pursuing a career in law. He wanted to be part of the political movement towards independence and then, once that was gained, to push for catholic emancipation without having the traditional resistance of Britain to contend with.

Dick returned to Dangan and set about persuading his father to support the decision he had made to stand for Parliament in the next election. He found he was pushing at an open door, for Robert quickly agreed to support his 22-year-old son's wish.

Throughout the 18th and 19th centuries Irish elections were colourful, corrupt and often very violent affairs. Galway as ever led the way in excess, and Richard Martin's escapades during his long political career only added to the folklore. An old refrain ran, 'He's not the man for Galway', meaning that the candidate did not live up to the usual representative, who was expected to have fought his duel by breakfast, commenced the daily surfeit of rum punch and claret, and hunted fearlessly with his hounds until nightfall, when he would entertain to such a lavish extent that he was permanently pursued by hapless bailiffs. Martin would live up to parts of the sterotype in years to come, but his first election at Galway was a relatively tame affair.

The electorate comprised Protestants who owned or leased land worth more than 40 shillings a year. Leaseholders almost always voted as dictated by their freeholder. Voters had openly to state their choice to the official in charge of the one voting station open in each borough. Most of the tenants on the Martin estate were Catholics and therefore disenfranchised from the system. The young candidate came last, with only

53 out of the 360 votes cast. There was, however, an alternative way of entering Parliament: purchasing one of the many corrupt boroughs that were openly for sale. Robert purchased the freeman Borough of Jamestown in County Leitrim for the sum of £2000, equivalent to almost half a million in current terms. Thus did Richard Martin become a member of the Irish Parliament, although his first experience of the role was to last only one day.

The Irish House of Commons was composed of 300 members. Each of the 32 counties returned two; the 117 Boroughs returned two, as did Trinity College, Dublin. There was an upper House that contained a varying number of spiritual and temporal peers. The Act of Supremacy debarred surviving catholic peers from taking their seats.

For centuries the British Crown, through government, had ruled Ireland by appointing a Viceroy, the Lord Lieutenant, assisted by a Chief Secretary who acted as the equivalent of Prime Minister, and often succeeded to the Viceroyship. This system was designed to ensure that any legislation unacceptable to Britain would not be passed. There was another failsafe: many of the representatives from the so-called 'rotten boroughs' had had their seats paid for by the British administration. A decade before, the Viceroy Lord Townsend had set a precedent by choosing to live in Dublin throughout his term of office. The incumbent Lord Lieutenant, at the time of Martin's entry to Parliament, was the ill-fated Lord Harcourt.

On 18th June 1776, Richard Martin, in the obligatory full court dress and powdered wig, took his seat in Parliament House. Dublin's twin houses of government were magnifcent buildings, their coffered ceilings adorned with extravagant Waterford crystal chandeliers. Today, as a branch of the Bank of Ireland, the buildings remain almost the same.

The opening session commenced with an issue outstanding from the previous administration: the contentious dispatching of a third of the Irish military to reinforce the British Army in America. Henry Grattan and his followers were set to oppose this practical support being sent to suppress the cause they openly favoured. Harcourt was not prepared to give the polemical Grattan the opportunity of galvanising support in the House for the American rebels. He promptly prorogued parliament, for an undetermined period, on the very day it assembled.

Harcourt's action reflected the panic beginning to permeate the government at Westminster. The King had ignored General Howe's warning and instructed North to take whatever military measures were needed to quell the wayward Americans. The immediate problem was to find a sufficient armed force within the already overstretched British military. The strength of the army on paper was less than fifty thousand; 16,000 were in England and Scotland, 12,000 in Ireland, 9,000 in various garrisons in India, Africa, the Mediterranean, and the West Indies and some 8,000 in America. Pay was low, and in order to find recruits standards had dropped; pardons were offered to malefactors who enlisted. George turned to his native Hanover for the solution, recruiting five regiments of mercenaries for British garrisons in the Mediterranean, and releasing the troops there to be dispatched to America.

Early in 1776 the British Government, in an attempt to put further pressure on the colonists, passed the Prohibitory Act, forbidding all trade with the rebellious

Americans, and declared a blockade of the American coast. This was the final straw for the moderate element within the colonial ranks. Not all colonists wanted to break away from Britain, just as there were many British politicians who did not want to force the issue. Many Americans did not share Howe's pessimism, although Washington's ability to organise the patriot troops was beginning to be recognised by the Congress assembled in Philadelphia.

On 7th June 1776 Richard Henry Lee moved the following resolution: 'That these colonies are and of right ought to be free and independent states; that they are absolved from all allegiance to the British Crown, and that all political connection between them and the state of Great Britain is and ought to be dissolved.' Six of the thirteen colonies opposed the resolution, fearing that a formal declaration, especially before any foreign alliances had been concluded, would trigger a full-scale British invasion. But news of the British economic sanctions turned conciliatory members of Congress, and a committee, including Thomas Jefferson, was appointed to draft a formal statement outlining their grievances and the action they were taking.

On 4th July 1776, a month after Dick had returned to Galway bitterly disappointed by his first experience of Parliament, the Declaration of Independence, signed by all the rebel leaders, was published and the American fight for freedom had passed the point of no return.

*The Dublin Parliament building, engraving by James Malton*

Chapter 8

# Elizabeth

Though Dick returned to Dangan disillusioned by his interrupted entry into politics, Ponsonby and Grattan had asured him that the proroguing of Parliament was a temporary setback, underlining the pressure Britain was feeling from the Americans' unilateral declaration. Patience was needed.

By now Martin had acquired the reputation of intrepid duellist that would follow him through his life, and grow to legendary proportions after his death. Given that his father and great-grandfather had had similar reputations, and considering the culture that prevailed in the 1770s, it would have been surprising if Martin had not blazed with the best. Little is recorded about individual duels because they were technically against the law, but Jonah Barrington, a respected writer of the day, and a close friend of Martin in later life, suggested that approximately 300 duels of note took place in Ireland during the last third of the 18th century. Barrington discounted drunken posturing between rakes, choosing to focus on encounters based on real grievances, in which combatants genuinely intended to kill each other.

The general opinion is that Martin fought some twenty serious duels, starting in his youth and ending in tragedy in his thirties. Certainly the contest with 'Fighting' Fitzgerald has become the most widely known encounter. His father had taught Dick how to handle the short swords that were the traditional and favoured weapon in Galway but, by the time he went to Harrow, Dick was also a keen shot with a pistol. His reputation began while he was at Cambridge, and he increased his standing many times during his Grand Tour. Living now in Galway, the epicentre of duelling, gave him ample opportunity to enhance his status on the famous Field of Mars (now Merlin Park).

A legend is still told in Connemara that Martin, riding one day many miles into the bog-lands west of Dangan, saw the ghost of Nimble Dick appear out of the mist to hand him a duelling pistol. When Martin first had cause to use the gun, as he raised his arm to fire he could see a fine hair in his line of vision guiding his aim. On one occasion Dick saw that his opponent had the matching pistol and when both men fired the lead shot collided in mid-air. Whether it was this story that gave rise to his sobriquet, or the more obvious reason that a delicate finger was required to use the mechanism of a duelling pistol accurately, by now he had acquired the nickname 'Hair-trigger Dick'.

Martin did not emerge unscathed from such encounters. In later years, when preparing for combat, he employed a ritual to unnerve his opponents: unbuttoning his shirt to reveal a large scar, the mark of a previous meeting, he would point to the wound, look his opponent in the eye and say in his deepest Irish brogue, 'Your target, Sir!' He found that his reputation never left him, and was a distinct advantage throughout his political life. 'Hair-trigger Dick, the legendary duellist from Galway' was a far more impressive calling card in Dublin political circles than 'the young member for Jamestown'.

By the summer of 1776 Dick had more on his mind that duelling and politics. He had fallen in love. The object of his desire was the beautiful Elizabeth Vesey. He was besotted with her, and she was to break his heart.

Robert Martin had established a connection with the family when he had married a Vesey following the death of Dick's mother. Elizabeth Vesey was the niece of Dick's stepmother. The Veseys were not a tribe of Galway, coming from neighbouring County Mayo, but Elizabeth's father was heir to Lucan House, one of the most impressive mansions in Dublin. The family can be traced back to the Archbishop of Tuam and Elizabeth was raised on the renowned clergyman's estate, Holymount. By marrying into it, Dick also became related to the two great Irish banking dynasties, La Touche and Dawson. These connections would provide him with a financial lifeline in years to come.

Besides being beautiful, Elizabeth was intelligent, well educated, witty and had a passion for the arts. She was already an accomplished writer and painter. Elizabeth saw the dashing young Richard Martin, with his reputation as a crack shot, and his worldly experience, as an equal. Both families considered the marriage more than acceptable, and Robert negotiated a dowry of £5000. Dick would be provided with an annual income of £1500 and Elizabeth an income of £600 in the event of Dick's death. A lump sum of £600 would be paid to any child that outlived the couple. The marriage took place on 1st February 1777, a few days before Dick's twenty-third birthday, on the Vesey's estate, and was attended by the social élite of Connaught. The couple moved into Dangan, but had plans to find a home of their own.

Dick was disinterested in the financial side of the marriage. He already displayed a complete distain for money matters, an attitude which, along with a cavalier handling of his finances, would stay with him throughout his life. Vast sums were to pass through his hands but, with little actual business acumen, a tendency to give money away, and a ferocious ability to spend it, he would live most of his life in colourful insolvency.

While Dick awaited an opportunity to re-start his ambitious political career, local trouble was brewing for the Martins. A new family had emerged to take power in Galway Town. The Dalys were not one of the original fourteen families but had quietly been establishing power within the Corporation. Dennis Daly was now a Member of Parliament and the Mayor of Galway. He had a virtual stranglehold on the system, with all key appointments given to friends or family. Robert Martin had been voicing concerns about the monopoly for quite a while and the resulting feud between the Martin and the Daly families continued for another fifty years.

Martin and his bride were invited that summer to attend the summer assizes at Clonmel, about 100 miles to the south-east. The assizes in any large Irish town were a major social occasion, when the travelling judiciary along with their wives and entourage would descend to administer justice to wrong-doers whose crimes were too heinous for local magistrates to deal with. Alongside the hangings and floggings, a round of banquets and balls would occupy the social élite of the town.

The assizes at Clonmel had an added agenda. Duelling had become so rife and anarchic that the authorities could not continue to turn a blind eye to the resulting casualties. Some formal structure must be put in place. Martin, by now recognised as the leading exponent of the art in Ireland, was invited to attend a meeting of legal minds to draw up a set of rules governing conduct in duels. All gentlemen must adhere to the resulting 'Thirty-Six Commandments' if they wanted to avoid arrest for murder.

By now Parliament had been given a date for recall. Lord Lieutenant Harcourt, who had so frustrated Martin the previous year, had died. Considering Dick's later championing of animals, he had died an ironic death, trying to rescue his favourite dog, which had fallen down a well. His replacement, the Earl of Buckingham, was loosely related to Elizabeth: his brother-in-law was married to her first cousin.

Assured by Ponsonby and Grattan that there would be no further false starts, the young couple, both natural socialites, prepared to move to Dublin for the duration of Parliament. They took a house in fashionable Kildare Street, opposite the lavish mansion built 30 years beforehand by the Duke of Leinster. Leinster House serves today as the seat of the Irish Government.

Dublin had continued to develop since the time when Dick had stayed there for extended visits with his parents. The population of the city had now reached 150,000, making it second only to London within the British Isles. The town planners in the second half of the 18th century were visionary designers. In 1757 the Wide Streets Commission became responsible for completing the enclosure of the city with the North and South Circular roads, and the modern layout of the quays. Sackville Street Mall, 900 yards long, 150 broad, and lined with elm trees, stretched north to the famous Rotunda. A new and wider road joined Essex Bridge to the Parliament building. The commissioners were ruthless in the delivery of their grand plans. Residents in old property who would not move had their roofs ripped off.

Wealthy peers built grand urban mansions such as Belevedere House, Moira House, Clonmel House and Aldborough House. The homes of the wealthy were adorned with furniture from England, where Wyatt and Adam were the fashion. With ample demand, luxury manufacturing industries flourished. Huguenot craftsmen

*Leinster House, engraving by James Malton*

*The Rotunda and New Rooms, engraving by James Malton*

produced fine silverware, Wedgwood opened showrooms on College Green and Dublin became famous for the production of highly decorative coaches.

The Martins flung themselves into extravagant upper-class life. Dick's childhood experiences and upbringing held him in good stead and with Elizabeth equally skilled in social graces the Martins fitted into the élite Dublin circles with ease, attending a never-ending string of functions. The pivot of every social circle was the Viceroy and, through their connection with Buckingham, the Martins were amongst the guests at the many levées and balls held at Dublin Castle. The diarist Mary Herbert wrote, 'Nothing can be so gay as Dublin is . . . the Castle twice a week, the opera twice a week, with plays, assemblies and suppers to fill up the time.'

Masked balls were the most popular activity. Guests would visit various noble homes to have their costumes admired en route to the ball proper, revisiting the open houses until dawn broke. As many as 2000 people attended functions at the Rotunda and marvelled at the spectacular firework display that concluded each festivity. The climax of the season was the grand Ridotto Ball, held in the music hall in Fishamble Street, where guests could inspect the elaborate murals of waterfalls, hills and painted villages. Five hundred guests would dine on 'every style of cooking, from that of the plain viands of our ancestors to the appetite-provoking culinary arts of France.'

If respite from the demands of urban life was needed, wealthy Dubliners took themselves south along the coast to Blackrock, where a bathing house had been built, and on pleasant evenings carriages would gather to observe the fine views back to the city. Many aristocrats, such as Lady Arabella Denny and Lord Clonmel, had magnificent second homes along the coast. To the north, Drumcondra boasted exclusive teahouses and public gardens. Further afield lay the Wicklow Mountains where the Martins enjoyed weekends with Elizabeth's relatives, the fabulously wealthy La Touche family.

Fashion had become loud and gaudy, and two of the leading dandies were Dick's first cousins, the Lords Trimlestown and Gormanston, who had moved to Dublin to partake in the prevailing extravagance. Trimlestown was noted for his scarlet and black hunting caps, Gormanston for a light blue silk suit. Gentlemen wore knee breeches and three-quarter coats, liberally festooned with lace. Tightly corseted ladies preferred cloaks of gold and silver, embellished with elaborate feathered hats.

While no doubt enjoying the social side of Dublin with his young wife, Dick had a serious political agenda and eagerly took his place at the lavish State Opening of Parliament on 14th October 1777, when the Lord Lieutenant, in ceremonial dress, delivered the opening speech.

Buckingham had sensed the depth of the Grattan-led support for American independence and knew there would be considerable resistance to sanctioning the dispatch of 4000 Irishmen to join the British campaign against the rebels. He omitted any mention of the crisis in America from his speech, which delivered from the throne was deemed to be the King's words. Grattan in his response welcomed the Lord Lieutenant's diplomacy, stating that he 'approved of the silence from the throne from a delicacy to the feelings and circumstances of individuals'. He would much have preferred to have been given the opportunity of attacking a contentious speech with his already prepared response, supporting the American cause and likening the position of the colonists to that of the Irish. The Lord Lieutenant was not reflecting the stance of George and his sycophantic cabinet, who were now totally committed to retaining America by force and had enjoyed initial but short-lived success against the Patriots.

Immediately following the Declaration of Independence, Washington moved his army towards New York, and took up positions on Long Island and Brooklyn Heights. By now General Howe's troops had been reinforced from Britain and he assembled 25,000 men, the biggest army ever seen in North America, on nearby Staten Island. Howe attacked the Patriot position on Long Island with his naval force but the winds were against them and the British withdrew. Washington, realising his vulnerability, retreated into New York city and from thence into the Hudson Valley to regroup and if necessary fight a guerilla war.

Howe now made a number of errors. He decided against pursuing Washington, preferring to march towards the constitutional heart of the Patriot cause in Philadelphia. Looking to secure the state of New Jersey as he progressed, he dispatched troops in a haphazard fashion to remote townships. Washington knew that if Philadelphia were taken while Patriot confidence was at such low ebb, the war would be lost. Without the strength to attack the advancing British front he chose instead to retake the occupied village of Trenton, taking the small British garrison by surprise. With an astute understanding of the importance of propaganda he hastened to Philadelphia ahead of Howe and paraded the captured British soldiers. The effect of this stunt was out of all proportion to its military importance, restoring confidence and boosting morale within the Patriot hierarchy.

On hearing the news of Trenton, Howe dispatched Lord Cornwallis to avenge the defeat, but Washington foiled the attack, gaining a famous victory at Princeton. The British lines to their front were now not secure and, with the onset of winter, Howe stopped his advance short of the colonial stronghold. While the British officers spent a pleasant social season in New York, the Patriots dispatched Benjamin Franklin across the Atlantic to seek French support for their cause.

Reports of Howe's failure to capture Philadelphia enraged King George. North and his Government were coming under increased pressure from dissenting voices within Parliament and the press. Charles James Fox, a friend of Grattan and a man who would succeed to the highest office and be a thorn in the King's side for many years by supporting catholic emancipation, now led the Opposition.

The American campaign was proving a financial millstone around Britain's neck. There was little room to squeeze more tax out of businessmen, who were already siding morally with the colonists' fight for independence. A letter addressed to North appeared in the influential *Gentlemen's Magazine,* attacking him for not listening to the Americans who, 'before they took up arms in defence of their liberties had presented the most humble petition that injured parties could present.' It went on to accuse the Prime Minister that his 'impolitic Junto are sacrificing the flower of our troops and exhausting the wealth of the nation to remedy their own misconduct.'

George and his luckless Prime Minister needed to appease the powerful lobby within British trade and manufacture, which was effectively footing the military bill to regain the colonies. Ireland, as ever, was an easy target. Laws were passed to ban the Irish export of cattle, grain woollen and glass products. Everything else exported to England bore a heavy import tax although English exports to Ireland were tax-free, so that a flood of English products surged into Ireland.

The pressure from Fox made the King more stubborn to crush the American rebels. He banished all moderate counsel from his advisers. Angry at what he saw as Howe's incompetence, George took the fateful decision to play a hands-on role in the military campaign. When the spring of 1777 arrived, Burgoyne, the commander of British troops in Canada, was ordered to move down the Hudson Valley towards New York where, in theory, he would join forces with Howe and isolate the New England states. Howe, meanwhile, was ordered to march in the opposite direction to take Philadelphia. Washington knew that he was powerless to stop Howe taking the city, and turned his army to head off Burgoyne in the north.

Howe was now aware of the ill-considered advance of his subordinate from Canada, and after securing Philadelphia set off to provide reinforcements. Terrain and weather conspired against both his progress and his ability to communicate with Burgoyne, who had reached as far south as Saratoga, fully expecting Howe to be there to meet him. As the autumn rains began to fall, Washington spotted his chance and, with the benefit of troops who knew how to operate in dense woodland, inflicted overwhelming casualties on Burgoyne's demoralised army. The Patriots had won the first major battle of the war.

Washington accepted Burgoyne's surrender on 17th October 1777, three days after the state opening of Parliament in Ireland. When news of the American victory arrived in Dublin the winter season was in full swing. Amid the whirl of masquerade balls, everyone speculated on how Grattan would use British embarrassment as a platform to push for Irish independence.

# Chapter 9

# A Small Step

After its false start, 'Grattan's Parliament' got down to business in the winter of 1777. Grattan's followers were sometimes known as the 'Patriot party'. As their name suggests, they openly sympathised with American independence, but they also embraced liberal tendencies similar to those of the Whigs, currently in opposition at Westminster. Grattan had been instrumental in encouraging Martin to enter politics when he did, and Dick broadly subscribed to his policies, but he chose to retain his personal independence and remain outside the group. This was typical of the maverick position he was to adopt throughout his long parliamentary career, as he sided with individual causes rather than parties.

His ambition being the achievement of catholic emancipation, he saw an independent Ireland as the catalyst for this. Yet the months before the commencement of Parliament, spent mixing socially with other politicians, had alerted him to the level of corruption throughout the administration. It gave him an immediate crusade to fight for. Martin, who had a disdain for all things financial, was offended by prevailing practices such as lucrative positions secured by bribery and favour, and public funds openly diverted to private individuals.

He chose corruption in general, and the Collector of Customs in Cork specifically, as the targets of his maiden speech. His belligerent reputation attracted more attention, as he rose to his feet, than was normally reserved for debutants to the parliamentary floor, and his attack on the holder of the Cork sinecure, who had adhered 'steady to the banners of corruption' was an unusual and provocative subject. Eyes focussed firmly on the new Member, as he went on to condemn other colleagues and even likened George III to the beneficiary of an insurance fraud!

'The King, unfortunately for this country, is not very much interested in the embezzlement of the public revenue. His situation resembles that of a man whose goods and chattels are insured for more than they are worth. If the servants commit depredation, or his house is set on fire, he recovers more than he could have lost, a system which for some time past has rendered it unnecessary that he should be provident of the Public Revenue. The supply has always been made up two-fold to him. If he has been so corrupt as to bribe the majority in Parliament . . .'

The Speaker, who had listened to Martin's audacity in amazement up to that point, called the young Member for Jamestown to order, but the mark had been made. Martin would attempt frequently to address this hitherto taboo subject, but his opening speech had already made a number of powerful enemies with long memories.

Though astonished by this attack on their dubious practices, the Irish Parliament's attention was soon diverted to the reaction of the King and his lame-duck prime minister to the British defeat at Saratoga.

Lord North's immediate response was to try and resign. He wrote to George pointing out his 'Majesty's service requires a man of great abilities, who can choose decisively, and carry his determination authoritatively into execution . . . I am certainly not that man.'

George had no intention of replacing North, especially as the only credible candidate was the opposition leader Charles Fox, who had viciously attacked him in the debate immediately after Saratoga. The King, however, had accepted the seriousness of the military setback and realised France was not going to miss such an opportunity to kick Britain when she was down. He still arrogantly clung to the belief that 'a majority of Americans still wished to be his subjects, that the rebels must sooner or later sue for peace, and he would then be able to show that the parent's heart (was) still affectionate to the penitent child.'

Plenipotentiaries were dispatched to America to negotiate. Britain was prepared to recognise Congress, suspend all objectionable Acts of Parliament, give up all rights to tax the colonies and to consider admitting American representatives to the House of Commons. America was offered virtual internal home rule. The condition was that the Declaration of Independence be withdrawn. No doubt if Britain had taken this conciliatory stance a year earlier, most colonists would have considered it a victory for their cause, but Washington's success, coupled with Franklin's news from Paris, had injected fresh confidence into Congress and the British diplomats returned to London empty handed.

Two months after Saratoga, Louis XVI had entertained an ambitious plan that involved France's catholic ally Spain invading Ireland, while the French simultaneously mounted a full-scale invasion of Britain, thus taking full advantage of a British army depleted by deployment in America. Louis considered the scheme too risky and instead publicly declared that France recognised the independence of America, signing a treaty of alliance with Congress. The British ambassador was expelled from Paris and France formally declared war on Britain.

King George had to make a choice about America. He could accede to her position and accept her independence, withdrawing troops to repel any attack from France against Britain's mainland or her territories, or he could fight on. He took the latter course, replacing General Howe with Sir Henry Clinton, who was instructed to stop treating the rebels as subjects who could be regained after hostilities had ceased; instead they were enemies to be fought with ruthless intolerance. The War of Independence was entering its last phase.

When George became aware of the aborted Franco-Spanish plan to invade Ireland he at last realised how vulnerable Britain was with her catholic-populated back door. He put aside the commitment of his coronation oath and looked for the smallest concessions necessary to retain Irish loyalty. He addressed two issues: firstly, the repression of civil rights was doing little to engender support for the crown from Catholics; secondly, both catholic and protestant Irish traders harboured grievances over the strong protection their British competitors had been afforded.

The attempt to redress economic sanctions was a total disaster that fell between two stools. It failed to appease the Irish, and it sparked riots in England. The Irish were to be allowed to export certain goods to the colonies, but exclusions remained on wool, cotton garments, all hats, glass, hops, gunpowder and coal. Export duties remained on goods bound for Britain and restrictions continued to be applied to imports from America. Not surprisingly, the Irish reaction was apathetic and Lord Lieutenant Buckingham, with heavy understatement, reported that the measures were 'scarcely received with gratitude'.

Reaction in the English manufacturing heartland was less restrained. Riots broke out in Manchester and Leeds, and fearing that they would spread to London the British Government repealed the trade relief measures. Apathy in Ireland now turned to growing resentment.

Balancing concessions to Catholics was even more difficult for the King and his government. Britain was not only vulnerable to catholic support for France in Ireland: Scotland too had a large catholic population; and so in May 1778 a Catholic Relief Bill was proposed in Westminster, aimed at encouraging papist Scotsmen to enlist in the Army. Political resistance was minimal, since the Whigs were traditionally for religious toleration and the Bill, with opposition support, became law within weeks. The message was clear: the British Parliament was receptive to the measures: it was King George who was the stumbling block.

The Bill had been very moderate in its concessions, and nobody within government was expecting the reaction that followed, from protestant extremists in England. Since the days of the Stuarts many Protestants had lived in fear of a bloody papist conspiracy to overthrow the Crown and now, with the very real danger of invasion by a catholic country, rumourmongers moved into top gear. It was reported that 20,000 Jesuits were hidden in a network of underground tunnels beneath the Thames and were awaiting orders from Rome to flood London. Another story emerged that a group of papists had poisoned all the flour in the city, so that for weeks all bread had to be tasted first by dogs.

The most vocal scaremonger was Lord George Gordon, the President of the London Protestant Association, who organised 50,000 supporters to march on Westminster. Widespread rioting followed. Troops were used against the rioters and over 800 were killed.

Against this backdrop, the government tasked its counterparts in Dublin to draw up an Irish version of the Act. The main agenda was always to give away as little as possible to keep Catholics loyal to the crown. The secondary agenda was to protect the Protestant landowners who of course, under the current voting system, controlled Parliament by virtue of controlling the majority of individual members.


The Irish spring session of 1778 was wholly taken up with the Catholic Relief Act. Debate was vigorous and Martin involved himself fully. He was already developing the style of parliamentary speaking he would retain all his life. While the period is known for the lengthy oratory of the likes of Grattan and Burke, Martin limited himself to brief but cutting comment. He was a master of the short, pithy statement, heavy on irony and usually using a throwaway line delivered in a heavy Irish brogue, that would have been just as effective in modern-day televised exchanges as in the fora of the day. Usually successful in making his point, the sarcasm was occasionally misunderstood and Martin's regular use of humour prevented some commentators from taking him too seriously. Throughout his life, Dick would use humour to disarm people.

The argument in the House concerned where to draw the line of concession. Martin took a simple and extreme stance: there should be no line, and emancipation should be total and immediate. Whether he was being naive about the dynamics involved, or clever in arguing for an extreme knowing that the middle ground would then appear more harmless, is uncertain.

By the end of May, Parliament had decided. Catholics would still be debarred from owning land but could take out leases of up to 999 years, provided they swore an oath of allegiance. Gavelkind law was repealed, meaning that inheritance within families was now the same for both Catholics and Protestants. Martin, though complaining that these measures had not gone anything like as far as he wished, voted for the Act. Catholics in general welcomed the reforms and many made public shows of their abiding loyalty to the Crown.

By now General Clinton had taken command of British forces in America. His strategy was to turn the Colonists against themselves. To do this he needed to move his campaign to the southern states, where the majority of loyalists were, and in April 1778 a large contingent of British troops left New York for the southern port of

*The Irish House of Commons in 1780, from the painting by Francis Wheatley.*
*Henry Grattan (standing, right) urges the claim of right for the first time.*
*Richard Martin is third from the left in the back left-hand row.*

Savannah, 50 days' march away. In the mean time twelve French ships had set sail from Toulon across the Atlantic, to take New York.

Losing New York would have been disastrous for the British and, when Clinton heard news of the French naval plans, he turned his men around and headed desperately back across New Jersey, suffering many casualties on the way as they encountered Washington's buoyant army. Clinton arrived in New York on June 18th, the very day the first French ships appeared off the American coast.

Admiral Howe, the brother of the superseded British commander, who had replaced the playboy Lord Sandwich in charge of the fleet, engaged the French outside New York harbour. After a two-week naval battle, the French were forced to accept defeat and made sail toward British interests in the West Indies.

Henry Grattan and his supporters, including those on the fringe such as Martin, took stock of their achievements at the end of the first parliamentary session. The Irish had implemented the Catholic Relief Act without any of the problems that Westminster had encountered. The Irish House of Commons had a sense of identity not experienced for a long time, King George and his government were increasingly vulnerable, and independence for Ireland was becoming more than a mere dream.

On balance, Martin thought the last nine months had seen some progress, although given his disposition to seek immediate solutions it was woefully short of what he was committed to achieve. He found the parliamentary system slow and cumbersome but was beginning to understand the more subtle workings of politics. At this stage he was not aware of the enemies he had made, nor how long their grievances would last.

Dick and Elizabeth, who had entered so fully into social activity in Dublin, returned to Dangan with more than just weary constitutions as a result of the winter months. Elizabeth was pregnant. But the first of many family tragedies was about to strike the couple: their first child was stillborn.

# Chapter 10

# Under Pressure

Elizabeth recovered at Dangan during the summer of 1778. Sadly the loss that the Martins had experienced would not be their last. Five more children would be stillborn or die in the very early stages of infancy. Elizabeth also had at least one miscarriage.

Possibly due to the focus on family that Elizabeth's pregnancy had given him, or because of the fact that Robert was now in his mid-sixties, Dick spent much of the summer with his two young stepbrothers, Robert and Anthony. Just as his father had taught him, Dick now showed the boys how to handle swords and pistols, the young brothers no doubt in awe of having the most famous duellist in the country as their tutor.

Dick also spent long periods talking with his father about his experience in Parliament. They agreed that, though independence was increasingly likely, there was a very real possibility of a French or Spanish invasion. This might give Ireland catholic masters, but at what price? Ireland would be the theatre of a bloody war. The Martins may have been reluctant Protestants, fighting for catholic rights, but they were also Irishmen. Father and son debated for weeks whether their preference was for protestant-controlled independence or catholic rule by a foreign power.

At the beginning of autumn Dick and Elizabeth, now rested and becoming bored with the tranquility of Connemara, left Dangan to attend the winter 'season' in Dublin. Elizabeth had a passion for the theatre, and the many new plays that were due in the capital that winter beckoned her. Dick was anxious to pick up where he had left off in Parliament six months before.

The effects of the trade barriers imposed from London, and the bitterness at their partial removal and quick reinstatement, had combined to unite the Irish people in resentment. Many saw the rebellion in America, which had been attributed to over-zealous taxation, as an enactment of their struggle. The sheriffs and commoners of Dublin, followed by Liberal clubs and radical Whig societies in other cities such as Belfast, voted for addresses of congratulation to the American rebels. There was a revival of interest in the satirical works of Swift and Molyneux. Clergymen began preaching sermons seasoned with warnings against fighting the American 'brothers'.

The embargo on the export of Irish foodstuffs was justified by Britain as a disincentive to war profiteering. The people of Ireland maintained that it only served to keep their country in a constant state of depression. Martin threw himself vigorously into the debates that raged on the issue. Eventually the pressure led to Lord North setting up a joint committee of members from Westminster and Dublin, to look at how interests of both English and Irish trade could be accommodated.

The Irish Parliament, as merely an extension of Westminster, was expected to deliver the policies laid down in London. However Grattan and his supporters, with their assiduous arguing of the American cause, were beginning to achieve resuls, and the issues of troop supplying and financial support for the war were not having an easy passage. The 'Patriot' party, totally supported in this session by Martin, scored a significant success when Parliament tried to oppose their plan to replace the 4000 Irish soldiers sent to America with German mercenaries. To Grattan and his followers this was a major indication that the Irish system had begun to grow teeth.

The problem remained of how defenceless Ireland had become, and how susceptible to invasion. To the protestant Irish Parliament, invasion and rule by a foreign power was as abhorrent as it would be to any Englishman. Forty thousand British soldiers were now engaged in America and it was estimated that Ireland was defended by a third of the troops necessary to repel an enemy.

The Irish landowners put forward a solution. Owners of the larger estates should recruit small armies from their tenants and arm and equip them out of their own pockets. There was to be no overall command unless war or invasion necessitated it. Parliament would have no costs to meet but neither would it have any control. Both Buckingham and the British government were extremely apprehensive about the plan, but the only alterative was to leave Ireland insufficiently defended. The decision to allow the volunteers to form up was justified on the grounds that it was a protestant force, and infinitively preferable to foreign occupation.

The network of Volunteer Corps grew at a phenomenal rate. By the beginning of 1779 thousands of men had been recruited across the country, and huge pride in the movement was established. Each corps had its own colours; scarlet, green, blue or orange tunics were elaborately adorned by silver and gold lace. The gentry took advantage of the military experience many of their tenants had gained in the Seven Years War, and well structured chains of command and training were put in place.

Each body of men had an emblem and motto but the Volunteer Corps as a whole shared the emblem of a crowned harp, symbolizing a motto to rally the entire country: 'Loyalty and independence'. At face value an oxymoron, this summed up everything the Volunteer Corps purported to stand for: loyalty to the British Crown but with a desire to be independent of its governing.

Individual corps democratically elected their officers, and the Galway Independent Volunteers looked no further that the dashing Richard Martin, with his celebrated reputation for fearlessness, to be its Colonel. The corps was embodied, with Martin as its leader, at a packed assembly in Galway on 31st May 1779. It was nothing like the Home Guard that stood waiting for an invasion of Britain during World War II. From inception the movement was intended to be a political force in which each corps made its own constitution and resolutions.

*A Volunteer*

Martin, his reputation now augmented with experience of politics and public speaking, addressed his troops. He proposed that the first resolution of the Galway Volunteers be that Poyning's Law be totally abolished and the Irish Parliament liberated from British government. It was passed noisily and unanimously. Martin went on to propose a more immediate and practical measure: all members of the Corps to buy only Irish manufactured products, and a list to be published of people not supporting this policy. This patriotic stance quickly spread across the region.

The fledgling Galway Volunteers took up most of Martin's time and energies during the summer of 1779. A structure of command was established and the men were armed and trained. With the Martins' reputation as lavish socialites, the corps quickly became the pivot of social life in the city.

When Dick and Elizabeth returned to their second home in Dublin, ready for the start of Parliament and the winter season, the Volunteer movement had grown to over 50,000 men and had galvanized patriotism throughout the country. The question was, patriotic to what? Grattan and his growing number of supporters clearly wanted to be free from the constraints of British government, but the issue was, whether or not Ireland should follow the republican model Americans were fighting for? Grattan put forward the more moderate case that Ireland should seek political independence but remain loyal to the British crown. The rationale was that this would be achievable, whereas Britain, regardless of the outcome of the American war, would never countenance a country on the doorstep that they had no control or influence over. Grattan made a number of powerful speeches during the 1779/80 session, but the government, retaining power in the House by the use of patronage, always succeeded in repulsing his attacks.

France had decided that invasion could only be accomplished if the people of Ireland, and more importantly the armed Volunteer army, supported it. Now firmly in league with the Americans, France sent Edward Bancroft, a wealthy merchant and friend of Benjamin Franklin, to Ireland to gauge the feeling of the country. He returned with disappointing news. Irish Catholics had been pacified with recent concessions and the Volunteers appeared loyal to the British Crown.

Resistance to Grattan's 'Patriot' party was becoming more vitriolic. Understandably the protestant landowners who had been rewarded with wealth and power within the current system were not going readily to embrace any kind of change. They rallied behind John Fitzgibbon, later to be rewarded for his stance by being made Earl of Clare. Fitzgibbon's argument was brutally honest: as he succinctly put it in a parliamentary speech, 'The act by which most of us hold our estates was an act of violence . . . an act subverting the first principles of the common law in England and Ireland.' In other words Fitzgibbon was openly admitting that many Protestants had gained their land by force, and force would be necessary to maintain their control. Independent of Britain, Irish Protestants would not have sufficient resources to keep the catholic majority at bay. Fitzgibbon accused Grattan of posturing in the fashion of a colonial nationalist, playing a very dangerous game of mirroring American patriots, but, as he and a number of loyalists kept pointing out, Ireland was not America.

Grattan, who was not a significant landowner himself, had reassured people like Martin that his vision of an independent Ireland included admitting Catholics to the political system. The immediate priority, however, was to demonstrate that Ireland would not put up with the economic recession she was currently forced to endure.

The British government by now realised that they had let a genie out of its bottle in the guise of the Volunteer movement, who were now using the prevailing trade measures as their rallying cause. A force of 50,000 armed men, albeit proclaiming loyalty to the Crown, could not be ignored. Lord Lieutenant Buckingham was spending most of his time sending London dire prophecies that chaos would ensue unless economic concessions were made.

In October 1779 the Speaker of the House, flanked by rows of Volunteers presenting arms to add dramatic effect, proceeded to hand a resolution to the Lord Lieutenant. It read: 'That it is not by temporary expedients but by free trade alone that this nation is now to be saved from impending ruin.'

A month later, on 4th November, when tradition dictated that William of Orange's birthday was celebrated in Dublin with great pomp, the Volunteers made another dramatic gesture. Thousands of them congregated around the statue of William in front of Parliament House and placed on a cannon a placard that read 'Free Trade or . . .' A printed pamphlet was distributed around the city reading, 'No illuminations, no rejoicings, until the English Parliament shall do away all its acts that in any manner affect this country, and our constitution is made free.'

Three weeks later Parliament turned up the pressure by delaying the handing over of tax revenues. The Prime Sergeant, Hussey Burgh, made an impassioned speech explaining the action. Beating his chest as he spoke, he claimed that Britain had placed Ireland in a state of 'Egyptian bondage'. He stated, 'The words penalty, punishment and Ireland are synonymous. The English have sowed their laws like serpents' teeth.' Although Burgh was immediately sacked, North and his government caved in. Laws were rushed through Westminster ending the crippling embargos. Ireland would be allowed to export wool, woollen cloth and manufactured glass and to trade freely with the colonies.

It was a tremendous victory for Grattan, the Irish Parliament and the Volunteer movement. Grattan seized the opportunity to strike again. On 19th April 1780 he placed a Declaration of Independence before the House. The document asserted that the Crown of Ireland would always be annexed to that of Britain. There were two nations 'united by one Sovereign and indissolubly connected by ties of interest, loyalty and freedom but that no law on earth except the King, Lords and Commons of Ireland was competent to make laws for Ireland.' Grattan knew that his declaration would go no further within Parliament but he had made a clear statement of intent and within weeks the country was uniting under it.

The reason that the 'Patriot' party's efforts would at best gain approval in the Irish Parliament only to be halted at the next stage of the legislative process, was the archaic Poyning's Law, that had for nearly 300 years allowed Irish law to be controlled by the British Parliament, the Privy Council and ultimately the King. Barry Yelverton, a close colleague of Grattan and a friend of Martin, followed up the Declaration of Independence with a Bill to modify the power of veto held by Westminster

Martin fully immersed himself in the ensuing debate. He had by now developed a method of pre-empting an opponent's argument. In supporting the proposition that

Ireland needed to control its own legislation he stated that this was 'a truth so self-evident as to need no demonstration'. Before an opponent could argue the contrary he commented wryly, 'Indeed self-evident truths may serve to demonstrate, while they are themselves hardly demonstrable.'

One faction in Parliament felt that the whole debate was pointless, as Britain was on the verge of repealing Poyning's Law in any event. Martin was somewhat sarcastic in his response, saying, ' Can the requisition of the Commons be an injury and prevent the sisterly affection of Britain on our behalf?'

While supporting the argument put forward by Grattan and others that the British parliament had no intention of allowing Dublin to control itself, Martin stated pointedly that it would 'be prudent to go into the framing of this Act, [as]certain as we are of a refusal on the other side of the water, that our legislation complies with the wishes of the constituents.' He added, 'Let the English administration have the censure of refusal.' There was no surprise when Yelverton's bill was defeated but the closeness of the vote, 105 for and 130 against, caused a shock wave. This was another victory for Grattan's strategy of fighting by attrition.

The 'Patriot' party and supporters such as Martin who were involved in the Volunteer movement had taken to wearing their military dress, including arms, in Parliament, much to the consternation of the Lord Lieutenant. Many corps of Volunteers issued their own formal statements commenting on events in the Dublin parliament. The Clanricarde Cavalry Corps, neighbours to Martin's Galway regiment, thanked him for his contribution to the independence debate. A motion, passed unanimously at a rally, thanked the Galway Colonel for his 'just and genuine approach', and his 'steady and uniform zeal for the liberties of this kingdom, both as a senator and a freeholder.'

The session came to a close in the spring of 1780 and the Martins returned to Galway for the summer. Dick was happy with the progress that had been made. Political pressure was mounting on Britain to make genuine concessions to allow Ireland more freedom and he was convinced that catholic emancipation would inevitably follow. The war in America had again turned against the British and now Ireland possessed a cohesive armed force, not subservient to British control, and committed to independence.

Martin used the summer months to strengthen his own Volunteer corps, and at a massed meeting a resolution was passed that reflected both the powerlessness felt by the Irish people and the increasing ability they had to redress it. The final clause stated that a 'whole people self-armed, self-paid' had the right of a 'free people to publicly declare their sentiments on measures by which they are affected.'

The Martins had suffered the further grief of Elizabeth losing another child, and stayed on in Dangan through the winter of 1780. Dick was becoming increasingly concerned for the health of his wife, and it appears that she had a miscarriage soon after. With his father now approaching seventy, matters on the estate also needed attending to. Prudent financial management, however, was not one of Martin's strengths. He and Elizabeth were living extravagantly even by the standards of the time. They maintained a large house in Dublin and Elizabeth always insisted on a high degree of luxury wherever she lived or travelled. Being a Volunteer colonel was a costly role in its own right. Whereas tenants could usually be squeezed when necessary, this was never an option pursued by the Martins.

Dick did not miss much political activity by staying in Galway when Parliament reconvened for the winter session of 1780-1. There was a feeling of being in limbo while events in America came to a head.

Following the holding of New York against the French fleet, Britain had enjoyed a period of success in the war. General Clinton again attacked the southern states and succeeded in capturing Charleston in May 1780. Washington suffered a terrible blow when his trusted commander Benedict Arnold, who now was in charge of the strategically important fort of West Point on the Hudson, sold out to the British. For a sum of £20,000 Arnold offered the positioning, strengths and tactical plans of the Patriot army. To the great good fortune of the Americans, Major John André, the British spy who had completed the deal, was caught returning to the British command with the incriminating documents and was later hanged. Arnold continued the war, now as a British general. Washington found it increasingly hard to finance his army, and civil war broke out between Americans loyal to the cause of independence and those, especially in the south, who supported the British. 'We are at the end of our tether,' Washington wrote in the spring of 1781.

Meanwhile, France had persuaded Spain to enter the war, further threatening Britain's naval routes to America. Both sides needed the war to climax. This was to happen at the port of Yorktown, on the edge of Chesapeake Bay. General Cornwallis, the second in command of the British troops, had led the campaign into Virginia, which he saw as the heart and centre of the Patriot cause. If this state could be taken, with dissent in the south and Britain holding the north, the rebels would be beaten.

Washington's army, now augmented by the French, successfully engaged Cornwallis's forward troops and the British were forced to retreat to Yorktown. When the French navy was sighted, Washington amazed his followers by abandoning his normal reserve, jumping up and down and waving his handkerchief and hat. Forty French ships blockaded Chesapeake Bay. Five thousand British soldiers were trapped by three times their number of Americans and French troops but for two months held out against incessant bombardment. By 17th October 1781 only one British cannon remained in operation and a white flag was raised.

General Cornwallis surrendered, and the surviving British troops marched out of the ruins led by a band and piper ironically playing the melancholy strains of a song entitled 'The World Turn'd Upside Down'. Britain had lost her American colonies.

# Chapter 11

## Misunderstood

'Oh God, it's all over!' was Lord North's immediate response to hearing the news of the British surrender at Yorktown. His Cabinet colleague George Germain compared him to a man who had received a musket ball to the breast.

For Britain this was humiliation on an unprecedented scale. Martin's fellow-student, William Pitt, now in Parliament and destined for political greatness, condemned the campaign as 'the most accursed, wicked, barbarous, cruel, unjust, and diabolical war'. 'The expense of it has been enormous,' Pitt went on, 'far beyond any former experience, and yet what has the British nation received in return? Nothing but a series of ineffective victories or severe defeats.'

A motion was quickly put before the Westminster parliament censuring the Navy, and the government majority immediately collapsed. On 22nd February 1782 an opposition proposal was put before the House to abandon the war. The government managed to survive by one vote.

Ironically, it was now that North at last found the strength to bring the reality of the political situation home to his King. 'The torrent is too strong to be resisted. Your Majesty is well apprized that, in his country, the Prince on the Throne cannot, with prudence, oppose the deliberate resolution of the House of Commons.' He told the King of his intention to resign and this time, despite George making all manner of threats, refused to back down. The King's final comment as his loyal minister left the room was: 'Remember, my Lord, that it is you that deserts me, not I you.'

Parliament was in disarray, with nobody within the opposition able to step cleanly into North's shoes. The King was adamant that his *bête noire*, Fox, should not be First Minister, and favoured the Earl of Shelbourne, not because he liked or trusted the man, but on the grounds that Shelbourne had opposed North's government in isolation, and so presented less of a threat to the King's perception that the Crown was still autonomous. Shelbourne, however, was not the first choice of the Commons and eventually a loose coalition, led by the Marquis of Rockingham, appeared. Within months Rockingham was dead, a victim of influenza. George took advantage of this further confusion to engineer that Shelbourne became Prime Minister.

The American War of Independence did not officially end until the Treaty of Paris was signed the following year. The new country quickly established it's own identity and John Adams, who would later succeed George Washington as the second President, arrived in London in 1785 as the first American ambassador. On meeting King George he showed the utmost respect. The King in turn was candid with him.

'I will be very free with you. I was the last to consent to the separation; but the separation having been made and having become inevitable, I have always said, as I say now, that I would be the first to meet the friendship of the United States as an independent power.'

He then gave a very rare demonstration of humour. Changing the subject he quizzed Adams that there was 'an opinion among some people that you are not the most attached of all your countrymen to the manners of France.' It was business as usual: America was lost but France was still the traditional enemy.

The real significance of the aftermath of defeat in America was twofold. Britain had been shown that it could lose territory, not to another power, but by the territory itself deciding to break free. Secondly, up to that point British monarchs had sometimes to accept unpalatable decisions of government but now the House of Commons had used voting power to force the resignation of a prime minister appointed by the crown, and appoint their own replacement. The Prime Minister had become the leader of the House as opposed to the political representative of the monarch.

The talk in Dublin, during the spring of 1782, amongst Grattan, Martin and the growing number supporting independence for Ireland, was of the implications of the British defeat. The King was vulnerable without his puppet prime minister and the new government was anxious to avoid the mistakes of their predecessors. The timing could not be more favourable to wring concessions, but on the other hand Britain was not going to lose another domain, especially the one guarding her back door.

The concessions in trade restrictions had come too late to avoid Ireland sinking further into poverty. Despite the enthusiasm that greeted the repeals, industry had not attracted any significant investment, hard cash was in short supply and absentee landlords continued to milk their estates without any thought for the future. The distinguished political writer Arthur Young had published his observations on the Irish people, who, he wrote, 'mostly lived on a diet of potatoes, milk and whiskey and rarely enjoyed the luxury of shoes.' Young's work did, however, finish on a positive note, concluding that Ireland, with its availability of cheap labour and abundance of water power, had considerable commercial potential.

Three years earlier, Edmund Sexton Parry, now Speaker of the Irish House of Commons, had warned prophetically that the trade sanctions would be a 'general cause of distress in the economy and the people'. He forecast, 'Cruel and short-sighted laws would ensure that Ireland continued in a state of poverty.' Parry now turned to the matter of Ireland's control by legislation that favoured Britain. He reasoned that the Irish currently considered themselves as separate from the inhabitants of Great Britain. Were the 'fatal obstacle' removed, he argued, the Irish would be 'united as much in affection'. He warned that if Ireland was left under the current regime, 'Seeds of discord had been sown, and if suffered to take root they would soon overspread the land.' In blunt terms, if Ireland were not freed from her shackles the people, led by the Volunteer forces, would attempt to win the same outcome as their American cousins.

Lord Carlisle, who had recently arrived in Dublin to replace Buckingham as Lord Lieutenant, quickly saw the writing on the wall. Although his instructions when taking the post of Viceroy had been to maintain the British position regarding independence, he was soon trying to get his masters to appreciate the danger, writing to London that a repeal of the Declaratory Act was rapidly 'becoming wise'.

On top of the Irish drive for independence, a wounded Britain could not ignore the risks of its nearest colony being 80% populated by a people living under Draconian repression. Henry Grattan neatly summed up the dilemma: 'A Protestant colony or an Irish nation?'

R ichard Martin, an eternal optimist, must have been particularly confident during the latter part of 1781 that his hopes of catholic emancipation were shortly to be fulfilled. However not all of his energy was directed at politics. Elizabeth had succeeded in totally converting her husband to the drama, and Dick had given his beloved wife her own theatre by turning part of their Dublin house in Kildare Street into a private venue where plays, in which the Martins participated, were regularly staged. Elizabeth had previous experience of acting, but for Dick this was a new challenge to which he rose with typical energy and enthusiasm, demonstrating a natural talent.

Their interest in the arts brought the Martins in touch with a young man who was destined to have a strong impact both on their marriage and on the history of Ireland. Theobald Wolfe Tone was born in Dublin in 1763, the son of a protestant coachmaker.

*One of the few remaining 18th-century houses in Kildare Street*

His father's business was a casualty of the trade laws and the family was forced to return to their farm at Bodenstown, County Clare. Tone's ambition was to become a soldier but his father insisted he obtain a college education and in 1781 Tone entered Trinity College. An articulate and outgoing young man, he quickly developed an interest in the theatre through which he became close friends with the Martins, regularly taking part in the small productions staged at Kildare Street.

The Martins returned to Connemara for the Christmas of 1781 and soon afterwards Dick's status was further enhanced when the Lord Lieutenant made him

High Sheriff of the County of Galway. There were few day-to-day duties but it was the highest legal office in the town and to obtain the appointment Dick had been obliged to be called to the Bar at Trinity College. (His career as a lawyer in Ireland would be limited to one remarkable trial.) The fact that the post had been conferred on Martin as a result of his political connections in Dublin irked some of the local establishment in Galway, especially the increasingly powerful Daly family, who began spreading word that Martin had accepted the King's shilling and turned his back on the town.

Dick and Elizabeth were back in Dublin by January 1782, when the catholic question was due to be debated. The arguments were simple. Catholics were forced to live under outdated repression. Even if Protestants considered this régime fair, they should realise the inherent danger of repressing such a large majority. Protestants in favour of retaining the status quo relied on two points. If Catholics were allowed to acquire land it would only be a matter of time before they converted that privilege to exercising political influence. Furthermore, a relaxation of laws designed to prevent civil uprising would inevitably result in a Jacobite-type rebellion. In any event, many of the members of the Irish Parliament would be in danger of losing the property that had been confiscated from Catholics under the Acts of Settlement.

Before the debate was concluded, the Volunteers, egged on by Grattan, were again flexing their muscles. On 15th February, 143 corps of Volunteers from the northern counties met for a massed rally at Dungannon in County Tyrone. The men, all fully armed, marched as well as any trained army to be addressed by Grattan, who had taken the resolution adopted by Martin's Galway Corps the previous year and proposed an amended version, resolving: 'That a claim of any body of men, other than the Kings, Lords and Commons of Ireland, to make laws to bind that kingdom is unconstitutional, illegal and a grievance.'

Then, in a gesture that appears inconceivable at the beginning of the 21st century, 25,000 Protestants in Ulster went on to approve a further resolution, again proposed by Grattan, that there be a relaxation in the laws governing their 'Catholic brethren'.

The rally sent shock waves through both the Dublin and London administrations. There were now 100,000 armed, well trained and highly organised men in Ireland demanding not only independence for their country but also equal rights for Catholics. Grattan quickly sought to exploit the situation in Parliament. Always an animated speaker, he was positively hyperactive as he strode up and down the floor of the House. He declared that America was on the verge of being freed to become a great nation, while Ireland was being kept as a 'secondary state, engaged in a lingering contest for freedom, with some inferior Minister calling her fractious, making her corrupt and spending the last farthing of the Treasury to stifle the voice of the nation.'

Grattan moved that Parliament address the King, along the lines of the Dungannon declaration, for the right to control their own legislation. The House responded by voting to postpone the question. A few days later Henry Flood proposed a similar motion: it was defeated. Grattan realised that it was pointless to keep hitting the same brick wall without further weight behind the attack. He suggested that members use the forthcoming regional assizes as an opportunity to gauge the opinions of their constituents, confident that the people would back his 'Patriot' party.

Martin rose to speak in support:

An honourable gentlemen has told you he thinks the Assizes may produce unanimity. I think nothing can be more effectually binding upon the constituents. Nothing could coerce me so strongly as those instructions. As he thinks it will be the sense of every country it will be better to postpone it. I do not favour this claim by giving a negative to the motion, nor do I pledge myself after the Assizes to supporting it.

It was hardly one of his clearest speeches, but he meant to say that if Parliament would not listen to its members then it must still listen to the people, and he would support what his constituents wanted, even if that meant voting against a bill he favoured. It was a convoluted way of saying he bowed to democracy, although he knew the people of Galway overwhelmingly backed the fight for independence.

The speech was not well received in his native Galway; especially by the Volunteer Corps. Almost unanimously they read it as a betrayal of the joint causes of independence and catholic emancipation. People in Galway did not trust the dealings of politicians in Dublin and the consensus of opinion was that Martin's new found loyalty to the British administration had been bought. His appointment as High Sheriff backed this slur, as the Daly family was quick to point out.

The Galway Volunteers, without referring to their Colonel, called an emergency meeting at the Tholsel, Galway on 17th March 1782, Saint Patrick's day. There was only one item of business: command of the Corps should be 'entrusted to none but men invariably attached to the rights of Ireland'. It was stated that Colonel Martin, by supporting the British administration 'had deviated from that line of conduct which induced us to give him command of this Corps.' The motion was carried. Martin had been disposed of and the Corps arranged to hold a further meeting on 31st March to elect his replacement. When news of his sacking reached Martin in Dublin, he was mortified. Angry that his men's loyalty was not strong enough to withstand a simple misunderstanding, he made plans to depart for Galway to put matters straight.

Two hundred Volunteers met a fortnight later, again at the Tholsel, to elect their new Colonel. To their surprise, Martin entered the room and demanded to be allowed to address the meeting. He first pointed to his impeccable and long record of supporting Ireland's claim for independence. He reminded his men that he had voted for Grattan's Declaration asserting in the House that, 'No law of any kind made in England could be in force in this country.' He went on to outline what his recent speech had advocated: taking notice of, and voting in line with his constituents whether he agreed or not, was what he had really meant. He pointed out that he had, only days before, as High Sheriff, called a meeting of the Grand Jury, gentlemen, clergy and freeholders of Galway County, to support the Dungannon resolutions, hardly the actions of a man who now supported British control. At the end of his impassioned speech Martin, still seething over the questioning of his motives and honour, left the room.

A revised motion was put to the assembled Volunteers. With only one Daly voice opposing, they voted to re-elect Martin as their Colonel.

# Chapter 12

## An Actor's Life

Although back at the head of the Galway Volunteers, Dick was still angry and saddened that people in his home town had seen fit to question his loyalty, and the accusations of having sold out to the Dublin establishment hurt him deeply. With the expectation of a general election later in the year, Dick thought it in his interests to stay in Galway and rebuild some bridges, even though the struggle to wring concessions from England was coming to a head in Parliament.

Furthermore, Elizabeth had suffered another miscarriage, having lost at least three children in, or soon after, childbirth. The Martins were desperate for children but the doctors now advised that the couple's lifestyle in Dublin was not conducive to bearing them. In 18th-century Ireland, childbearing carried inherent risks and Dick knew his wife had been lucky to survive her pregnancies. Elizabeth was persuaded to take up residence at Dangan, a prospect which, with her love of the arts and high society, did not much please her.

Martin's two stepbrothers had entered their teens and, now that Robert was an old man, required a full-time tutor. Martin decided to offer the post to Wolfe Tone. He and his wife had come to know and like the young man during the previous winter in Dublin and Tone, now twenty, had good cause to seek employment outside the capital: he had acted as second in a duel between two students at Trinity, in which a youth called Anderson had been killed. The college had expelled all those involved, but to Martin this incident held no stigma, and Tone was highly intelligent, well educated, and witty. Dick felt that he would provide not only excellent tutorage to his stepbrothers but also intellectual company for his wife during the long periods when he was absent. He gladly hired Tone as a private tutor and invited him to move into Dangan.

Satisfied that he had repaired his reputation in Galway and settled Elizabeth, albeit reluctantly on her part, into Dangan, Martin returned to Dublin for the final weeks of the parliamentary session, which seemed to promise that the work of the last seven years was about to come to fruition.

Over in London, Parliament was in the middle of a constitutional crisis. The buzzword throughout the British press and the coffee houses of London was 'reform'. Prime Minister Shelbourne, with no party backing nor any real support from the King, was hanging on to office by his fingernails. For the last two years of the American débacle, the influential and eloquent Irishman, Edmund Burke, who represented the constituency of Westminster, had been attacking the corrupt electoral system. Public and press laid the blame for losing, or even bothering to fight to keep America in the first place, at the door of Parliament, and Burke's views on its improvement were now being listened to. The Irishman pointed out that the House of Commons was hardly representative of the nation. The concept of democracy was the cornerstone of the new American constitution; Burke was touching raw nerves in both the British people and the growing number of reforming politicians.

William Pitt joined his cause. He had found his political feet. His father was now receiving posthumous recognition as a great prime minister, who would never have allowed the American fiasco to happen. Pitt backed Burke's attempts to change the electoral system and stamp out its inherent corruption.

By April 1783 Shelbourne could survive no longer and was replaced by William Cavendish-Bentinck, 3rd Duke of Portland, who only months before had taken over from Carlisle as Lord Lieutenant of Ireland. He returned to London with first-hand awareness of how powerful the Volunteer movement had become and how much grassroots support they enjoyed. After five administrations in two years, with the fall-out from the American war still ringing loud, and a buoyant France looking to kick her old enemy while she was on the floor, the last thing Britain wanted was an organised rebellion in Ireland. Envoys were dispatched from London to have private talks with Grattan, to see how much was being asked and establish how little need be given.

The two leaders of the 'Patriot' cause, however, were on the verge of a serious rift. Grattan believed that repeal of the hated Poyning's Law, and the removal of many of the repressive laws that Catholics had lived under for centuries, must be considered a victory. London had indicated to Grattan that all he was asking was deliverable. Flood on the other hand felt it was not enough. He had taken a keen interest in the reform debate raging in Westminster, and pointed out to Grattan and other 'Patriot' supporters including Martin, that even if Britain allowed the Dublin parliament to make its own laws, control could and would still be exercised through the corrupt system that prevailed in Ireland. He also felt strongly that nothing short of full catholic emancipation was acceptable.

By the time that Martin arrived back in Dublin, matters between Grattan and Flood had approached a bitter head. He had become increasingly closer to Flood over the last two years but still greatly respected Grattan. His initial reaction was to side with Grattan, supporting him in the House by describing one of his rousing speeches as 'a production of consummate wisdom and great deliberation'. He went as far as criticising Flood, saying that, 'The Honorable Gentleman is not the advocate of Ireland.'

Within weeks Martin had performed a complete u-turn, convinced that Flood's fears of backdoor control were totally valid and anything short of complete emancipation for Catholics was selling short, when compromise was not called for. This would not be the last time that he would move between completely opposed views. Unlike many politicians he did not consider this as a weakness, more a virtue to be able to see alternative positions. Critics would accuse him of being easily influenced and unreliable.

This time, knowing that Britain had already agreed in private to his position, Grattan rose to state,

'I have had to admire by what inexplicable means and steady virtue the people of Ireland have proceeded, till the whole faculty of the nation is now braced to the great act of her own redemption. I am not very old, yet I think I remember Ireland when she was a child. I have watched her growth with anxious wishes. I have beheld with astonishment the rapidity of her progress from industry to arms, from arms to liberty.'

The Declaratory Act was repealed and Poyning's Law, after 289 years, was modified, with the British parliament specifically renouncing its claim to legislate for Ireland. Gardiner's Bill was also passed, allowing Catholics to purchase land, and many of the minor but contentious laws, some dating back to Cromwell, were repealed. Catholics, however, were still barred from entering Parliament. It was far short of total emancipation.

Grattan responded by stating, 'We do assure his Majesty that no constitutional questions between the two nations will any longer exist which can interrupt their harmony.' Grattan felt a great victory had been achieved. He was wrong, and the next election proved him so. Ireland was legally an independent country, but the King was still represented by a Lord Lieutenant nominated by the British government, and the Viceroy selected and controlled the Irish executive, who in turn managed the patronage, the peers, sinecures and pensions that influenced the outlook and actual voting of many members. Britain still controlled the Irish parliament and Catholics had certainly not achieved equal civil rights.

Frustrated that a great opportunity had been wasted, Martin used the remaining months of the session to renew his crusade against corruption. His first target was John Fitzgibbon, the future Lord Clare, a man who made no attempt to hide his bigotry against Catholics. Two new lucrative posts, the Attorney and Solicitor to the Queen, had been created by the Lord Lieutenant to reward loyalty and buy further support. Fitzgibbon was making a speech elaborating on the purpose of the posts; Martin leapt to his feet and interjected, drawing on his best west coast brogue to add emphasis to his sarcasm, 'I do beseech the Honourable Gentlemen to suspend his judgment till he is appointed to one of them.'

At this time Martin became curiously involved in the appointment of a new Counsellor to the Commissioners. An elderly man called Coppinger, who had few assets and little income other than the salary provided, had filled the post for many years, but had become too old to retain it. Martin does not appear to have had a close relationship with Coppinger but, presumably in the spirit of humanity, decided to intervene. The post was to be filled by his old Cambridge friend, George Ponsonby. Martin pleaded with Ponsonby not to force the old man out of office. When this did not work he took to addressing Parliament about the situation, reserving the longest speech he was ever to make in the House for this subject, and concluding with the impassioned plea, 'Poor Coppinger! He is deprived of his place! He is ruined!'

When Fitzpatrick, the Chief Secretary, second only to the Viceroy, pointed out that Coppinger was too old and infirm to carry out the role credibly, Dick demanded that a pension be given. He even offered to have his property taxed to help provide it. In another speech he threatened to wear out the Castle pavement and carpets until the administration agreed to right the injustice. Turning on his old friend Ponsonby he likened him to a man that could only be found in 'some dank cells of the darkest dungeon'. Only a 'wretch with a savage heart' would accept the post.

After Martin finally threatened to go to London and personally address the King, Fitzpatrick conceded and arranged compensation for the old man. The way that Dick had thrown everything into the cause, even threatening to end an old friendship, was quite extraordinary, bearing in mind he did not appear to have more than a passing interest in the matter, but it was indicative of how he was always capable of pitching himself into a crusade without any thought of the consequences to himself.

By early summer Parliament had been prorogued, and a general election was to be held that autumn. Dick returned to Elizabeth at Dangan and found her frustrated by the country lifestyle and missing the attractions of Dublin, with no company other than Wolfe Tone to amuse her. However, Dick, had been putting a plan into motion that would provide Elizabeth with what she missed most from Dublin: a theatre.

Martin had acquired a small plot of land in Kirwan's Lane, near to Galway's main quay and on the site that had once been occupied by his ancestor's mills. He had paid for the building of a little auditorium, without boxes but designed to hold 100 people on its sloping floor. Touring theatre troupes did not usually frequent Galway but Martin had persuaded the leading Irish actor, Robert Owenson, who had been trained in London under the famous David Garrick, to form a permanent repertory company based at the new Kirwan's Lane Theatre.

Owenson was not asked to stage the first production. Martin, who quite rightly

*Site of the theatre in Kirwan's Lane, Galway*

regarded himself and his wife as accomplished thespians, was to star in *Douglas*, the historical Scottish tragedy, supported by the farce, *All The World's A Stage*, due to be performed on the opening night of Friday, 8th August 1783. In the tragedy, Colonel Richard Martin was to take the role of the villain, Glenalvonin Douglas, with Elizabeth playing the heroine, Lady Randolph. In the farce Martin was to play the leading role of Sir Gilbert Pumpkin and Elizabeth his stage wife, Bridget.

The supporting roles of Lord Randolph in *Douglas* and the butler Diggery in *All the World's a Stage* were to be played by Wolfe Tone. Tone had grown out of the youthful awkwardness he had displayed when the Martins first became acquainted with him. He was now a handsome, almost effeminate-looking young man. Elizabeth had been coaching Tone with his acting and helping him overcome the difficulty he had pronouncing his Rs. The constant rehearsals, which necessarily had to be undertaken without the absent Dick, had brought them close together. At this point, Martin had no idea how close.

The opening night of the Kirwan's Lane Theatre was the social event of that summer in Galway. Tickets could have been sold many times over. The much sought-after stage seats cost the princely sum of £1 2s 6d. A pit seat was priced at 4 shillings and 4 pence. Ladies were asked not to wear hooped skirts, so that more people could witness the performance. Dick had also leased a large residential property near to the theatre, where the Martins could entertain their guests and which would serve as Dick's Galway town house for many years. It is now the famous Tigh Neachtain pub.

Both plays were a great success. The Martins and Tone received generous acclaim from both critics and audience. No-one could have suspected the irony in Tone playing the part of a suicide, who died exclaiming, 'I have tried a thousand times and never could kill myself to my own satisfaction.'

With the theatre open and Elizabeth hopefully relieved from tedium, Martin turned his attentions to the forthcoming election, in which his opponents were Daly, a close friend of Henry Grattan, and Trench. Martin's term as Sheriff had ended and the independent freeholders of Galway County had formally expressed their thanks to 'Colonel Martin, our late Sheriff, for his just, upright and active conduct while invested with that important role'. However the damage done to his reputation earlier that year by Daly was still to take effect.

The election got off to a typically rumbustious start with Martin, through the *Freeman's Journal*, accusing Daly of creating new freeholders to boost his votes at the ballot. Martin had himself tried this trick, persuading many of his catholic tenants to take protestant oaths in order to gain their vote. The Rector of the Cathedral of St Nicholas was accused of preventing Martin's people from taking the oath, while granting it to 'the perjured vassals of Daly'.

To place their votes, qualifying freeholders had physically to attend the one voting station in Galway. Martin was greatly disadvantaged, due to the majority of his tenants living in remote corners of Connemara. In the absence of proper roads, they had to be shipped into Galway and housed at his expense.

When the polls closed, after seven weeks, Martin came only third to Daly and Trench, and therefore was out of Parliament. The financial burden of the election had been enormous for all concerned and Martin, with the additional cost of opening the theatre, had spent and borrowed well in excess of what was prudent. His insolvency was a state from which he would never escape.

When the picture of the election results throughout Ireland became clear, it was apparent that the Lord Lieutenant's administration had actually succeeded in strengthening control of Parliament. Flood's worst fears had been confirmed. Two hundred of the 300 seats in the House had been returned by only a handful of eligible voters. Some boroughs had only one person qualified to cast a vote. Half of the members were on government salaries and all of the powerful large boroughs were loyal to the Viceroy.

Along with Martin, another personal victim of the election had been Flood himself, who had lost his seat. The two men met to discuss the implications of what had happened. With Grattan out of favour as a result of what with hindsight appeared capitulation to the British, Flood had decided that the Volunteer movement was now to be his voice. Martin, with his highly influential Galway Corps, and Flood with Volunteer connections throughout the country, needed quickly to organise a show of defiance.

Meanwhile, the British government had arrived at a conflict of interest between the system they had installed to control Ireland, and the fight for parliamentary reform on the mainland, a cause that by now had brought William Pitt to power.

The factors at play during the aftermath of the American war had brought the process of government to the edge of collapse. The complacency of the public that had prevailed for most of the 18th century was shattered. People were looking at the root causes of the disaster and it was apparent that the problem, as in Ireland, lay in the 'rotten' boroughs. To add to the chaos the King's almost Machiavellian interference, constantly playing one faction against another, had resulted in a lack of control or power within parliament. This also meant fundamentally weak government, which, combined with a monarch who was less than able in the art of war, created the very real danger of playing into the hands of the French, who were still keenly looking to press home their advantage.

The time was ripe for a real leader to emerge. The King, though stubborn, was not stupid; he realised that Pitt was the man, and within weeks of Parliament reconvening after the 1783 election, appointed him Prime Minister. His first few months in office tested the novice to the full as he came under immediate pressure from the ousted Charles James Fox. But with the support of the King, and a head that belied his years, Pitt survived and began to grow in strength and power. The King warmed to his new First Minister, whereas Fox grew closer to the King's heir, George, Prince of Wales, with whom he shared a hedonistic outlook, and growing frustration with the incumbent King. This fault line would fissure British politics for years to come.

Within weeks of the election, Henry Flood had managed to coordinate the entire Volunteer movement at a National Convention in Dublin. The powerful Ulster Corps had already passed a resolution at a rally in Dungannon calling for parliamentary reform. Dick wrote to Lord Northington, the new Viceroy, stating that the changes called for were consistent with those favoured by Pitt for the 'other side of the water'.

He acknowledged the delicate position the Viceroy found himself in and accordingly Martin did not expect a reply to his letter, but was happy to receive any 'hints from your Lordship, with gratitude'.

On 11th November, 160 delegates representing the national Volunteer Corps met at the Royal Exchange in Dublin and marched in full uniform through the city, watched by thousands of onlookers, to the Rotunda, where they based themselves for the duration of the convention. Flood, who was suffering from a severe attack of gout and had to be carried into the building, addressed the delegates, saying that the objective of the assembly was to purify the system of representation. Parliament was asked to consider a motion that 'leave be given to bring in a bill for the more equal representation of the people in Parliament'. Flood took the opportunity, in a speech full of the emotion he could always command, to claim that it had been the Volunteer movement that had achieved free trade and made Ireland a nation.

The outcome was an anti-climax. The motion was easily voted out and the convention quietly dispersed. Flood had made an error of judgment. He had restricted the number of Volunteers by only inviting delegates, as opposed to full Corps, the rationale being that Parliament would not take kindly to being threatened. But with hindsight only fear of armed rebellion would have persuaded Parliament to change a system that favoured the vast majority of its members, and a show of strength might have brought a different result, shaming or frightening the House into reforming itself. Without the dynamic of a foreign threat to its very fabric, Britain was not going to respond favourably to political pressure from the Volunteer Corps. In the absence of results, the momentum behind the movement began to slacken.

For Martin it was a disappointment to find that the body within which he exercised influence had no real voice unless it became militant, a development he would in no way countenance. His personal finances having been severely dented by the election campaign, buying his way back into Parliament in the manner that he had originally entered was not an option. Flood, equally disappointed at the outcome of the Volunteer Convention, had decided to visit Britain to explore the possibility of gaining a seat on the mainland. Martin decided to join him with the same intention, hoping that his university links with the new prime minister would prove useful. Travelling to England, where he was to spend six fruitless months, he left Elizabeth to her own devices, and the company of Wolfe Tone.

# Chapter 13

# Fighting Fitzgerald

Dick Martin's political allegiance to Henry Flood was turning into a lifelong friendship, so that it was Flood who assisted Dick when he fought one of the most remarkable and entertaining duels in Irish history.

To the north of County Galway, and across Lough Corrib from Dangan and Birch Hall, lies County Mayo, described at the time by Jonah Barrington, the politician and sketch writer, as a thoroughly lawless part of Ireland. Two miles outside the county town, Castlebar, lies Turlough, home to the Fitzgerald family, descended from the great Geraldine clan who had been transplanted west of the Shannon by Cromwell. Like the Martins, the family had become 'Protestants of convenience' and continued ruling their lands in a feudal manner. Robert George Fitzgerald was their most infamous son.

His father had been a violent rake in his youth, and served in the Austrian army. His mother was the sister of the Earl-Bishop of Derry, but left her husband when Robert George was a small child, joining the court of the young King George III. The maternal side of his family would, on many later occasions, use their influence to extract him from serious trouble.

It did not take long for the youthful Robert George to acquire the nickname 'Fighting' Fitzgerald. Sent to school at Eton, he was in a coffee house when a fellow student was heard to remark that he could 'smell a Catholic'. Fitzgerald drew his sword and sliced off the boy's nose. In Paris, he ran a man through with his rapier for stepping on his dog.

Fitzgerald joined the British army and was posted back to his native Ireland, where he found that the culture of duelling meant he could blaze away to his heart's content. His regiment was stationed in Galway and, over the issue of a young woman shop assistant, he fought with a fellow officert and was shot in the head. A surgeon was summoned to trepan the wound and Fitzgerald, although semi-conscious and streaming blood, was more concerned to see that his toupée was spared. This injury was blamed in later years for his increasingly psychotic behavior, although some of the violent instability was probably inherited. His father, on hearing that his son was likely to die of this injury, ran his sword through the unfortunate messenger.

At his recovery, Fitzgerald, now an unbalanced bully, took to looking for any reason to quarrel, even to the point of standing in the middle of narrow streets in Dublin, challenging anyone who jogged him for immediate satisfaction. He carried a stout cudgel, which he called his 'rascal thrasher', to deal with immediate victims of his ungovernable temper.

Despite his lunatic tendencies he was highly intelligent, well educated, good looking and, having spent time at Versailles, he cut a dash in society as a dandy, resplendent with his hat, shoe buckles and sword ablaze with diamonds, his coat and vest tailored in gleaming French brocades and expensive velvets, a muff on his left arm and two emerald watch chains draped across his stomach adorned with lines of seals.

Fitzgerald married well and decided that it was time to take over the family estate. His father had made a settlement on the marriage, but reneged on it. Fitzgerald Junior made a successful application to the Court of the Exchequer to make him custodian of the family estate until the debt was paid. He immediately evicted his father and took over as squire.

Fitzgerald and Dick, who was six years his junior, met at around this time, having a number of mutual acquaintances in both the west of Ireland and in Dublin. The Volunteer movement had just been formed and Fitzgerald was envious that Dick had been elected Colonel of the Galway Volunteers, whereas he had been overlooked for the same honour in Mayo.

His response was to form his own quasi-volunteer army called the Turlough Guard, which comprised various assorted fugitives, jail-breakers and deserters. Outside the structure of the Volunteer Corps, but providing Fitzgerald with a troop of armed men to command, he used the Guard entirely for his own purposes. When a Dutch ship was wrecked off the Mayo coast Fitzgerald took the opportunity of commandeering six cannons, which he used to fortify his house.

By this stage his behavior had moved from eccentric to deranged. He took to keeping pet bears and delighted in dressing them up to pose as travellers on the Castlebar to Dublin stagecoaches. Normal hunting was not proving dangerous enough and so he insisted that this activity took place at night. At first locals thought the troop of torchlit horsemen was a supernatural spectacle but they soon dismissed the midnight call to hounds as merely 'mad Fitzgerald going hunting in the night'.

It must be acknowledged that although Fitzgerald was a criminal lunatic, he was also a commendable landlord. By draining bogs he made inhospitable land capable of bearing wheat. He built a clothing mill, providing employment in a deprived area, and his tenants were happy to ignore his violent and insane actions, which in any event tended to be channelled toward other members of the gentry.

Up to this stage Fitzgerald had paid more attention to Dick than Dick had to him. It irked Fitzgerald that 'Hair-Trigger Dick' was acknowledged as the finest duellist in Ireland. Fighting and winning twenty or so duels, incurring only minor wounds, had earned Dick his fame. Fitzgerald had fought more duels, but had lost most of them, suffering many appalling injuries in the process. His main talent appeared to be to avoid being killed. However an incident was about to happen that would put Fitzgerald into Dick's pistol sights.

Dick, at this stage, was still on friendly terms with Lord Altamont and the Browne family who lived at Westport House, just outside the town of Westport and about ten miles from Fitzgerald's estate. Westport House was (and still is) one of the grandest houses in Ireland, and the Brownes, it may be noted, were staunch supporters of the political status quo.

Besides wanting to be Colonel of the Mayo Volunteers and recognised as the most celebrated duellist of his generation, Fitzgerald jealously coveted Martin's membership of Parliament. He had once stood for election but, despite parading around the streets of Castlebar for three days lavishing money on voters, he had been beaten by Dennis Browne, Lord Altamont's younger brother.

One morning in 1780 Fitzgerald rode to Westport House and strode up the long flight of steps leading to the imposing front door.

In Richard Martin's own words, as recounted by Sir Jonah Barrington:

George Robert Fitzgerald, having a deadly hate to all the Browne family, but hating most Lord Altamont, rode up one morning from Turlow to Westport House, and asked to see the big wolf-dog called the 'Prime Sergeant'. When the animal appeared, he instantly shot it, and desired the servants to tell their master that 'until the noble peer became charitable to the wandering poor whose broken meat was devoured by the hungry wolf-dogs *he* would not allow any such to be kept.' He, however, left a note to say that he *permitted* Lady Anne, Lady Elizabeth and Lady Charlotte Browne, each to keep one *lap-dog*.

News soon reached Dick in Galway. The senseless killing of an innocent animal, which he himself had known and been fond of, filled him with rage, while the insults to his friends indicated by his use of italics above, prompted him to revenge. His immediate reaction was to seek out Fitzgerald and fight him, but this was impossible. It

*The steps at Westport House*

would have implied that Lord Altamont and his brother were cowards. Dick decided to bide his time and seek an alternative remedy at the first opportunity.

Fitzgerald was not long in providing one. Relations between him and his father had been far from harmonious since the old man had been evicted from his home. Robert George had no heir of his own and was afraid that his younger brother, Lionel, could one day inherit the estate. Therefore he wanted his father's will changed in his favour. No doubt embittered by the treatment he had received from his son, the father adamantly refused. Fitzgerald junior then became more pragmatic in his persuasion, imprisoning his father in a cave and chaining him to a pet bear for good measure.

Lionel, predictably taking umbrage at his father's treatment and armed with a writ of Habeas Corpus, commanding the release of the old man, personally arrested his brother while he was sitting on the Bench at Ballinrobe Assizes, frog marching him to the cells.

Having heard of the forthcoming trial, Dick spotted his chance to pick a fight. Coincidentally, earlier that year, he had been called to the Irish Bar in order to assume the post of High Sheriff in Galway. He had no intention of practising law, and the only brief he ever accepted was for this action against Fitzgerald, waiving the normal fee to ensure he would get the case. The stage was set at Castlebar Assizes for Dick to come face to face with his enemy.

Remesius Lennon, whom Dick later described as a 'battered old counsellor' was defending Fitzgerald. He based his case on the somewhat dubious argument that his client's father was one of the worst men living and that it would be unjust to censure any son for confining such a public nuisance.

Dick countered by agreeing that the father had committed many crimes, and closing his submission he turned to look directly at Fitzgerald and said,

'But the greatest crime against society and the greatest sin against heaven that he ever perpetrated, was having begotten the traverser.'

Fitzgerald rose to the bait and from the dock said,

'Martin, you look very healthy, you take good care of your constitution, but I tell you that this day you have taken very bad care of your life.'

It was enough. Satisfied that this exchange was more than enough to instigate a duel without any reflection on the honour of the Altamonts, Dick rested his case. He had hoped that the outcome would be the immediate release of the old man and that Fitzgerald, having satisfied the court on this point, would be set free, so that Dick could engage him then and there in a duel. Fitzgerald however, after being found guilty, refused to comply with the order of the court and was promptly sentenced to three years' imprisonment.

Two days later the Fitzgerald militia sprang their leader from jail. Riding through the town firing his pistols in the air, on his return to Turlough he was greeted with bursts of cannon fire. This blatant act of lawlessness was too much for the Lord Lieutenant. He dispatched a company of horse, foot and artillery from Dublin to recapture Fitzgerald and dismantle the fort at Turlough.

Fitzgerald had collected his father from his subterranean prison and, with a troop of his yeomanry, made for nearby Clew Bay. This magnificent part of the coast is dotted with numerous islands, providing many hiding places. Here he boarded a small fishing boat with his father and set sail. His plan was to force the old man to swear that he had been imprisoned of his own free will. With little alternative, Fitzgerald senior agreed to his son's demands and the two of them returned to shore and immediately departed for Dublin, passing the approaching troops travelling in the opposite direction.

On arriving in Dublin the father immediately bolted to a friend's house and refused to reiterate the statement he had made when confined in the small boat. Fitzgerald, with a ransom on his head, was soon recaptured and thrown into Newgate prison. His mother's powerful family began pulling the necessary strings and six months later he was released. Dick, who had closely followed these events, could continue his pursuit of the duel he craved.

Fitzgerald was making no effort to carry out the threat he had boldly made from the dock, although at one stage Dick had diverted a journey through Castlebar and made his visit to the town clearly known to his prey.

It was now the autumn of 1784 and Dick had recently returned from his six-month trip to England, unsuccessful in finding a parliamentary seat. His intention, instead of travelling immediately on to Elizabeth in Galway, was to stay in Dublin for a short period while he explored the possibility of gaining a friendly seat in parliament. He had settled back quickly into the swing of Dublin social life and like many of his friends was looking forward to seeing Mrs Crow perform in *Belvidera* at the Playhouse Theatre. When he took his normal place in the front row of the stage-box he looked behind and saw Fitzgerald. Making apologies to his guests Dick removed himself and went to sit next to a surprised Fitzgerald, asking him if he had anything to say.

Fitzgerald replied that he considered Dick to be the 'Bully of the Altamonts'. This was enough of an insult for Dick's purpose and he said that Fitzgerald would be hearing from him in the morning, the usual jargon meaning that a formal duel was to be arranged. In defiance of etiquette at the theatre Fitzgerald unexpectedly lashed out there and then, aiming a blow at Dick's head with his cane and quickly departing from the box. Dick went to give chase but became entangled in a curtain. With assistance he freed himself and found Fitzgerald standing in the lobby.

Fitzgerald shouted, in front of what was now a large crowd, that he had struck a blow of challenge and that Dick would soon have his satisfaction, whether 'being shot or run through the body'.

In accordance with procedure, Dick waited to hear from Fitzgerald the following day but nothing was forthcoming. Dick decided against dispatching a friend to make the arrangements as he had begun to realise that Fitzgerald was unhinged and would probably attack the go-between. He elected to watch his enemy's house for the next few days. When recounting this whole incident nearly 50 years later to his friend Jonah Barrington, who was writing his memoirs, Dick wrote that he 'could not uncage the fox'.

A man called Lyster, an acquaintance of Dick's and a cousin of Fitzgerald, approached Dick and offered to break the stalemate and make the necessary arrangements. Dick, frustrated at Fitzgerald's evasion, reluctantly accepted the offer, which led to the unfortunate Lyster being badly beaten by Fitzgerald, who was promptly arrested. In court Fitzgerald maintained that it was the go-between who had picked the fight and he was merely defending himself. This time the court believed his version of events and he was discharged.

Fitzgerald was now adopting the role of the challenged and accordingly could select the venue for the duel. Not surprisingly he chose Castlebar, expecting Dick to decline venturing to a town where his banditti ruled the streets. Dick, however, immediately accepted and set out with Henry Flood, an accomplished duellist in his own right, as his assistant.

On arriving in Castlebar they stayed with Lord Lucan. Dick awaited the arrival of his duelling pistols, which he had entrusted to a servant who, it turned out, had got drunk en route and forgotten where he was going. Knowing Dick's dilemma, which he may well have had a hand in, Fitzgerald was walking the streets of Castlebar with members of his mob, shouting taunts and taking substantial bets on the outcome of the duel.

After another couple of hours Dick could wait no longer and, grabbing a crude pair of holster pistols from his servant, he set out to find Fitzgerald. He finally confronted him in the street and asked him to draw his sword. Fitzgerald claimed that he was lame and the pavement uneven. Dick flung a switch into Fitzgerald's face and challenged him to move to the nearby barracks.

Fitzgerald turned up with a case of pistols in his hand. Dick was still having to rely on what he described as 'wretched tools' after having tested the old pistols and found them to have anything but a hair-trigger. The long drawn-out feud was about to come to a climax.

Dick took up his position against a projecting part of the barrack wall and, holding his ungainly horse pistols, invited Fitzgerald to come as close as he pleased. This form of duelling called for tremendous nerve from the combatants, as the one who fired first had to make sure he hit his target or else expect an unpleasant outcome. When (according to the account) their pistols were practically touching, they both fired. Fitzgerald missed, but Dick's shot hit Fitzgerald squarely in the chest and he fell to the ground exclaiming 'Honour, Martin, honour!' meaning he accepted defeat.

Dick, graciously allowing Fitzgerald time to recover, replied, 'If you are not disabled I will wait as long as you choose.' As Dick waited, Fitzgerald, true to character, fired a second shot from his prone position, this time hitting Dick, who although wounded managed to fire his second pistol, scoring another direct hit on his opponent's body.

Dick was helped by Flood to a nearby doctor's house where the wound, at first thought to be serious, was found to be slight and easily dressed. Convinced that he had twice shot Fitzgerald in the body, Dick dispatched his doctor to find out if his opponent was still alive and if so, the extent of his injuries. He was surprised when Fitzgerald himself returned within an hour and, with no apparent hurt, demanded that the duel continue a few days later at nearby Sligo.

Dick turned up on the appointed day, this time armed with his own weapons. Fitzgerald failed to show, and it was now that Dick found out the real reason for his miraculously quick recovery. He had been wearing concealed armour. On hearing this Dick concluded that the feud was beneath his dignity as a gentleman and that the matter was at an end.

This was the beginning of the end for Fighting Fitzgerald. Now shunned by the upper class for cowardice and cheating, his behaviour became increasingly anarchic. He turned his attention to the gallant and popular Colonel Patrick McDonnell, head of the Mayo Volunteers: a post he felt was his by right.

Fitzgerald concocted a plan that involved a warrant for McDonnell's arrest, issued by a corrupt magistrate. Armed with this spurious document Fitzgerald and his ramshackle army, led by a fellow psychopath called 'Scotch' Andy Craig, captured McDonnell, who was out riding near Turlough with two of his men. After holding them prisoners for a night, they set up a mock ambush, to give Scotch Andy the excuse to kill McDonnell and his fellow officers as they allegedly made their escape.

A rat was smelt, and Fitzgerald and his cohorts were arrested. Scotch Andy turned King's evidence in return for a sentence of life imprisonment, and incriminated Fitzgerald as an accessory to murder.

The trial was held in the summer of 1786 in Castlebar, now firmly under the control of the King's army and the Mayo Volunteers, who were anxious to avenge their colonel's death. Fitzgerald's house was ransacked, he was badly beaten while in jail, and all his fine clothes were stolen. Great public attention was focussed on these events, with numerous influential and powerful people travelling from Dublin to the small Mayo town. Bets were taken on whether Fitzgerald's uncle would procure his release in time.

It was now that Dennis Browne fully gained his revenge. He was a member of the Grand Jury that convicted Fitzgerald and sentenced him to death. It was rumoured that, in his other role as High Sheriff, on the day the hangman took three attempts to dispatch Fitzgerald, Browne kept the reprieve in his pocket.

*Irish wolfhound*

# Chapter 14

# Fatherhood?

After six months in England fruitlessly seeking a parliamentary seat, and with the longstanding feud with Fitzgerald finally out of the way, Dick returned to Elizabeth at Dangan, ignorant of how the relationship between his wife and the revolutionary-to-be had developed during his absence.

The only clues to the affair between Elizabeth and Theobald Wolfe Tone lie in Tone's diary, published many years later. It would appear that at the start the beautiful and intelligent woman, who undoubtedly enjoyed flirting in general, was bored with life in the country and began to play a dangerous game with the young man. An infatuated Tone quickly recognised what was happening. He wrote:

> As I preserved, as well as felt, the profoundest respect for her, she supposed she might amuse herself innocently in observing the progress of this terrible passion in the mind of an interesting young man of twenty; but this is an experiment no woman ought to make.

Tone had matured both physically and mentally during his employment at Dangan. Now tall and slender with lively, bright eyes, the only remnants of his adolescence were acne scars. He displayed a charm to both men and women that would stay with him until his tragic death. He talked quickly and with great animation. His passion for culture and the arts was infectious. It was only a matter of time before Elizabeth crossed her own boundaries and fell in love with him, although Tone would never admit that the affair 'overstepped the bounds of virtue'.

Richard Martin was a man of vision, capable of throwing himself simultaneously, with passion and boundless energy, into many different causes, roles and activities. This type of person rarely sees what, in hindsight, was so obviously under his nose. If Martin had harboured any suspicion that Elizabeth was unfaithful he would have been honour bound to seek satisfaction from the other party involved, in the traditional manner. However, when Martin again took up residence in Dangan during the autumn of 1784 he appears to have happily renewed his friendship with Tone, unaware of the passions lurking in the background.

This period at Dangan was deeply impressive for Tone, and possibly may have affected the course of Irish history. Tone was born a Protestant and his family had held that faith for centuries, not converting merely for the sake of convenience. During his time on the Martin estate, tales of Jacobite rebellions from Robert and passionate reasoning from Dick may well have influenced his thinking.

On his return to Galway, Dick immediately had something new to preoccupy him. He was preparing for the arrival of his friend Henry Flood in his capacity as a General of the Volunteers. Martin's Galway Corps were to receive Flood with due recognition for his gallantry and patriotism. The scale of the event was enormous and the formalities lasted for three days, culminating in the entire Galway Corps marching in full dress uniform, accompanied by a band and with Martin, newly promoted to the rank of Major General, at their head.

Given the anti-climactic events of the previous year, this pomp and ceremony, without real fervor or focus, was representative of the new role of the Volunteer Corps. They had missed the opportunity to achieve independence and had now become merely an excuse to dress up and posture. Their influence in Irish politics was waning.

Britain had resigned herself to losing her American colonies and had quickly built new bridges with the independent nation. France, suffering internal turmoil that would, within five years, result in revolution, presented no immediate threat. Moderates, who now included the former firebrand Grattan, had been appeased by the concessions made and the stage was set for a period of calm in both British and Irish politics.

Pitt had turned his attention to rebuilding the British economy, which had been shattered by the efforts in America. He had quickly established a relationship with the King that suited both men. George felt he was in control and Pitt believed he had autonomy to run the country. Until the King succumbed to his first bout of madness, Pitt relied on a strategy of boring the opposition into submission. Fox took a long-term view of his aspirations to power, using the time to ingratiate himself with the future monarch and fellow playboy, George, Prince of Wales.

Martin realised that he was not missing a lot by being out of politics. With his father now too old to run the estate, he decided to take a much more hands-on role. His finances were in a perilous state. Lavish spending, running a second home in Dublin for seven years, the costly election and opening a theatre to provide his wife with amusement, had taken its toll.

It was now that Elizabeth told her husband that she was again pregnant; but with so many miscarriages and stillbirths in the past this would have been rather a cause for concern than happiness. Ignoring the advice of her doctors, Elizabeth continued to throw herself into the drama, starring, along with Dick and Wolfe Tone, in a number of new productions.

Dick was based in his home town for the foreseeable future. His status as a lawyer and former sheriff qualified him to become a judge on the Connaught legal circuit. It was this role that led to the most tragic event in his life, but one that probably saved the life of Wolfe Tone and later certainly spared a wealthy English businessman.

James Jordon of Resolven, Dick's cousin, boyhood friend, and travelling companion eleven years before, had settled into a traditional legal career and was practising in western Ireland. He had for years held a grievance that his widowed mother had not properly attended to the education of his sisters while he had been abroad with Martin. Dick was saddened to observe that there was by now a permanent rift between Jordon and his mother.

The Connaught circuit, made up of solicitors, barristers and judges, met regularly for formal dinners. These were far from sober events and on this particular occasion Jordon was very much the worse for drink. Dick, throughout his life, was never a heavy drinker, a minority virtue in 18th-century Ireland but one that probably directly contributed to his success as a duellist. The conversation between the cousins somehow turned to the subject of Jordon's sisters' education. Dick defended the absent mother, saying that his cousin should show her more respect. What should have been a private family argument was now being carried out in front of the local legal establishment. Jordon felt that Dick had insulted him and demanded satisfaction. Martin desperately tried to pacify his angry, drunken cousin, but he remained adamant. Jordon repeated his challenge and Dick had no option but to accept it.

Jordon had no great reputation as a duellist and the confrontation could only have one outcome. The following day messages were passed between the cousins. If Dick had insulted or offended Jordon, then he offered his unreserved aplogy. This was not sufficient for Jordon, who needed the apology to be made in front of all those who had witnessed the previous night's argument. This being impossible to achieve, a duel was now unavoidable.

They met in a field near the public road at Green Hills, half way between Castlebar and Westport. In one last attempt at avoidance, Martin arrived unarmed. Jordon was determined to have his honour and insisted Dick use one of his pistols. The cousins faced each other. Martin fired first, aiming low in a desperate attempt merely to wound his old friend. The shot struck Jordon in the upper leg and the duel was over, Dick relieved that it had not had a fatal outcome. He was wrong. An infection set into the wound and a week later Jordon died.

Martin was beside himself with grief. He was witnessed soon afterwards in the grounds of Castlemacgarrett, the home of his friend Lord Oranmore. Walking almost in a trance and holding a carving knife in the manner of a pistol, Martin wailed, 'No! I could not have missed him. Poor Jordon, I could not have missed you!' 'Hair-Trigger' Dick had fought his last duel.

T he following February Elizabeth gave birth, prematurely, to a baby daughter. After the tragedy of numerous past deliveries, this child survived and was christened Laetitia.

Soon afterwards a strange incident occurred at Dangan. Two men broke into the house and attempted to arrest Martin, who was in the company of Wolfe Tone. The men were sent packing but it was immediately after this episode, as Martin tried to find out the background to an attempt to arrest someone of his status, that Martin and Tone fell out. Tone hastily left Dangan, never to return. Writing about the affair with Elizabeth he described it as a 'passion of the most extravagant violence'.

There are a number of questions about this part of Martin's life that may never be answered. Did Tone sleep with Elizabeth? Was he the father of Laetitia? Did Martin ever suspect? If he did, perhaps the tragic duel with Jordon saved Tone from death at Martin's hand. Were the men who broke into Dangan in the employ of Tone? Whatever the answers, the Martins' marriage survived and Dick was apparently as devoted to his wife as ever. There was no question of him rejecting Laetitia as a daughter.

Now, with Dick's family resident in Dangan, Robert moved to Clareville, a fine house in Oughterard, ten miles from Dangan in the direction of Connemara. Dick was

*Clareville in winter.*

now fully engaged in the running of an estate that stretched as far as the coast, 50 miles to the west. Much of the terrain was wild bog and harsh mountains that only a gifted horseman, native to the area, would dare venture into.

Arthur Young, writing in 1780, described the plight of the Irish peasantry:

A long series of oppressions, aided by very many ill-judged laws, have brought landlords into a habit of exerting a very lofty superiority, and their vassals into that of an almost unlimited submission: speaking a language that is despised, professing a religion that is abhorred, and being disarmed, the poor find themselves in many cases slaves even in the bosom of written liberty.

A landlord in Ireland can scarcely invent an order which a servant, labourer, or cottar dares to refuse to execute. [A cottar lived in a cottage owned by the landlord and worked for him in return.] Disrespect or anything tending towards sauciness he may punish with his cane or his horsewhip with the most perfect security. A poor man would have his bones broke if he offered to lift his hand in his own defence. Landlords of consequence have assured me that many of their wives and daughters have been sent for to the bed of their master; a mark of slavery that proves the oppression under which people must live.

Martin, like his father, could not be more diametrically opposed to this stereotype. He knew all his tenants by name, even those living in the remotest corners of the vast estate. He spoke to them in their native Irish. He was fair in respect of rent, understanding the harsh terrain they worked, and only charging an amount that the land could realistically generate. Widows were allowed to stay in their homes without paying rent. Protection was provided against any form of outside pillage. Disputes between tenants were fairly arbitrated.

The Martin estate, sparsely populated and unproductive, and run as it was along such tolerant lines, could never have sustained its owners in the style they wished. There was, however, a supplementary source of income: smuggling. The coastline of the estate stretched for over 100 miles, with numerous small coves and inlets. A multitude of little islands close to the shore provided refuge and cover. With the bogs and mountains preventing the authorities getting close to the action, smuggling had always been prevalent. Drink and tobacco were brought in, and Irish goods such as woolen products and butter, prevented by trade barriers from leaving via normal export routes, passed in the opposite direction. The Martins took no active role, but chose to turn a blind eye in return for a healthy commission, either in cash or in contraband, mainly fine French wines and brandies.

The holder of the chief franchise was one George O'Malley, who controlled the illegal import-export business from a small inn at Ballynahinch. This would eventually become Dick's family home when personal financial misfortune forced him to put impassable miles between himself and his creditors. Now it was a small hostelry, well situated in the centre of the smuggling activities that took place through what are now the towns of Clifden and Roundstone. The authorities in Galway were well aware of what was going on; a letter was sent to Dublin stating that 'Mr. Martin's command of smugglers and fishermen cannot be less than a thousand.' But a combination of Martin's high standing in the city and the thanklessness of sending soldiers into the wilderness to police this local industry, allowed it to continue unabated.

Martin also differed from the traditional protestant landlord in that he made no attempt to stamp out catholic worship and education. The hedge schools and churches that still operated throughout Ireland, constantly in fear of discovery and reprisals, were unnecessary in Connemara, where the faith was allowed to flourish with Martin's blessing, to the extent that a thriving Carmelite friary was situated a few miles from Ballynahinch.

There was, however, one practice, endemic at the time, that appalled Martin and would increasingly affect his actions. The day-to-day treatment of animals was, by today's standards, barbaric. Animals that were uncooperative, usually because of malnutrition and exhaustion, were beaten unmercifully. Outside work, common pastimes included badger baiting, cock and dog fighting. Moreover there was a dreadful quasi-political practice endemic in Ireland, of maiming cattle which were being reared to supply the Royal Navy with beef. Martin increasingly took strong measures if he saw any inhumane act taking place. His form of justice would, over the years, become more prevalent and more formalised.

On October 4th 1785, Elizabeth gave birth to a son who was named Thomas Barnewell, the middle name being in memory of Dick's late mother. This time there was no question as to who the child's father was: future portraits would show Thomas to have the distinctive Martin nose. Although Dick was to have a turbulent relationship with his eldest son, the latter inherited his father's humanitarian principles and approach to his tenants.

The following year saw Martin's old Cambridge roommate, Charles Manners, the former Marquis of Granby and now Duke of Rutland, succeed to the role of Lord

Lieutenant of Ireland. The Martins were only too pleased to use the opportunity of reaquainting themselves with him and the social life in Dublin, taking a small house to accommodate their extended visits to the capital.

Rutland decided in the autumn of 1787 that, as Viceroy, he should undertake a tour of the west coast. Dick readily offered to be his host and made arrangements for the visit. Typically of Martin's style, the intinerary was demanding and intense. The highlight was to be the restaging of *Douglas* at Kirwan's Lane Theatre, with the role of the hero this time being played by Dick's sixteen-year-old stepbrother, Anthony. Martin would play his usual part: the villain, Glenavon.

The punishing schedule Martin had arranged called for him to meet his old friend at Elizabeth's family home at Hollymount. Rutland arrived worn-out after a twenty-mile ride from Westport. He retired soon after dinner complaining of a severe pain in his side. The following morning he felt better and declined Martin's suggestion to see a doctor. The tour continued 25 miles to the Dalys' house at Dunsandle and then on to Galway.

As a prelude to the performance at Kirwan's Lane, Elizabeth read an address to the Viceroy, penned by her husband. The play itself was well received as ever and the party continued to Dangan, where a lavish banquet had been laid on. Martin and Rutland left at four in the morning for a journey back to Dunsandle. Within days Rutland, having returned to Dublin, was dead, the cause attributed to a chill caught in the late-night ride from Dangan. Dick had lost another close friend.

His finances were in an increasingly parlous state. Credit could not be extended any further against an estate barely capable of servicing the interest. Martin's life reveals an extensive list of talents, but business acumen was not among them. Creditors were becoming impatient and Dick was now on the verge of bankruptcy.

Temporary salvation appeared in the form of the first of many hopeless business ventures that would promise much but deliver nothing. Copper had been found on the estate, near to Maam Bridge. First reports indicated a rich vein of high-class ore.

In keeping with his ideas of Irish self-suficiency, Martin resolved to exploit the find. With ceaseless energy and infectious enthusiasm, he threw himself into the venture. By the summer of 1788 he wrote to Earl Temple, the new Lord Lieutenant, informing him that the veins of solid ore were 'so tender as to work without powder'. He concluded that he was sending some specimens of it and 'some other fossils which I dare say you will think are curious'.

It would be some years before the flaw in this business plan became apparent. It was impossible profitably to transport the mined copper to the sea. But at this stage the business, fuelled with Martin's optimism, kept his many creditors at bay.

# Chapter 15

# A French Affair

The year 1788 saw Britain fall into a constitutional crisis. King George and his Prime Minister had settled into a workable relationship. Neither man particularly liked the other but, over the five years since Pitt came to office, mutual respect had been established. Pitt had presided over a period of calm for Britain both internally and, remarkably, in foreign policy. The Irish Parliament had been appeased with only limited concessions and the Volunteer Corps were adopting a much less threatening role. The British economy had been rebuilt, albeit refinancing the National Debt by selling a substantial part of it to the Dutch.

Pitt thought he had planned for most contingencies, but he had not foreseen that the King might go mad. In the summer of 1788 George suffered a severe bilious attack. As ever, his posse of physicians made differing diagnoses, ranging from lead poisoning to gout. The King ignored all of them and went off to Cheltenham to take the waters. While staying at the spa, he began demonstrating strange behaviour, bustling about the town, raising his hat to passers-by and going into the houses of complete strangers, talking to them as if they were old acquaintances.

On returning to Windsor his physical and mental condition deteriorated rapidly. He would not sleep for days on end and began speaking in a strange loud, rapid tone, constantly repeating himself and shouting 'What! What!' and 'Hey! Hey! Hey!' On some days he returned to his old self, others he spent in complete delirium. He claimed he could see his native Hanover through a telescope and was convinced a flood had destroyed London. At a dinner on 5th November he attacked the Prince of Wales, although this was not necessarily attributable to his illness.

Pitt urgently sought advice from the best medical team he could assemble. Their opinions ranged from the King's condition being temporary and treatable to permanent madness or death within weeks. Whatever the illness was, the Prime Minister could no longer hide it from parliament. The Whig opposition saw it as the opportunity they had waited for, to grab power.

Fox had cultivated a close friendship with the heir to the throne. Prince George was now twenty-six, and harboured his own aspirations. He had never enjoyed a good relationship with his father. The King lived to a strict moral code and despised his son's hedonism and spendthrift nature.

Fox knew that if the Prince came to power Pitt could be usurped, so he pressed in Parliament for action to be taken. He argued that, if the King was incurably insane, then the heir must be formally appointed Regent, with all the powers of the monarchy. In Ireland a separate row erupted. Henry Grattan led the call within the Irish parliament that a Prince Regent should have no power in Ireland.

Fox won the day in the Commons, and the Regency Bill was passed on 12th February 1789. Days later, just as the Lords were about to give their approval, word came from the royal palace that the King had made a full recovery. Modern medicine has diagnosed the King's condition was probably porphyria, a disease whose symptoms could be construed as madness. He would suffer again from these apparent bouts of insanity but was now fully recovered and enjoying a tremendous wave of sympathetic public support, while the Prince of Wales sulked in his Brighton pleasure dome.

From Connemara, Martin watched the crisis unfold with great interest. He had witnessed the lost opportunity to maximise progress toward catholic emancipation when Britain was under pressure from the war in America and from the powerful Volunteer movement. He had been frustrated by the next few years, when nothing politically appeared to be happening. A new king, or at least a virtual monarch with a new government, might break the stalemate. Dick was becoming bored with being a combination of landlord, mine owner and theatre impresario. He desperately wanted to get back into politics.

The year 1788 also saw Elizabeth give birth to another boy, who was christened St George. The Martins' existence at Dangan was not ideal for either Dick, frustrated in his political ambitions or Elizabeth, equally frustrated socially. But a dramatic change in their life was about to happen, forged from necessity.

The copper mines were still not producing an income. The estate remained unprofitable. Debts had become unmanageable and creditors were closing in. Bankruptcy law in the 18th century was straightforward and brutal. If you could not pay your debts you went to a debtor's prison until you could. There was a simple but extreme solution. In the spring of 1789 Dick moved with his wife and children to France, beyond the reach of his creditors. He still had every confidence that the copper mining venture would deliver financial salvation but he needed some breathing space. He retained this Micawber-like attitude to money, always assuming that something would turn up, until the day he died. Martin had family connections in France: his first cousins Jenico and Martin, the younger brothers of Lord Gormanston, lived there. However, France in 1789 was not the ideal place to take a young family.

Supporting the patriot cause in America, combined with inept government, had left France bankrupt. The French constitution resembled the British insofar as there was a monarchy and a government. The catholic King Louis XVI lived in opulent splendour at the Palace of Versailles. French aristocrats maintained a lifestyle similar to that of their equivalents in Britain, but with one distinct advantage: they paid no tax. The fiscal burden was firmly placed on the peasant and middle classes. A particularly harsh winter in 1788-9 pushed the lower classes to desperation. The cause was in fact the exact opposite of the rallying cry of the American Patriots; the French aristocracy should have no representation without taxation.

There were obvious similarities between France and Ireland, each with an élite upper class and an impoverished peasantry, but the differences were far greater. France had no foreign master and was populated, ruled and governed by Catholics. Martin held deep-rooted sympathy for the American cause and supported the French underclass in their desire for equality, but his move to France was from financial necessity, not political idealism.

Martin went ahead of his family. It was an arduous journey for a man travelling alone, let alone the woman and three children who followed behind. It entailed a coach to Dublin, boat to Liverpool, coach to the port of Dover, another boat and another coach, eventually arriving at the home of his cousins in Lille. The Martins, although technically bankrupt, chose not to settle quietly in this medium-sized market town and by early summer had moved on to Paris where they rented a house in the fashionable district of St Phillipe du Roule. Here another cousin of Dick's, Count Patrick D'Arcy, an eminent scientist, had lived until his death.

The Martins had no problem adapting to a scene very reminiscent of their circle in Dublin. There were no amateur dramatics to take part in, but the social calendar was filled with dinners and balls. The Gormanstons enjoyed the highest connections and the Martins were soon acquainted with a group that included Jacques Necker, the Prime Minister, who had put forward a radical financial plan which was favoured by the emerging 'Third Estate', the representatives of the 'non-privileged' who were pushing to oust the ruling aristocracy. Dick and Elizabeth were frequent visitors to dinner parties hosted by the Neckers, where the conversation amongst the assorted philosophers, bankers and politicians was dominated by speculation on how events in the country would unfold.

Spasmodic rioting had broken out across France, and when the government met at Versailles on 5th May, the Third Estate put forward their plans for greater representation and an end to fiscal immunities for the aristocracy. As in the Irish parliament seven years before, the privileged few refused to vote for their own demise. Necker could see the writing on the wall and counselled the Third Estate to be patient and the ruling classes to make concessions. He advised his king to assert his authority to break the deadlock in favour of change.

Louis responded by sacking his prime minister. The French people reacted angrily and violent demonstrations took place in Paris, calling for Necker's reinstatement. By now the policies of the Third Estate had been taken up by the masses. The French Revolution was not driven just by a revolutionary few but by the momentum of the population rallying behind those who had had the audacity to call for change.

The Third Estate now formed a National Assembly and on 11th July King Louis sent Necker into exile. This was the flashpoint. The following day a mass rally took place in Paris, where an angry mob paraded through the streets holding a bust of the ousted Prime Minister. Law and order quickly collapsed when the commander of the Paris garrison withdrew his troops from the city.

The mob spent the next day arming themselves and, on the morning of 14th July 1789, a cry went up, 'To the Bastille!' The infamous Parisian prison was stormed by a mob headed by an Irishman, Colonel Blackwell. This event had little practical significance, since it only contained seven prisoners, but just as the Boston Tea Party had come to symbolise the start of rebellion, so did the storming of the Bastille.

Within days King Louis visited the city to meet representatives of the National Assembly, thereby recognising their existence. Necker was immediately recalled and power was passed to the electors, who set up a municipal council. The real effect of what had happened in Paris in the summer of 1789 would not be felt for another year, but the flame of revolution had been fanned in peasant communities throughout France and would result in the King and most of the aristocracy being slaughtered at the guillotine. Unlike the rebellion that was to follow in Ireland ten years later, the French Revolution was not about religious, nationalist fervour; it was about a desire for order and an end to class distinction.

After the excitement of events in July, Paris society resumed its course, and the Martins continued their pleasurable, but somewhat shallow, existence until the following March, when Dick received the news he had been hoping for. An English company wanted to invest in the Connemara copper mines. Dick immediately left for London, on 3rd March 1790, to conclude the deal, accompanied by Joseph Casteaux, a valet who had been in the Martins' employ for the last ten years.

Dick arrived in London, anxious to secure the investment that would allow him to collect his family and return home to Ireland. Negotiations took a few weeks but eventually terms were agreed and contracts dispatched to Martin's hotel for his signature. Dick was impatient to conclude matters and get back to France. When the contracts finally arrived at 10 in the evening, he had a coach waiting to take him that night to Dover.

Dick was coming down the steps of the hotel to get into his carriage when an old friend called to him. He had news that Pitt had called a snap general election on 27th May. Martin also made a snap decision. He instructed the carriage to take him to Liverpool instead, whence he would travel on to Galway with the intention of regaining his seat in Parliament. The decision was to cost him his marriage.

Back at Dangan, having gained the necessary respite from bankruptcy, Martin prepared for the forthcoming election. His opponents for the two seats were an old foe, Dennis Daly and a new one, Skeffington Smith. The election followed the normal pattern, with candidates hurling accusations of skullduggery and cheating at each other and then all proceeding to rig the outcome. Having his voters spread over Connemara again disadvantaged Martin and he was struggling from the start of the campaign.

When the polls closed Dick had trailed in a dismal third, with 28 votes to Skeffington Smith's 99 and Daly's 109 votes. He immediately made it known that he would petition parliament as soon as it reconvened, claiming that he had over 100 supporters who had wrongly been disallowed from casting their votes, Daly had received 80 illegal votes and in any event Skeffington Smith was a non-resident and inegible to stand for election. The petition failed.

D eeply frustrated, Dick, now turned his attention to retrieving his wife. His finances were repaired sufficiently to allow him to remain in Ireland within reach of his creditors. He wrote to Elizabeth telling her to prepare to return with the children to Dangan, and that the manservant Joseph was already en-route to Paris to assist with the arrangements.

He hardly expected her reply. Elizabeth had become involved in organising the Fête de la Fédération, a Parisian celebration to mark the first anniversary of the storming of the Bastille; she would leave soon after. Another letter then explained that she had left Paris on 20th August but that she was delaying her return to Ireland with a stay in London.

Finally the loyal servant, Joseph, arrived back at Dangan with the hideous task of breaking the truth to his master. Elizabeth had fallen in love with a man called John

Petrie, a wealthy English plantation owner who had been in the circle of Martin's acquaintance in Paris. Petrie had accompanied Elizabeth back to London, where she was now resident in his house in Soho Square. It later transpired that Joseph had begged his mistress to return to her husband, even offering to leave the couple's employ to prevent Dick knowing of her indiscretion.

Martin's first reaction was total disbelief, which forced Joseph to reveal the graphic details of what he had witnessed taking place between Elizabeth and her lover. Dick's heart was broken. He had adored Elizabeth from the moment they had met. He had undoubtedly forgiven her for the indiscretion with Wolfe Tone and was prepared to do the same again. He wrote to his wife begging her to return home, putting her actions down to a temporary aberration, when tempted by a rich and unscrupulous adulterer.

Dick only finally accepted he had lost his beloved wife when he went to London and, posing as an Eastern pedlar of silks, gained entrance to Petrie's house. There he found Elizabeth in the arms of her lover. Petrie was terrified that 'Hair-Trigger' Dick would take the course of action expected of a man whose honour could not have been more soiled. Had the infidelity taken place before the tragic duel with his cousin then Petrie's life expectancy would probably have been no longer than the following dawn, but Dick took a different course of action. He would seek redress in a court of law.

Martin later put Elizabeth's adultery down to unfair temptation. He wrote to the intermediary who had passed correspondence to Elizabeth when she first began living with Petrie that 'the riches of the East are at her command and if that can procure her happiness, may that fountain never be exhausted. The mention of one who for fourteen years lay constantly in her arms does not seem generous.' He added that her behaviour must have been attributed to 'a deranged mind'. Wolfe Tone, writing of the Petrie affair in his diary, laid the blame firmly at Martin's door, attributing Elizabeth's behaviour to desperate loneliness, caused by her husband's continual distractions and long absences.

Now accepting the reality of his loss, Dick made arrangements for his three small children to return to Dangan. There was never any question of them remaining with their mother. Though heartbroken, he still had his pride to retain.

He returned to Paris for one last time and at the end of September threw a banquet of such magnitude that is was reported in the *Dublin Chronicle*:

> The entertainment consisted of every delicacy the season could afford or art produce. Dinner was served up under one hundred covers, in a sumptuous style of elegance and hospitality, which did honour to the character of an Irishman. The dinner and wines, which were of the choicest description, it is said, cost Mr. Martin upwards of 600 louis d'or.

Among Martin's guests was Lord Thomas Erskine, the former Attorney General to the Prince of Wales and a future Lord Chancellor. He was to become a lifelong friend, and crucial to the success of Martin's animal rights legislation. However, the next time they met, Erskine was defending Petrie in court.

# Chapter 16
## A Criminal Conversation

The four years following the loss of Elizabeth were the darkest of Dick's life. He returned to Dangan emotionally devastated, his political ambitions again frustrated. Despite the mining deal providing temporary respite, he remained on the verge of bankruptcy. Kirwan's Theatre was now a mockery of the past: he sold it. (It was subsequently closed in 1795.) His attention was taken up with his young family, now motherless, and the continuing pursuit of making his copper mines pay. To complete his unhappiness, as he was preparing to leave for London to attend to the unpleasant formalities stemming from his wife's affair, he received news that his close friend Henry Flood was dead.

Dick arrived in London two weeks before the Christmas of 1791 for the beginning of the Criminal Conversation action he had taken against Petrie. Eighteenth-century British law permitted an injured party in a case of adultery to claim damages from the third party, providing the infidelity could be proved.

The case of Martin v Petrie was heard on Thursday 15th December at the Guildhall before His Honour Judge Kenyon and a special jury. Mr Bearcroft represented Martin, the plaintiff: Dick's friend Lord Erskine defended Petrie. Martin's advocate rose to outline his client's case. He was claiming a sum of £20,000. Mr Bearcroft felt that when the jury heard the facts of the matter they would have little choice but to award this sum against a man of 'very ample fortune'.

Bearcroft continued. The plaintiff was from the most respectable of families. His Irish estate, although vast in size, was currently encumbered with debts of £25-30,000. Martin had married Elizabeth in 1777 and, considering how modest her dowry had been, Bearcroft reasoned that it must be concluded Martin's motive for marrying her could only have been 'the affection he entertained for this woman'. Bearcroft conceded that many couples claim untruthfully to exist happily and comfortably together, but he intended calling witnesses to testify that the Martins had lived together 'in a manner that was a model for all other married people'.

He explained to the jury that the couple had had nine children, three of whom survived. They had lived in Ireland until the move to France at the beginning of 1789. Bearcroft outlined how Martin had been called to London on important business and from there had been obliged, having given promises, to return to Ireland and stand for Parliament. Martin had made both separations reluctantly.

While her husband was away, Elizabeth had become acquainted with the defendant, Petrie, who, Bearcroft claimed, 'endeavored by all possible means to ingratiate himself into the affections of this lady; and at last, as the jury will hear from the witnesses, matters were carried to the most indecent heights.' After receiving word from Martin that he required her return to Ireland, she chose to remain in Paris for the anniversary celebrations. She then travelled to London accompanied by Petrie and put up at the Royal Hotel in Pall Mall. When Mrs Martin discovered that her brother had

# AN

# A C T

## TO

Diffolve the Marriage of *Richard Martin*, Efquire, with *Elizabeth Vefey*, his now Wife, and to enable him to marry again; and for other Purpofes therein mentioned.

---

**HUMBLY** fheweth, and complaineth unto Your Moft Excellent MAJESTY, Your true and faithful Subject *Richard Martin*, of the Town of *Galway*, in the Kingdom of *Ireland*, Efquire;

**That,** in the Month of *February*, One thoufand Seven hundred and Seventy-feven, Your faid Subject was married to *Elizabeth Vefey*, Spinfter; and that they lived and cohabited together as Man and Wife, from that Time until fome Time in or about the Month of *May*, One thoufand Seven hundred and Ninety; and there is Iffue of the faid Marriage now living Two Sons and One Daughter, all of whom were born during fuch the Cohabitation of Your faid Subject with his faid Wife:

**That,** in the faid Month of *May*, One thoufand Seven hundred and Ninety, the faid *Elizabeth Martin* entered into, and hath fince carried on, an unlawful Familiarity and adul-

A

terous

terous Converfation with *John Petrie*, of *Sobo Square*, in the County of *Middlefex*, Efquire; and that in or about the Month of *November*, One thoufand Seven hundred and Ninety, the faid *Elizabeth Martin* eloped with the faid *John Petrie*, and hath ever fince lived and cohabited in Adultery with him:

**That** Your faid Subject, in or about *Trinity* Term, One thoufand Seven hundred and Ninety-one, brought his Action in the Court of *King's Bench* at *Weftminfter*, againft the faid *John Petrie*, for fuch Criminal Intercourfe and adulterous Converfation with the faid *Elizabeth Martin* as aforefaid, and hath obtained Judgment in the faid Action for Ten thoufand Pounds Damages:

**That** Your faid Subject exhibited a Libel in the Confiftory Court of the Bifhop of *London* againft the faid *Elizabeth Martin*, and on the Firft Day of *March*, One thoufand Seven hundred and Ninety-three, obtained a Definitive Sentence of Divorce from Bed and Board, and mutual Cohabitation, againft her the faid *Elizabeth Martin*, for Adultery with the faid *John Petrie*:

**That,** fince the Month of *May*, One thoufand Seven hundred and Ninety, Your faid Subject hath never had any Accefs to or Perfonal Intercourfe with the faid *Elizabeth Martin*; and the faid *Elizabeth Martin* hath, ever fince the faid Month of *May*, One thoufand Seven hundred and Ninety, conftantly continued her unlawful Familiarity and adulterous Converfation with the faid *John Petrie*, and they the faid *John Petrie* and *Elizabeth Martin* now live and cohabit together as Man and Wife; and that, on or about the Twentieth Day of *February*, One thoufand Seven hundred and Ninety-two (which was long after Your faid Subject wholly ceafed to cohabit and live with the faid *Elizabeth Martin*, or had any Accefs to her) there was born of the Body of the faid *Elizabeth Martin*, One Child, who has been baptized by the Name of *Emily*:

**That** the faid *Elizabeth Martin* hath, by her adulterous Behaviour, diffolved the Bond of Marriage on her Part, and your faid Subject ftands deprived of the Comforts of Matrimony, and liable to have a fpurious Iffue impofed upon
him,

unexpectedly returned to London, she saw fit to move to her aunt's house in Clarges Street. Bearcroft deduced that this was to prevent her family discovering the affair she was conducting with the defendant.

Bearcroft now produced a letter from Petrie to Elizabeth, which he read to the jury, placing great emphasis on the opening words, 'My adored and adorable Eliza'. The letter contained detailed instructions on how Elizabeth might elope with Petrie without being discovered by her now suspicious brother. She was to leave her aunt's house, taking no more than 'one servant and a small bundle'. From there she was to hail a coach to take her to the Strand, where Petrie advised her to walk on a little, go into a shop and buy a 'trifling article'; then take another coach to the Adelphi hotel, 'altering her dress, blackening her eyebrows with burnt cork and applying rouge to her cheeks'. After diverting into another shop, she should then hail a third coach to take her to the end of Westminster Bridge and walk to the other side, where Petrie would meet her.

Petrie also was married, and the letter concludes that regarding Peggy (his wife), Elizabeth must 'judge for the best. It is necessary for your interest and happiness that I should appear clear of suspicion on this occasion; and safety to us both is now the sole consideration.'

Bearcroft concluded his character assassination of Petrie by saying that the letter proved him a 'man of considerable parts and abilities, and who most shamefully took advantage of the necessary absence of Mr Martin, for the purpose of seducing his wife.' Satisfied that the jury must now be convinced that adultery had occurred, he turned to the question of damages, telling them he had every confidence they were 'men of sense, men of honour, and men of feeling' and he was convinced that at their hands his client would receive 'compensation which substantial justice requires'.

Lord Erskine's reply was confined to admitting that the Martins married in 1777. Bearcroft now called his main witness, the valet Joseph Casteaux.

Joseph started by confirming he had worked for the Martins since 1779 and from the time that he knew them, 'in his life, he had never seen married people live more happily or affectionately.' He described how fond they were of their three surviving children and how whenever he had seen the couple part, if only for a matter of two or three days, it was always with the same affectionate manner. When Mr Martin returned from such an absence, Mrs Martin would run down the street to embrace her husband.

Bearcfroft now recalled his witness to events after Martin had left his wife in France. In June of the previous year Joseph had been instructed to travel from Galway to Paris and give Elizabeth a letter from her husband, but he observed that his mistress did not receive it with her usual enthusiasm, 'reading one half of it and then throwing it down on the table'.

Joseph confirmed that by now Petrie was a daily visitor to the house, usually remaining until about 3 or 4 in the morning. One night Joseph had looked into the room where Elizabeth and Petrie were and saw his mistress lying on a sofa with Petrie sitting very close to her, one hand in a very 'indecent situation', the other around Elizabeth's neck. When asked, Joseph replied that Petrie was kissing her. He afterwards saw the couple in bed together.

The servant recounted a conversation he had had with Elizabeth and the defendant, showing the concerns the couple felt about Martin's reaction if he became aware of the affair. Elizabeth thought that her husband's pugnacity was subdued by the killing of Jordon, but she needed to be sure. She quizzed Joseph about whether there had been any incident in the recent election between her husband and another man. 'Is it likely to be a serious business?' she asked Joseph. He replied, 'Madam, I cannot say whether it is settled or not, but I hope it is.' Elizabeth enquired, 'Do you think, Joseph, it will be settled without fatal consequences?' Joseph answered that he hoped it would. Elizabeth continued, 'So you think they will not have a meeting?' to which Joseph replied 'You know, Madam, my Master is a gentlemen who never gives offence to any man, nor puts up with any insult without relenting it.'

Petrie, who if he had any sense was probably at least a trifle nervous about the possible outcome of the seduction, then questioned Joseph. 'Oh, then, Mr Martin is a violent man?' Before 'Hair-Trigger' Dick's valet could reply Elizabeth interrupted with a strange proverb, possibly alluding to the tragic incident with Jordon: 'There is a saying among the lower classes of people,' she said, 'That a pitcher which goes often to the well is broken at last.'

Lord Erskine's cross-examination of the servant was limited to two points. Why had he not told his master earlier of the alleged affair? Joseph replied that he did not think Martin would have believed it even if 'an angel had come down from Heaven and told it.'

Had Joseph interfered with correspondence between Mr Petrie and Mrs Martin? The valet confirmed that he had. In desperation he had challenged his mistress with the two letters he had intercepted from her lover, addressing her, 'Madam I know all your secrets and tricks. You have dishonoured your husband and his family as well as your own; but if you will return to the Master, I will give you back your letters.'

Bearcroft now called the rest of his witnesses. Margaret Cummins, another servant of the Martins', who had been with them for nine years, testified that she 'never saw people fonder of each other.' Joseph Blake, a Member of Parliament for Galway said that he 'never knew a couple that seemed to be more happy.'

Most damning to the defendant was the evidence of William Dolman, a waiter at the Ship Tavern in Brighthelmstone [Brighton]. Dolman claimed Petrie had slept with Elizabeth every night she stayed at the inn, adding she had the appearance of pregnancy.

Erskine rose to make his case. In fairness to the advocate it was not the easiest brief of his distinguished legal career and as *The Times*, reported he 'made the most of the slender materials that were put into his hands.' He acknowledged that the plaintiff's case had been most ably and powerfully stated. Wisely Erskine chose to admit his client's adulterous act and Petrie 'hung down his head and was extremely sorry.' Rationalising his client's actions, he laid part of the blame at Martin's door, reasoning that he should not have left his wife in Paris, without any 'female friend to be her companion'. Paris at the time was a 'scene of total confusion' which no husband should have wished on his wife. Martin certainly should have sent for his spouse when he knew that he was to return to Ireland and fight an election. Erskine maintained that a candidate's wife should 'make her share in the toils of an election, where female aid was often of the greatest consequence.'

He went on partly to excuse his client's actions by pointing out that Petrie had not been a friend of Martin; certainly he had not put Elizabeth in Petrie's care and therefore no trust was deemed to have been placed in him. Petrie had broken none of 'the sacred rites of hospitality'.'The best security of the honour and virtue of a woman is the prudence of the husband.'

Turning to the task of minimising the financial fall-out from his client's infidelity, Erskine pleaded that Petrie's wealth had been grossly overestimated. The agents Messrs Turner and Company could show that his wealth was completely tied up in an estate in Tobago and given the 'unhappy situation of affairs there' any value was highly suspect. Martin on the other hand was a 'man of fortune'. The reality of the position was that extravagant damages would simply have the effect of banishing the defendant to a foreign country, leaving his innocent family and children in ruin.

Judge Kenyon now addressed the jury. He thanked them for paying such close attention to the evidence they had heard and, with a strong implication that the matter was as open and shut a case as they were likely to hear, told them that no doubt they had 'already drawn their conclusions and it is probable that nothing I can say can alter the judgment you have formed. But still from the expectations of the parties, it is my duty to say something.'

Moving on to the issue of damages, he dismissed the argument that just because a man cannot pay then the amount should be reduced. If such a plea were to be accepted, then every defendant would say the same thing. He doubted the claim by Petrie that his wealth had little foundation, pointing the jury to the fact that he had a house in a fashionable area of London and another substantial property in Essex.

Was Petrie sorry for what he had done? Had he brought forth the fruits of sincere and genuine repentance? Kenyon rhetorically asked the jury, answering his own questions by pointing out, 'This criminal adulterous flirtation still exists.' Petrie and 'this lady still live in the face of day, in a public place resorted to by people of all ranks, and by their example contribute more to debauch their age.'

The judge's tirade against the helpless Petrie now waxed lyrical. 'Another circumstance is, that he has the infirmities of human nature hanging about him. But to quote the lines of the poet:

> Having waste ground enough to build upon,
> Why should we raze the sanctuary walls,
> And plant our mischief there?'

With thick irony, bearing in mind the role Wolfe Tone had played in the marriage, Kenyon stated that Martin 'and his lady have lived together, and he has been the father of nine children.

'This was the fixation of the parties till the plaintiff was precipitated into his present position by the villainy of the defendant. Mr Martin has lost his nearest and dearest relation in life; his children have lost a protector, and now, from the situation of the mother, doubts may be raised of their legitimacy.

'Gentlemen of the jury, it is you who are the guardians and protectors of the peace of families, it is you who are the sanctuaries of honour and of moral obligation, it is to you that the plaintiff appeals for justice. He has laid his damages at £20,000. You will give him what you think proper, though no pecuniary satisfaction can ever restore the wounded peace of his mind.'

The jury withdrew for twenty minutes and when they returned to the courtroom their verdict of 'guilty' was no surprise. They had however chosen to halve the amount of damages, awarding Martin the sum of £10,000 (worth in 21st-century terms approximately £300,000). Petrie paid in cash within days of the hearing.

Martin stayed in London no longer than he had to and, after receiving the compensation awarded, he set out on the long journey to Holyhead and thence to Ireland. The case had attracted tremendous publicity, which it is tempting to compare to modern coverage of the sexual peccadilloes of celebrities. There had been remarkable coverage in the press, with *The Times*, which ran details of the trial the day afterwards, forced to extend its coverage to two full pages ten days later, due to the matter being the 'subject of much conversation'.

The lonely journey home gave Dick ample time to reflect. Lord Erskine's words were ringing in his mind. He had neglected Elizabeth. Undying love had not been enough for her; she had needed him to be there for her. Martin was capable of launching himself with passion into many things at once, but Erskine and Tone were right: he had overlooked the love that was closest to him. The fact that much of what Erskine had said, albeit in order to benefit his client, rang true, allowed Dick to forge a deep and productive friendship with the man in years to come.

Quite why Martin had proceeded with the action is difficult to understand. At heart he was a private man and indeed no-one would take pleasure in having such personal details made so public. At a time when much emphasis was placed on honour, making his humiliation known in all corners of society was a perverse course of action. To put himself in the position of re-living the previous year must have hurt Martin deeply. If his motive had been to disgrace both Petrie and Elizabeth, he had succeeded; they would spend the rest of their lives as social outcasts. Even after the trauma of killing his cousin, it would have been so much easier to settle the matter with Petrie in one immediate, simple and violent encounter.

One thing is certain: his motive was not financial, although the sum received would have provided him with resources he desperately needed. On leaving London, Martin instructed his coachman, Thady Harte, to convert the £10,000 into small change. He then told the bewildered servant to throw the mass of coins from the coach as it rumbled along the route. When Harte came to Martin some weeks later for his wages, Dick asked him, why he had not kept some of the money back for himself? Harte replied that if his master considered it wrong to keep it, then so did he.

# Chapter 17

# Martin's First Law

**B**ack in Dangan, Martin took stock. Elizabeth was gone, leaving him to bring up the three small children. There was no prospect of a quick return to politics and, although a natural optimist, he had to accept that the copper mines were never going to produce an income. Once again his many creditors were closing in. Fleeing to France was no longer an option; Martin had to seek sanctuary closer to home, and he found it in the wilds of his own estate.

Ballynahinch lies 50 miles to the west of Galway city; the 30 miles onward from Oughterard, where Robert now lived, was then only passable along a path winding through treacherous bogs and over the rocky Connemara mountains. It was this wilderness that Martin put between himself and captivity in a debtors' prison. Only a skilled horseman with detailed knowledge of the terrain could find his way through.

The small inn Robert had built on the shores of Ballynahinch Lake had been intended, with little prospect of passing trade, to accommodate the healthy smuggling industry so rife along the nearby coast. The setting is one of stark beauty alongside the Owenmore River and dominated by Ben Lettrey, a 2,000-foot conical mountain that towers above the remote location. Ballynahinch already had secured its place in Irish history. In the middle of the lake to the rear of the house there is a small island that still hosts the remains of a medieval castle.

It was here that Grace O'Malley, the pirate queen of Connaught, lived 250 years prior to Dick taking up residence. O'Malley had pillaged the Elizabethan ships plying their trade along the west coast. Her reputation made her the perfect bride for Donal, then head of the ferocious O'Flaherty clan. When Donal was murdered, Grace took over as ruler of his lands, forcing the English to accept her power. She visited the court of Queen Elizabeth, the two formidable women meeting as equals, and conversing in Latin. Ballynahinch was to add a bloody footnote to the story. In 1586 Grace's son Owen, now leader of the clan, captured the English Captain John Bingham who had unwisely ventured into Connemara, murdering the officer and eighteen of his men.

Martin himself was now living the life of an outlaw, rarely venturing into Galway for fear of being served with a bankruptcy writ. The only line of credit he could still rely on was from the smuggler George O'Malley, a descendant of the pirate queen. Another of Martin's shady contacts was Patrick Curly, a former servant at Dangan who now presided over a money-laundering operation between the Irish and French black markets. Most of Martin's staff at Ballynahinch were fugitives, grateful to work for little or no money in return for a safe haven.

Not surprisingly, the more zealous of the King's administrators in Galway began taking a closer interest in the former Volunteer Colonel and High Sheriff, now living a lawless existence in the furthermost parts of their jurisdiction. The role of chief zealot fell to Mansergh St George, an officious magistrate who had long held the Martins in

*Ballynahinch, viewed from downstream*

suspicion. A vendetta followed, reminiscent of the saga fifty years previously involving St George's predecessor Stratford Eyre and Dick's father.

St George reported to the Government in Dublin that, 'Connemara is the asylum of outlaws, deserters and persons escaped from justice, the stronghold of smugglers. Mr. Richard Martin resides there and conciliates the garrison with presents of liquor and provisions.'

By the beginning of 1794 the magistrate had decided that something needed to be done about Martin. He managed to find a process server who was either stupid or fearless enough to venture into inimical Connemara; but when the poor man returned it was with tales of Martin attacking him with a sharp instrument concealed in a stick.

A few days later, possibly in an attempt to clear the matter up, Martin interrupted St George as he presided in the Galway magistrates' court. Dick was promptly arrested and thrown into prison. He did not have to languish there long. He still had many friends in the city and, swelled by a small mob of his tenants who had arrived from the estate, the impromtu army sprung his release. Thenceforth, St George concluded that tangling with Martin was not worth the effort.

One other creditor, Eustace Stowell, undiscouraged by these events, decided that he would press for payment of his debt. Confronting Martin, and not being satisfied by the compromise he offered, Stowell challenged his creditor to pay him fully in cash, or provide personal satisfaction. Martin resigned himself to foregoing his self-imposed retirement from duelling and accepted the challenge. He later wrote of his pre-dicament, 'Though Soloman was a wise man and Sampson a strong one, neither of them could pay ready money if they had it not.'

The men met at the appointed hour and place, and faced each other with pistol in hand. But now Stowell concluded it was probably better to be owed money by 'Hair-Trigger' Dick than try to recoup the debt in this fashion. As the men took aim Stowell dropped his gun exclaiming,

'Mr Martin! Mr Martin! A pretty sort of payment this! You'd shoot me for my interest money, would you?'

Martin replied, 'If it is your pleasure Mr Stowell, I certainly will; but it was not my desire to come here, or to shoot you. You insisted on it yourself, so go on if you please, now we are here.' Stowell saw the sense in Dick's original offer of payment and the parties left the scene on amicable terms.

Despite his frustration at being forced to watch the political stage from a distance at which influence was impossible, Dick must have drawn some satisfaction from events that were stirring outside Connemara. This time it was Martin's old friend and former rival in love, Wolfe Tone, who was playing the leading role.

After his abrupt departure from Dangan, Tone had returned to Dublin, where he completed his studies at Trinity College. Later he studied for the Bar in London and, after dallying with the notion of joining the British Army with a bizarre plan of conquering the Sandwich Islands, he instead took up political pamphleteering. Though his first publication called for a celebration of the French Revolution, it was his famously seditious 'Argument on Behalf of the Catholics of Ireland' that caused the greatest stir. Tone argued that Ireland had no national government, being under British control, and the only way to counteract this was with sweeping parliamentary reform and full catholic emancipation.

Possibly influenced by his time with Robert and Dick at Dangan, and certainly by his friend Thomas Addis Emmet, Tone helped to form Societies of United Irishmen. These were middle-class debating organisations that strove to work upon public and parliamentary opinion. They called for political reform and equal civil rights for Catholics. At one stage extending the vote to women was discussed, but members quickly agreed that this radical step was impractical.

Tone also assumed the role of secretary for a new body, the Catholic Committee, which united many of the leading Catholic leaders and held a large convention in Dublin during December 1792. The Committee called for the total abolition of the remaining penal laws. More surprising was the further action taken. The Committee by-passed the Irish parliament and dispatched a delegation directly to Pitt in London.

The old firebrand Grattan also joined the clamour for reform and independence, along with a resurgent Volunteer Corps. The reality however was that neither King George nor his prime minister would have made any concessions because of this pressure alone. Events on a wider European front were accelerating in a direction that would help the Irish cause.

After a faltering start, the French Revolution had moved into top gear. Huge numbers of the aristocracy were being executed. On 21st January 1793 Louis XVI was beheaded. A group of fervent leaders had now emerged from the Third Estate with Citizen Robespierre as leader. The ambitions of these men did not end at the French border. Ten days after the fall of the monarchy, France found herself at war with both Holland and Britain. The governing body had no experience of leading a military campaign but Robespierre had found a young artillery lieutenant who had been responsible for the capture of the royalist fortress of Toulon. His name was Napoleon Bonaparte.

Pitt now addressed the House of Commons.

The contempt which the French have shown for a neutrality on our part most strictly observed; the violations of their solemn and plighted faith; their presumptuous attempts to interfere in the government of this country and to arm our subjects against ourselves, to vilify a monarch, the object of our gratitude, reverence and affection, and to separate the Court from the people; does not this become, on our part, a war of honour, a war necessary to assert the spirit of the nation and the dignity of the British name? We are at war with those who would destroy the whole fabric of our constitution. In such a case as that in which we are now engaged, I trust that our exertions will terminate only with our lives.

Behind the scenes Pitt advised his King that he would again have to compromise his coronation oath to secure Britain's back door. France's revolutionary cries of 'Liberty, Equality, Fraternity, Justice and Humanity' were falling on receptive Irish ears. British intelligence was reporting that the French had established links with revolutionary elements in Ireland. Reluctantly George agreed to another raft of concessions. Although catholic pressure needed to be acknowledged, the Irish Parliament, which had become increasingly complacent since Flood's death, chose not to push at this open door.

The result was the 1793 Relief Act that at last gave Catholics the right to vote, subject to owning a freehold valued at 40 shillings. Further concessions included the right to bear arms, take commissions in the army below the rank of General, enter Trinity College Dublin, sit as grand jurors and hold certain offices in local government. These measures were not enough for the Catholic Committee, who again called for total repeal of the penal laws. They immediately presented a petition to the House calling for Catholics to be allowed to enter Parliament. As if to say 'enough is enough', the government reacted to this by trimming back the concessions.

Wolfe Tone now decided to forge his own links with the new French administration, putting Ireland on the path of one of the bloodiest events in its history.

On 7th August 1794 Robert Martin died peacefully at Dangan. He was eighty-four years old. Robert had been a violent man in his youth and was undoubtably guilty of murdering an unarmed British officer all those years ago. But he was also a man of great vision, fair to people within his control and a good father to his children. His paternal advice to Dick on how catholic emancipation could and could not be achieved was about to be proved right in dramatic and tragic circumstances.

Dick had been running the estate for a number of years, so his father's death made little practical difference save in one important aspect. The Patent that had been granted to Nimble Dick Martin from King William in mysterious circumstances 100 years beforehand now passed to his great-grandson. Martin could now legally control his own army, a useful resource to a man with so many debts, but the truly far-reaching consequences would stem from the inherited right to hold his own court, administering whatever justice he saw fit for people living within his small empire.

The influences of his mother and aunts, combined with the teachings of Samuel Parr and Robert Sumner. were about to become law. Martin's tenants were by now aware of his views on the maltreatment of animals. The world was a hard place for domestic creatures in the 18th century. Poor, sometimes starving people, desperate to wring the last ounce of effort from their assets, beat working beasts until they dropped. Dogs were feared for the rabies they might be carrying and hunted down without mercy. Cocks and badgers were subjected to unmitigated pain in the interests of sport.

Had an average man, even as master of his estate, begun advocating kindness to animals, he would have been regarded as a sentimental madman. However this was 'Hair-Trigger' Dick, whose fearsome reputation had by now been elevated to almost mythical heights by years of his deeds being told and retold. He naturally commanded a respect which influenced the behaviour of his tenants.

Martin began formalising the law he had practised *ad hoc* since returning to Connemara. Until now he had relied on the power of his presence and reputation to deal with miscreantts. But the Patent allowed him actually to arrest them and bring them before a court at Ballynahinch with Martin as the sole judge and jury. If found guilty of cruelty they were sentenced to a short, but thoroughly unpleasant stay at Martin's private prison: Grace O'Malley's partly ruined pirate castle standing in the middle of Ballynahinch Lake. Changing his role from judge to jailer, Dick rowed the disgruntled prisoners to their dank and inhospitable accommodation, taking the opportunity of the boat journey to counsel them into better ways of treating defenceless creatures.

Martin's legal measures still had a long and tortuous road to take before they could be applied outside his domain, but his brand of justice, administered under the inherited medieval powers, was the initial impetus behind all modern animal welfare legislation.

*Grace O'Malley's castle, Ballynahinch lake*

# Chapter 18

# Harriet – and Rebellion

The success of Martin's Criminal Conversation process meant that Elizabeth's adultery was proven and the legal path now cleared for formal divorce. But before the Act to dissolve the Martins' marriage could be passed there was another hurdle to overcome. An Ecclesiastical Court had to approve the separation. For this to happen the plaintiff must agree to enter into a bond not to marry again during the lifetime of the divorced spouse. Most divorcees saw this as a purely notional commitment and remarried anyway. Whether or not Dick fell into this category is a matter for speculation. Within two years of the affair with Petrie, Elizabeth was dead, having given birth to her lover's child, a girl named Emily.

Elizabeth's death solved Dick's dilemma. He had met the second and last love in his life. Harriet Evans was the daughter of Hugh Evans, an army surgeon in the Fifth Regiment of Dragoon Guards, and Mary Thomas, a vicar's daughter from the southern English county of Hampshire, the family's head being Lord Carberry. By the time Dick met Harriet she was a widow: her husband Captain Robert Hesketh, an English naval officer, had died the year before.

Fifteen years younger than Dick, Harriet shared many of Elizabeth's qualities. She was attractive, intelligent and extremely well educated. Unlike the wandering Elizabeth, she reciprocated Dick's devotion. Since being widowed Harriet had returned to her family home in Cashel, County Tipperary. This was a prosperous area with welcoming landscapes, very different from the Connemara wilderness which became her home after the wedding at her father's house on 5th June 1796.

The war with France was now raging. Bonaparte had galvanised the French army, conquering Italy and forcing the Emperor of Austria into surrender. At the onset, Britain had pulled together a fragile alliance with the Low Countries, Prussia and Spain. By 1797 Prussia had joined Austria, anticipating that with Napoleon's support Poland and Russia would fall. The Spanish, fearing they had picked the wrong side, threw their hat in with the French. The Continent belonged to France and, with the Royal Navy on the verge of mutiny, and continental ports closed, Britain's control of the seas was looking increasingly tenuous.

British panic can be measured by the government's reactions. The writ of Habeas Corpus, which protects the right of an accused person not to be imprisoned without trial, was suspended throughout Britain, although not in Ireland at this stage. A new Treason Act was brought in, to allow imprisonment of anybody criticising the constitution. Any lingering press support for revolutionary French ideals disappeared overnight.

Under mounting pressure, Pitt deemed it sensible to form a coalition government that included Lord Portland, the former Viceroy of Ireland and William Wentworth, who as Earl Fitzwilliam was second-largest landowner in Ireland after Richard Martin.

The British government viewed Ireland as their Achilles heel in military terms. It was well known that radicals such as Wolfe Tone had strong links to the French. Fitzwilliam proposed himself as the man to calm Irish disquiet and was dispatched to Dublin as Lord Lieutenant.

Fitzwilliam's plan to keep the loyalty of Ireland was simple, and would no doubt have been successful if allowed to run its course. After consulting Henry Grattan and George Ponsonby, he immediately promised Catholics full emancipation. Within two months he had been replaced, his brief sojourn merely stirring up an already angry hornet's nest, while more and more moderates moved towards sedition.

It was in this increasingly fractious climate that a fault line opened in the north of Ireland that exists to this day. Fifteen years after the Volunteer rally in Tyrone, where thousands of Protestants had demanded fairer laws for their catholic brothers, sectarian violence broke out.

Protestant Ulstermen had for centuries been as poor as their catholic neighbours but felt that at least they maintained superiority by virtue of the penal laws. Arming Catholics and allowing them on to the political ladder had been a cause for concern. In the inevitable economic downturn that occurs in times of war, the linen trade became increasingly cut-throat. Protestants and Catholics responded by forming secret societies to protect their work. It was only a matter of time before, driven by the combined motives of financial self-protection and simple paranoia, groups each side of the religious divide clashed. Trouble flared in County Armagh, where protestant groups succeeded in getting the upper hand, at the 'Battle of the Diamond', near Lougall. Old Orange and Jacobite wounds were reopened and on 12th July 1796, 5000 Orangemen regrouped at the Diamond to celebrate both their recent victory and the previous one 100 years beforehand at the Boyne.

In the remotest part of Connaught, Harriet Martin was settling into her new way of life. She had immediately taken to the role of stepmother to Dick's three children, all still under twelve.

Martin had no hesitation in welcoming the trickle of refugees that began arriving from the north, letting them settle on plots of land without the burden of rent. When news of the benevolence awaiting them in Connemara became known, the trickle turned into a stream. During an extraordinarily harsh winter, Dick and his new bride opened the doors of Ballynahinch, providing food and shelter, and turning their home into an overpopulated refugee camp. Martin immersed himself in the problems of his guests and when spring arrived he provided men to help with the building of meagre but adequate housing.

All the components of revolution were beginning to come together. From the troubles in the north there emerged a very different organisation of United Irishmen. What had started as a peaceful lobby group had been taken over by radicals. and disillusion had set in when the realities of the Relief Act, managed by the British government through a Protestant administration, became apparent.

The radicals began organising themselves along military lines, described by a contemporary in 'A Memoir of the origin and progress of the Union':

The military organisation of the United Irishmen had no existence until the end of 1796; and was, as nearly as could be, engrafted on the civil. In order to avoid giving alarm, it continued to conceal itself as much as possible under the usual denominations. The Secretary of a society of twelve was normally the petty officer; the delegate of five societies to a lower baronial, when the population required such an intermediate step, was usually the captain; and the delegate of ten lower baronials to the upper baronial or district was most commonly colonel. All officers up to colonel were indispensably elected by those they were to command, but at that point the interference of the societies ceased and every commission was in the power of the executive only. As soon as a sufficient number of regiments were formed in any county the Colonels were directed to transmit to the Executive the names of three persons fit in their opinion to act as Adjutant-General for that county; of those the Executive chose one, and through this organ all military communications were made to the several counties.

Martin was a prime candidate to take an active senior role in the United Irishmen. His catholic sympathies were known, he had the experience of being a Volunteer Colonel, an established and armed yeomanry was under his command, many United Irishmen were already being harboured, and the remoteness of his location would have protected the rebel preparations. He chose not to go down this road.

France saw an opportunity to exploit her enemy's weakness further. Encouraged by Wolfe Tone's advice that the Irish people would be receptive to an invasion, William Jackson, a French agent, visited Dublin to meet United Irishmen leaders. He had brought a fellow agent with, him but this man was in the employ of British intelligence and Jackson was arrested and charged with treason. He chose dramatically to take his own life while standing in the dock.

The spotlight now turned on Wolfe Tone, who had had dealings with Jackson. The legal evidence against him was patchy and he still had friends highly placed in Dublin Castle. Accordingly he was permitted to emigrate to America, but this destination was a ruse and he immediately travelled back across the Atlantic to France, where he began plotting the invasion of Ireland.

The Royal Navy had successfully placed a blockade preventing French attacks on the mainland but did not have the resources to extend this protection to the waters surrounding Ireland. Tone had been planning the invasion with two of Napoleon's senior generals, Carnot and Hoche, the latter tasked with leading the initial naval attack, assisted by Tone who intended, on landing in Ireland, to broker the invasion plans with leaders of the United Irishmen.

The French fleet, delayed by dockyard deficiencies, finally set sail from the Atlantic port of Brest on 14th December 1796, carrying 14,000 troops. Tone had been given the French rank of Adjutant-General, and travelled with General Hoche on the chief of staff's ship. Six days later the fleet were sighted off Bantry Bay, on the south-west coast of Ireland. The plan was to land there and immediately march on Cork, Ireland's second city, which was protected by a garrison only half the size of the invading army. The alarm was quickly raised across the country and in Connemara Martin revealed his hand; he was not going to support Tone and instead offered his yeomanry to the parliamentary army. He was not a sympathiser with the French Revolutionary movement, which was hardly pro-catholic, and had executed priests along with aristocrats. Then again, perhaps his attitude to Tone contained a personal element.

It was now that General Hoche rued the delay in sailing. Fierce winter storms rolled in from the Atlantic, scattering the French fleet along the coast. The wind and snow continued for a week, by which time reinforcments had arrived in Cork and the Royal Navy was approaching from the east. With no chance of reassembling his fleet as a cohesive unit, Hoche gave the order to return to France.

Life on the Martin estate quickly returned to what passed as normality, and on 25th March 1797 Dick and Harriet were blessed with their first child, Richard. Although Harriet loved Elizabeth's children as hers, the birth of Richard cemented what was to remain a blissful and lasting marriage.

The following year a cousin of Dick named Thomas Martin died. Thomas had lived in America and served as Quartermaster for General George Washington during the War of Independence, before returning to Galway. It is likely that Dick had visited him during his travels with James Jordon.

Martin's finances, although far from healthy, had improved to the extent that he could set foot outside Connemara without being thrown into a debtor's prison. He still harboured a burning ambition to return to politics, more so after Tone's abortive attempt to achieve catholic emancipation, and he was given his chance when a General Election was called in July 1797. This was to be the first election in which land-owning Catholics would be allowed to vote and the guaranteed support from his estate must have decreased Dick's apprehension at fighting a campaign with virtually no financial backing.

Despite his new catholic voters, Martin lost to St George Daly and his old friend George Ponsonby. The route back to Parliament started from an unexpected direction. John La Touche, a member of the wealthy banking family related to Martin's former in-laws, the Veseys, vacated his seat in nearby Lanesborough for Martin to occupy.

On 9th January 1798, after a forced absence of sixteen years, Richard Martin again took his seat in the Irish Parliament. The country was in turmoil. Radical United Irishmen were regrouping and planning further action. British troops, using emergency powers, were billeted with Irish families in an attempt to suppress rebellion pockets before they could be coordinated. Tone, who had blamed bad luck and weather for his previous failure, ignoring the fact that he had not ostensibly attracted much support, was planning a second invasion with his French allies.

The United Irishmen were beginning to achieve a much higher level of success among the peasantry across Ireland. A song, 'The French are on the sea says the Shan Van Vocht' (old woman) was being sung across the land. By February 1798, revolutionary organisations comprised over 280,000 members. What Fitzgibbon, now Earl of Clare, described as 'a deluded peasantry aided by more intelligent treason' was actually on the point of explosion.

Parliament rushed through further acts to pave the way for quick suppression. Habeas Corpus was suspended in Ireland, and an Insurrection Act was passed whereby a 'proclaimed district' could impose curfews and give magistrates sweeping powers to search for arms. The army enthusiastically used this law for raiding settlements suspected of rebel tendencies.

The more moderate Whigs in Parliament, supported by Martin, argued that, as in the past, concessions would neutralise the radicals. But moderates on both sides were not being heard. The United Irishmen believed that the time had come finally to oust the British. The British had decided that the boil needed lancing.

The outcome was decided, as is so often the case in armed conflict, by timing. The British had managed partially to infiltrate the hierarchy of the United Irishmen. Early in 1797 Thomas Reynolds, a member of the Leinster Provincial Directory, began feeding information to his paymasters. In March 1798 the Leinster Directory met, along with other senior members of the United Irishmen, at a house in Bridge Street, Dublin. The meeting was raided and all leaders, except for Lord Edward Fitzgerald, were arrested. Fitzgerald escaped but was hunted down and fatally wounded on May 19th. He was allowed to die in prison awaiting trial, his wounds left unattended.

The United Irishmen were simply not ready for the rebellion to start at this stage. Ideally it would have started the following spring, but with the realisation that the organisation was about to implode, the call to rise was given on 23rd May.

Activities were badly coordinated from the start. Skirmishes took place in the counties round Dublin but the rebels were quickly put down. The British army had successfully weakened the United Irishmen's reserves of arms in the north. It was in the south-western stronghold of County Wexford that the rebellion managed to take hold.

In stiflingly hot conditions the rebels, armed mostly with homemade pikes, took control of Wexford town and began marching both north and west. They were finally halted at New Ross and Arklow and regrouped at Vinegar Hill, near Enniscorthy. By now the United Irishmen in the north, led by Henry Joe McCraken, had been decisively beaten.

Rebel hopes hinged on French support arriving in time. Tone, caught equally unaware by the premature start of the rebellion, was desperately trying to organise French support but Napoleon's attention was focussed on directly engaging the British in the Mediterranean. He only saw Ireland as a diversion. Eventually Tone succeeded in assembling a French invasion force but it was too late: the rebels had been crushed in the brutal battle at Vinegar Hill.

Martin was thought to be a sympathizer with the rebellion, but his accusers were wrong. He supported many of its objectives but regarded armed rebellion as worse than fruitless. The uprising had seen frightful atrocitities inflicted by both sides, which must have sickened him. Men, women and children had been shot, piked, tortured and burnt alive, and he must have dreaded such carnage invading his poverty-stricken lands. He turned his energies to pleading in Parliament for mercy for the rebels. He vigorously called for amnesty for the 600,000 Irishmen who had fought for independence. When the government agreed to allow pardons, Martin continued to argue that they were not being implemented and that rebels continued to be imprisoned.

The corpse of the rebellion however, still twitching, was given resuscitation by the belated arrival of the French. On 22nd August, they landed at Killala in County Mayo, not far up the coast from Martin's estate. Led by General Humbert they marched quickly to Castlebar, the former stronghold of Fighting Fitzgerald. Dick's two surviving Jordon cousins joined them, along with 5000 others. After taking Castlebar the plan was to march on east of the Shannon, where resurgent rebels from the north would meet the French army. French reinforcements were en route from Brest.

In the meantime Lord Cornwallis, now Viceroy and an experienced military campaigner, had assembled a large force and was converging on the alliance of French and United Irishmen. Though aware of the great odds against them, Irish and French fought spiritedly at Ballinamuck, but the eventual outcome was defeat. The French soldiers not killed in battle were afforded full prisoner of war protection, the Irish rebels hunted down and slaughtered.

The Royal Navy continued to engage French ships close to the Irish coast and, some time later, on boarding the enemy's flagship anchored near to Lough Swilly, County Donegal, found Wolfe Tone, in his French uniform.

Tone was taken to Dublin, court martialled and sentenced to hang for treason. Awaiting execution, he made one final dramatic gesture. Tragically mirroring the actions of the forlorn victim he had played opposite Elizabeth Martin at Kirwan's Lane theatre so many years ago, Tone slit his own throat, although not cleanly, suffering a protracted death days later.

# Chapter 19

# Union

Fifty thousand Irishmen had lost their lives in the rebellion of 1798. The remainder of the people now held their breath waiting for what the aftermath would bring. But there were no Cromwellian reprisals. One problem facing the British Government was whom to blame. The leaders had almost all been radical Protestants whose main objective had been to achieve an Irish republic, albeit with full catholic emancipation. However not all Catholics had supported Tone and his fellow rebels. Ireland was in a complex state of confusion.

The army was bent on rooting out any pockets of insurgents that still existed, but by and large people innocent of direct involvement were spared. Rebels went into hiding, the Martin estate providing obvious sanctuary for hundreds.

Martin turned a blind eye to the fugitives who made a temporary home in his mountains and sought to help those who were brought before local justice. The most zealous magistrate in Ireland was Dennis Browne, 'Dennis the Rope', brother of Lord Altamont, the owner of the murdered wolfhound that Dick had gone to such great lengths to avenge. As the steady stream of captured rebels were brought before the courts, Martin pleaded for clemency, aided by juries who were reluctant to return the verdict of guilty against their countrymen. Furthermore, he gave shelter in Connemara to one famous rebel, Father Gibbons from County Mayo, wanted for, among other crimes, the murder of one of his jailers. Gibbons stayed hidden there until his death in 1840.

On the wider stage the period after the 1798 rebellion was comparable to the end of a card game. The pack now needed to be shuffled and dealt again. In London, Pitt saw an opportunity to implement a plan first suggested by his father: the union of the Irish and English parliaments. He and his cabinet realised that only having luck on their side had saved Ireland from French occupation. But events were turning in Britain's favour, not only in Ireland but also in the Mediterranean where a young admiral, Horatio Nelson, was aggressively tackling the French fleet.

Pitt (who only months earlier had uttered one of the greatest untruths in Parliament: that the new Income Tax was to be a temporary measure) decided finally to do away with the irritant of a puppet parliament in Dublin, and absorb it into Westminster. Union with the Scottish parliament had been a success and now events permitted Pitt to try the same with Ireland. To achieve his goal, he implemented a masterly plan whereby all parties were told what they wanted to hear.

There is no questioning that Pitt genuinely wanted full emancipation for Catholics; his actions two years later would prove this. But his first objective was to prevent King George realising that the catholic question was even on the agenda. When Pitt explained his plans for unification, George only saw the obvious benefits of finally removing a constant thorn in his side.

Pitt rightly did not anticipate any resistance from his own House of Commons, but needed the Irish Parliament to vote for its own demise. To achieve one of the greatest political three-card tricks in history, Pitt's cabinet put out two totally conflicting messages. Those who had opposed, or at least reluctantly supported, concessions to Catholics needed little reminding that, although one rebellion had been suppressed, another might not be. The unavoidable fact was that any Irish parliament ruled over a people that were overwhelmingly catholic. Protestants would be afforded better protection by one combined parliament, accountable to a population where Catholics were in a minority.

To those, including Richard Martin, who campaigned for emancipation, harsh reality was emphasised. The King, his government and therefore the Irish political subsidiary in Dublin Castle feared Catholics because they were the majority. A simple hypothesis was mooted. Ireland in isolation was five-sixths catholic, Britain as a whole was 80% protestant. If the parliaments were united then Catholics would immediately become a minority and therefore less of a threat: consequently their emancipation would in fact be much easier to achieve.

On top of this wonderful spin-doctoring, two other inducements were offered. Neither side was happy with its current position and saw little hope or satisfaction with the status quo. So why not support union, what was the downside? And, for those unconvinced by any of these arguments, there was always the time-honoured tradition of bribery.

The first thing to do was to ascertain the start point. Lord Lieutenant Cornwallis sounded out the most influential members of the Irish parliament. He reported to Pitt that opinion was equally divided on the issue. John Fitzgibbon, now Lord Chancellor, along with fellow anti-catholics such as Lord Beresford, felt that union would serve to neutralise the catholic threat. Advocates of an independent Ireland such as the Duke of Leinster and Henry Grattan were fervently opposed to such a large step back from full political independence. Cornwallis concluded that the key to successful union lay in convincing the substantial number of members, including the likes of Richard Martin, who were sitting on the fence.

On 22st January 1799 the Irish Parliament reconvened to debate the question. The major cities in Ireland had already taken positions. Dublin was naturally against it, since the demise of the government it hosted could only lessen its influence and trading potential. A whole mini-economy flourished on the extravagance of the politicians based in the Castle. Cork saw Dublin's problem as its opportunity, and supported union. Belfast was undecided, although the Orange orders were already strongly opposed to the move. Most significantly for Martin, the Galway Corporation had voted against union.

The first parliamentary debate on the issue lasted for twenty hours. By now Martin had concluded that emancipation would be eminently more likely in his lifetime if the Catholics were a non-threatening minority. However he made his position public not by arguing for hypothetical future benefits, but by criticising what had gone before.

His disillusionment with the Irish Parliament, built up since he had first entered the House twenty-three years before, was apparent from his speeches. When dissidents argued that retaining an independent parliament was critical to Ireland, Martin responded that the parliament these people were looking to keep was rife with 'incorrigible wickedness and corruption'

Martin went on to question why a rebellion had happened in the first place. Sir John Parnell, the Chancellor of the Exchequer, made a speech highlighting how the Irish economy had prospered since the granting of additional autonomy to its parliament in 1782. Martin replied:

'Since that period wealth has been more generally diffused through Ireland, than any other country; the poor have grown rich and there has arisen amongst us an agricultural yeomanry. If a country, Sir, that is poor, is increasingly beyond example in its agriculture and its commerce and yet becomes hourly discontented and at last breaks out into open rebellion against all its constituted authorities, what is to be done?'

Dick went on to call on those against union with Westminster to offer a better alternative. He acknowledged that there would be many, like him, who at first found the notion of giving up their parliamentary independence abhorrent, but he declared that, 'Some things which at first blush appear bad, not only cease to be so, but even become remedies when compared with greater disadvantages.' Drawing on the classics, he finished his contribution with a Latin quotation translated as

Here Phaethon lies: his father's car he tried:
Though proved too weak, he greatly daring died.

The marathon debate ended with a vote: 109 were for union, 111 against. Cornwallis, assisted by his new Secretary the young Viscount Castlereagh, now knew whom they had to convert and began the process of lobbying and bribing. The British government's reading of the position was that twelve more months were needed to bring a comfortable number of waverers into line. Lord Cornwallis personally assured Martin that emancipation would immediately follow union, a promise which Dick still bitterly recalled in a parliamentary speech 28 years later.

Martin's problem now was that his position was openly opposed to that of the majority of people in Galway, and immediately after the debate concluded he returned home. Harriet had not joined him in Dublin; she was pregnant again and was combining making a number of improvements to Ballynahinch with a new-found career as a writer.

Dick had formed a friendship with Castlereagh, which would survive many political differences over the years. The two men agreed on a plan to convert opinion in Galway, whereby Dick would spend the remainder of the year working on influential landowners, while Castlereagh attempted to convert Richard Trench, one of the Galway County Members who was strongly opposed to union at the start but now appeared to be wavering. In return for his support Castlereagh offered Dick a salaried seat on the Revenue Board and an assurance of safe return to parliament at the next general election. Both these offers must have been very welcome.

Assisted by his old friend Joseph Blake, another Galway County member, Martin set out his theory to local Catholics that union would best achieve their aim. With his reputation, gained over many years, as a man committed in principle and practice to the catholic cause, Martin received an accommodating reception wherever he went. By the end of the summer he was confident that public opinion had moved in his direction and a series of public meetings could now be held to back the union formally.

Castlereagh informed Martin that Trench was on the verge of shifting his support, but the member for Galway Town remained concerned as to how a volte-face could be achieved without him looking easily persuaded or worse, bribed. Martin was also encountering this problem with people he had been trying to persuade and wrote to Castlereagh that, when drafting resolutions for the forthcoming public meetings in Galway Town and County, the wording would be, 'A decided approbation of the measure and yet save the faces of those signatories who formerly expressed themselves against it.'

The wording put before the first public meeting in Galway on 2nd August 1799 made it clear that when the union of parliaments was first raised it had made 'an unfavourable impression' but after 'mature and deliberate consideration' it was now felt that this course of action would give both countries 'the blessings of connexion' and defence from the 'evils of separation'. Addressing the key issue of catholic emancipation in his final resolution, Martin's draft read:

> Resolved, that we look with peculiar pleasure to this measure, as it promises an admission to our Catholic brethren to the franchises of the Constitution . . . our most gracious and benevolent Sovereign, and a common and impartial Parliament, relieved from the embarrassing dilemma of right on one hand and danger on the other, will, we confidently hope, extend to this class of the Irish people, those privileges which they may then enjoy with perfect security, to the privileges and property of the other.

Martin was successful in gaining public support for union at the Galway Town meeting. All that remained was to achieve a similar vote at a meeting for Galway County, due to be held at Loughrea. Martin arranged for 60 influential freeholders from Connemara to attend. As the meeting prepared to vote, Dick's old foe Bowes Daly, a fierce critic of union, arrived with a mob that began pelting the building with stones. Chaos ensued and the meeting dispersed before a vote could be taken; however it was generally assumed that the outcome would have been pro-union, as the attendees had already heard from Trench that this was now where his support lay.

Although he was receiving favourable feedback from his Lord Lieutenant, the Prime Minister was increasingly faced with a dilemma. Anti-catholic supporters of union were asking for a categorical assurance from Pitt that the merging of parliaments would not lead to further concessions to Catholics. Members who favoured union because they believed it would result in catholic emancipation wanted more concrete promises that this would occur. Pitt kept all sides happy with a use of smoke and mirrors that any good illusionist would have admired.

He had already received a letter from the King making it absolutely clear that further concessions to Catholics were not open to consideration. Pitt, however, was not unduly worried, as he felt that with a united parliament, Catholics in a non-threatening minority, and an ongoing war with France, he would be able to bulldoze the monarch into allowing full emancipation. Pitt then cleverly let the content of the King's letter be known to those who did not favour emancipation, telling them that they could rest assured that the King would never budge from his coronation oath.

The line given to appease advocates of union plus emancipation (which now included Martin) was, not to make it an issue at this stage, as it would force the King unnecessarily into a corner. Better to wait until union was in place and then the Prime Minister would exert the strongest possible pressure on his sovereign to agree to something that now presented no further threat to the Crown. Pitt privately stated that he would make the Catholic question an issue of resignation if necessary, once union had been achieved. He assumed, of course, that he was now indispensable.

When the Irish Parliament reassembled on 15th January 1800, Westminster had already voted for union, by 236 votes to 50. A final series of debates and a vote on the issue was now to take place in Dublin. The opening debate started dramatically. Henry Grattan, too ill to stand for parliament at the previous election, and still a very sick man, had the day before secured the vacant seat of Wicklow and travelled through the night to make his entrance. Wearing his old Volunteer uniform, the former leader of the House made an impassioned speech for its preservation.

More and more speeches followed, none raising arguments that had not been heard a year beforehand. After hearing Grattan and many others remind the House of its heritage, Martin chose instead to look forward, asking how a group of Irishmen sitting as a minority in Westminster might serve the Irish people in a better manner than had been accomplished when they had been given a parliament of their own. He took the floor and said, 'We are a discordant, disagreeing band, liable to perpetual desertion; we must, therefore, pledge ourselves by such a bond as shall secure us from abandoning each other.'

The people of Dublin had cause above and beyond the loss of parliamentary independence violently to oppose the union. Even the strongest pro-union advocates could not deny that depriving the capital city of being the seat of parliament would bring severe economic depression to the area. The people of Dublin were not going to endure such losses without a fight.

Violent demonstrations were now taking place every day leading up to the final vote. In desperation a mob of nearly 1000 stormed the Castle looking for known supporters of the union. They immediately confronted one of the highest-profile politicians in question: Richard Martin.

Martin, never a man to take much account of danger, let alone run from it, confronted the angry mob and drew a small, one-shot pistol from his pocket. Cocking the weapon he faced the crowd and threatened that if anyone advanced 'six inches' towards him he would shoot them 'dead as that paving stone'. The crowd was stunned at Martin's nerve and, mindful of his reputation, no Dubliner in the mob was prepared to be the one person to lay down his life for the city's cause. After a stand-off of nearly a minute a cheer broke out for Martin's bravery, allowing him to walk away unscathed.

A few days later another crowd attacked Dick's carriage as he was leaving parliament. Martin escaped unharmed but one of the attackers, a man called Brocas, was arrested and brought before the bar of the House for sentencing. Martin successfully called for his release.

By now the British administration, after months of private persuasion and bribing, (£10,000 was paid to obtain the support of Martin's Hellfire Club colleague Buck Whaley), had arrived at the crosssroads. On 7th June 1798 the motion for union with Westminster was carried.

After two decades of serving within the Irish Parliament, Dick saw it as a toothless and corrupt body, hopelessly divided. Personally he stood to gain financially from the union, as he had promises of a sinecure, and by becoming a member of the parliament in Westminster he was afforded legal protection from his many creditors. But his support for the union had primarily been because he genuinely believed that his life's cause of catholic emancipation was more likely to be achieved by it. Within two years he would be bitterly regretting his own naivety

Both the sinecure and the protection were very relevant to Martin. By now he knew that the parties to the copper mine deal that had directly cost him his first marriage had, in fact, swindled him. Yet the precipice of personal bankruptcy was put into a more tragic perspective. Dick and Harriet's infant son Charles had not survived the first winter of the new century.

*View from Ballynahinch Castle*

# Chapter 20

# Westminster

The passing of the Act to unify the governments of Dublin and Westminster was celebrated with a lavish party at the home of Viscount Castlereagh in Phoenix Park, which the Martins attended. Two months later the House of Lords approved the Union and Dublin became a capital city without a government in situ. The British retained a scaled down administration there, still headed by the Lord Lieutenant, and Irish politics went into limbo for the remainder of 1800.

Despite a pressing need for the salary, Dick had resigned his post on the Revenue Board in good faith that his exertions to assist the Union would be rewarded with a new role when he took up his seat in Westminster. He was pleasantly surprised to be given a temporary post for the remainder of the year as one of the Commissioners for Stamps, which paid the grateful recipient £800 per annum.

Castlereagh was experiencing a problem in delivering to Dick the promised seat for Galway County that he so much coveted. Joseph Blake, who had agreed to relinquish his seat, changed his mind at the last minute. Cornwallis, still the Viceroy, stepped in quickly and offered Blake a peerage, allowing Dick to become the Member for Galway, albeit with no House to sit in until the Irish took their seats at Westminster the following year.

The Martins' grief at losing their young son had been tempered by Harriet quickly falling pregnant once more. The family began preparations for their imminent move to London. Dick's immediate priority was to concentrate on a new business venture following the collapse of the ill-fated copper mining scheme.

He still hoped that salvation lay beneath the Connemara soil. Minerals, including lead, pink granite, quartz, pyrites and more copper ore had been discovered in a mountain close to Oughterard, but more importantly the mines would be close to Lough Corrib, with its direct access to the port of Galway, a fundamental consideration for a mining operation, which had been overlooked last time. Dick's cousin Richard Kirwan was President of the Royal Irish Academy and recommended Monsieur Subrine, a mineralogist to the late King Louis XVI, to conduct surveys. The Frenchman confirmed the quality of the mineral seams and Dick, satisfied that their exploitation would materially assist his financial problems, turned his attention to other matters.

Since the days of Nimble Dick, the Martins had allowed catholic priests to operate throughout their estate. The best known of these was the firebrand Father Prendergast, who had taken an active role in the rebellion and was still a favourite amongst his fellow fugitives settled in the hills near Ballynahinch. The priest approached Martin and asked him if he would obtain an official pardon for himself and a well-known rebel leader, John Gibbons, also known as 'Johnnie the Outlaw'. Dick agreed to plead for Father Prendergast but felt that his fellow insurgent was a hopeless case.

The plea fell on the deaf ears of the Marquis of Sligo, as Altamont had now become. Martin had not done himself any favours by aligning himself with outlaws, and it was to cause him a high degree of trouble at the next election. Again, it demonstrated his almost total inability to think through the consequences of some of his actions.

Martin was now looking forward to taking up his new role as a member of the British parliament. He was full of confidence that catholic emancipation had at last appeared over the horizon, but there was also another, much lower-profile matter that had attracted his attention the previous year, and one in which he may well have had a distant hand.

Amid the major issues such as unification, and the full-scale European war that was still raging, a small but significant event had occurred in Westminster. Sir William Pultney, an English MP, had proposed a bill to ban the sport of bull-baiting. Pultney had asked for the assistance of Lord Erskine, Dick's old acquaintance from Paris and the lawyer who had represented the adulterer Petrie in court against him.

Another MP, Richard Brinsley Sheridan, an old school friend of Dick's, and fellow-devotee of Dr Parr, who combined his parliamentary career with being an accomplished playwright, drew on his dramatic skills to support the proposal in the House, condemning the sport as 'inhuman, cruel, disgraceful and beastly'. It could 'excite nothing but brutality, ferociousness and cowardice', and 'must debase the mind, deaden the feelings, and extinguish every spark of courage and benevolence.'

The reaction of the House of Commons to the previously unknown subject of animal rights was one of astonishment. Windham, the Secretary for War, and Canning, another Cabinet member, dismissed the bill on the grounds that the subject was below the dignity of the House to discuss. The bill fell at the first hurdle, but a political movement emulating Martin's private law in Connemara had begun.

Dick and Harriet planned to spend the winter in London, returning to Ballynahinch during the summer recess at Westminster. Travelling conditions had not improved since Dick's days at Harrow. The trip between Ballynahinch and London still took about a week, more if weather on the Irish Sea delayed the boat between Dublin and Holyhead. A first class ticket on the ferries only secured a curtain for privacy below deck, with the passengers having to provide their own food and drink.

The Martins' eldest child, Laetitia, now fifteen, remained in Ballynahinch with her half-brothers. Her younger brothers, Thomas and St George, now fourteen and twelve respectively, were placed in an English boarding school, Redlands, near Bristol. Dick and Harriet took up residence in Cumberland Place, a fashionable address close to Hyde Park and a short carriage ride from the House of Commons.

The first year of the 19th century saw Britain expanding its industrial revolution. Fashions had become moderately more conservative, partly due to an opportunistic tax Pitt had imposed on wig powder, and, since the fall of the aristocracy in Paris, London was now by far the most fashionable city in the world.

On the first day of January 1801 the one hundred Irish members took their seats at St Stephen's Palace in Westminster. Many held great hopes of a new period for Irish history and a time in the very near future that Protestants and Catholics would hold the same rights and privileges in all walks of life.

After the Irish Parliament had voted in favour of the principle of unification with Westminster, the task had been given to constitutional draftsmen in London to structure the actual statute, due to come into force on the first day of 1801. The devil was, as ever, in the detail, although the body of the statute remained in line with Irish expectations:

> Whereas in pursuance of His Majesty's most gracious recommendation to the two Houses of Parliament in Great Britain and Ireland respectively, to consider of such measures as might best tend to strengthen and consolidate the connection between the two Kingdoms, the two Houses of the Parliament of Great Britain and the two Houses of the Parliament of Ireland have severally agreed and resolved that, in order to promote and secure the essential interests of Great Britain and Ireland, and to consolidate the strength, power and resource of the British Empire, it will be advisable to concur in such measures as may best tend to unite the two Kingdoms of Great Britain and Ireland into one Kingdom, in such manner, and on such terms and conditions as may be established by the Acts of the respective Parliaments of Great Britain and Ireland.

Supporters of Catholic emancipation expected at least a statement of intent that it would be forthcoming in secondary legislation during this session of Parliament. There was nothing to this end within the accompanying Articles to the Act. What had been, however, been added to the Act some time between the ending of the Dublin Parliament and the official start of the unified Houses was Article 5, which read:

> That the Churches of England and Ireland, as now by law established, be united into one Protestant Episcopal Church, to be called The United Church of England and Ireland; and that the doctrine, worship, discipline and government of the said United Church shall be, and shall remain, in full force for ever, as the same are now by law established for the Church of England; and that the continuance and preservation of the said united Church, as the Established Church of England and Ireland, shall be deemed and taken to be an essential and fundamental part of the Union; and that in like manner the doctrine, worship, discipline and government of the Church of Scotland shall remain and be preserved as the same are now established by law, and by the Acts of the Union of the Two Kingdoms of England and Ireland.

As an endorsement of unification of the established Protestant Church in both countries it made logical sense, but the effect was irrevocably to alienate the Catholic Church. Wording the statute in a manner that described the United Church as 'an essential and fundamental part of the Union' meant that Irish Catholics were forced to pay dues to what they saw as an heretical institution.

For Pitt, his problems were that all his chickens were now roosting under one parliamentary roof. The Irish and English members who, for whatever reason, wanted no more rights granted to Catholics were obviously appeased, but those such as Martin, who had expected immediate concessions, were knocking on Pitt's door demanding their own satisfaction. Cornwallis and Castlereagh both reminded the Prime Minister of the promises and assurances they had made to persuade Irish members to vote for union. To his credit Pitt, true to his word, made it be known that he would if necessary make the matter an issue for resignation.

Pitt was confident he had made a good job of his term of office on both economic and war management terms. He had overlooked that King George was by now tired of his first minister and perfectly happy, after nearly 20 years, to contemplate a change of government. Pitt sought an audience with the King and formally raised the catholic question. He pointed out that Ireland was now controlled by Westminster. Irish Catholics did not present a threat and were more likely to do so if rights were not conferred, especially after the implications of unifying the Church became apparent to them. Catholicism was on the decline in England; the country had moved a long way forward from the days of rampant Jacobite plotting.

The King was having none of it. Pitt had misread the situation. George by now, despite his bout of madness, was the most astute and experienced politician in the country, and he was well liked by his subjects. He had come to the conclusion that it was time to recover control of his government.

Pitt needed cabinet support if there was to be a showdown with the King, but George out-manoevered him. At a levee on 28th January, with all the Cabinet in attendance, the King made his position clear. He viewed Irish Catholics as a threat to the security of the whole of Britain. The Royal opinion had 'not been formed on the moment' but had been 'imbibed for forty years.' If he had to, George would beg his bread 'from door to door throughout Europe' rather than consent to any measure that would be a betrayal of his solemn oath. For a group of politicians who by now could smell Pitt's blood, the most telling of the King's statements at the meeting was when he concluded, 'I shall reckon any man my personal enemy who proposes any such measure. The most Jacobite thing I have ever heard.'

George had backed his Prime Minister into a corner, and followed up the next day by dispatching the man already chosen to replace Pitt, to deliver the final move. Henry Addington, the current Leader of the House and a staunch anti-catholic, who had played a direct part in the wording of the Act of Union, personally handed a letter to Pitt from the King requesting that the issue of catholic emancipation be publicly abandoned.

Pitt had no choice in his reply but to repeat that the catholic question no longer posed a threat, and offered his resignation in the event that the King could not agree to back him in this matter. George of course merely replied on 3rd February 1801 that his coronation oath precluded him from acceding to Pitt's request and he was reluctantly forced to accept the Prime Minister's resignation. George had learnt one of the cardinal rules of politics: never make an unnecessary enemy. He was most gracious in his praises, addressing his written acknowlegment of Pitt's leaving with 'My Dearest Pitt'. More importantly, the King preempted any plotting on the part of his ousted minister by settling the substantial debts Pitt had accumulated during his nineteen years in office.

Cornwallis, Castlereagh and Canning had no choice but to follow Pitt's lead and resign. Pitt would soon rue forcing the catholic issue too soon after the unified parliament had commenced. He should have waited. Within weeks of the confrontation with the King, George had slipped into his second bout of madness.

Pitt's conduct cannot easily be explained. His main motive was to do away with the Dublin administration, which he felt was at least partly responsible for the 1798 rebellion. Catholic emancipation was not a crusade for Pitt, although he had undoubted humanitarian tendencies He probably genuinely considered that conferring equal rights on Catholics did not pose a threat and would probably prevent, or at least defer future problems. It was also a concession he needed to offer in order to secure enough support for the Union in Dublin. If he was aware that political circumstances, especially the King's obstinacy in adhering to his coronation oath, made the achievement of full rights for Catholics on the back of union impossible, then Pitt was guilty of perfidy, certainly to Cornwallis and Castlereagh. The likelihood was that he had taken a political flyer, as he had done before, but this time his arrogant belief that he would get his way was misguided.

M artin, within weeks of arriving full of hope at Westminster, was left bitterly disillusioned. Worse still, he faced having to explain the state of affairs to his constituents in Galway He reflected on the position and was realistic in his conclusion. Union was a fact and could not be reversed for the foreseeable future. Pitt had made private representations that emancipation was not a forlorn hope. The King was mortal and his adherence to his oath would die with him. George was now sixty-three, an old man by 19th-century mortality rates. He was also in bad health, above and beyond his recurring fits of madness. It was thought that if this bout went on for as long as the last then the Prince of Wales's supporters in the House, a group that did not include Pitt, would succeed in achieving a Regency Act, thereby giving immediate power to the heir to the throne.

Dick concluded that the future lay, if not immediately, certainly in the not too distant future, with the next monarch. Prince George was now nearly forty and desperately trying to lose the reckless, self-indulgent, womanising reputation he had gained during his youth. Dick soon became acquainted with the Prince, accustomed as he was to moving in the highest circles. Harriet, whose background, although upper class, had not previously exposed her to these lofty social heights, also effortlessly took her place in the spotlight.

Prior to leaving Ballynahinch, Harriet had completed her first novel, *Helen of Gloss*, published in four volumes by the London firm of Robinson. The novelty of this unknown Irish woman, already an accomplished author, was not lost on members of society and with her swashbuckling husband's infamous reputation preceding him, the Martins quickly became one of the most fêted couples in London.

Dick had converted his wife to the joys of the theatre and both were enjoying the wealth of thespian activity in London at the time. The famous actor Kemble played Hamlet, and Harriet, writing a review for a friend in Ireland, had no hesitation in praising the production but not the playwright. She wrote,

> The single defect I perceived was when he imposed secrecy on Horatio and
> Marcellus. At such a moment Hamlet could not, ought not to be a mimic; but this

fault is in the text itself. Kemble could hardly express it otherwise; but Shakespeare ought to have here conceived some of his fine imagined abjurations. He ought not to have put such sentences in Hamlet's way.

Her publishers were so impressed that this hitherto unheard-of lady had the nerve to criticise the Bard, that they began publishing her reviews. Harriet's pregnancy did not deter her from fully enjoying a social and professional life far removed from the isolation of Ballynahinch. In July she gave birth to a daughter, named after her.

If Dick had meant to court the friendship of the Prince of Wales, he did not have to bother. George had always held the leading Irish duellists in awe and was more than happy to seek the friendship of these intriguing newcomers. The Martins quickly became regulars at the many parties the Prince held at both his London palace and at Windsor castle. When showing Dick around the grounds of Windsor, George proudly pointed to the long drive leading through the Great Park up to the castle. Dick did not lose the opportunity of pointing out that the drive from his gatehouse in Oughterard, to Ballynahinch Castle, was in fact 30 miles longer!

Martin had resisted returning to Ireland bitter and disillusioned. He and Harriet were enjoying London life and, with his new found friendship with the royal heir, he was confident that one way or another the current king's reign would not last much longer, and hope for Catholics could be expected from the new monarch. He had also taken the opportunity of renewing an old friendship with Lord Erskine and his small group of animal rights campaigners in Parliament and he was beginning to form a notion that his legislation, for so long in place in Connemara, could now be implemented on a much wider front.

*The old coach house at Oughterard*

# Chapter 21

## No Sense of Consequence

By the end of February 1801 the King was displaying all the dreaded symptoms that had heralded his previous bout of madness, and attributing them to the stress of having to deal with the catholic question. He begged the Reverend Thomas Willis, the brother of his doctor, 'for God's sake save me from a regency'. William Pitt, who was now financially dependent on the Monarch's generosity, sent assurances that although he was out of power he would thwart the Prince of Wales succeeding prematurely to the throne and prevent the catholic issue ever being 'agitated' by others.

This time the Prince had not striven so determinedly to become Regent, but lowered his sights to Viceroy of Ireland, a request his father refused. The King spent the following year slipping in and out of his condition, leaving the running of his government to the new First Minister, Henry Addington.

Addington was a latter-day version of the helpless sycophant, Lord North. He only agreed to the King's request to become Prime Minister under sufferance. The son of a wealthy doctor specialising in the fashionable Georgian ailment of madness, Addington was a shy, introverted youth. He suffered from a stammer and therefore Parliament was a strange choice of career, probably influenced by his father who had been a close friend of Pitt the Elder.

His oratory hampered by his speech impediment, Addington took to developing an expertise on the rules of the House, serving on a number of committees. His father probably had a hand in getting him made Speaker of the House of Commons in 1789. The speakership had fallen into disrepute over the previous decade, culminating in Speaker Charles Cornwall keeping a supply of porter underneath his chair and sipping it noisily during debates. Addington turned out to be a good Speaker; he was popular and had a good knowledge of the workings of the House. He also brought a novel characteristic to the job: impartiality.

George no doubt chose Addington to replace the arrogant Pitt simply because the former would do as he was told. The new Prime Minister's first task was to put together a pinchbeck coalition cabinet, now without Greville, Castlereagh, Cornwallis and Canning, who had all resigned over the catholic issue. The Cabinet was immediately divided on how to proceed with the war against France. Henry Dundas, a senior member and a close friend of Pitt, wrote of their divisions:

> Some of us are of the opinion that the response to Europe and the security of Great Britain are only to be obtained by the restoration of the ancient royal family of France, and that every operation of war and every step to negotiation which does not keep that object in view is mischievous and will ultimately prove to be illusory. Some of us are of the opinion that although we ought not to consider the restoration of the ancient royal family as a *sine qua non,* we ought not to treat with

a revolutionary Government, and that the present Government of France is of that description. Some of us are of the opinion that whatever has been the foundation of the present Government, it has established within its power the whole authority, civil and military, of the country, and that we are not warranted to reject the negotiations with a Government so constituted and *de facto* existing. Some of us are of the opinion that although we ought to negotiate with the present rulers of France, we ought only to do it in conjunction with our Allies, particularly the Emperor of Germany, it being the interest of this country closely to connect our interests with his. Some of us are of the opinion that if ever it was practicable to influence by force of arms the interior Government of France, that time is past.

Privately, Dundas thought Addington a political lightweight. He wrote to Pitt:

It is impossible for me not to whisper into your ear my conviction that no arrangement can be formed under him as its head that will not crumble to pieces almost as soon as it is formed. Our friends, who, as an act of friendship and attachment to you, agree to remain in office, do it with the utmost chagrin and unwillingness, and the feeling they are embarking in an Administration under a head totally incapable to carry it on, and which must of course soon be an object of ridicule, is uppermost in all their minds.

Meanwhile, Martin was growing impatient at not being financially rewarded. He knew that his early backing of the Union had helped build a basis for support amongst the neutrals in Dublin. Moreover he had worked tirelessly in persuading Galway to change its stance. He felt it was now payback time, especially as broken promises were littering the ground at Westminster.

Martin still held the salaried post of Commissioner of Stamps, but a minor act passed in July 1801 meant that he would have to relinquish this office at the next election. He wrote to the Chief Secretary of Ireland pointing this out. His resentment quickly grew as he saw former colleagues from Dublin being amply rewarded for much less support and certainly not placing their personal reputations so firmly on the line as he had done.

When nothing materialised from the Chief Secretary, Martin approached the Lord Lieutenant, asking to be made Governor of Galway. His request was refused, as was a further request for an appointment to the Privy Council.

Not for the first time, Martin's precarious finances were on the verge of toppling him into disaster. The mineral mines were not producing an income, and the lifestyle that Martin naturally felt obliged to adopt in London was not coming cheap. As a member of the British House of Commons, Martin was afforded protection from his creditors for just as long as he retained his position. But how the voters of Galway felt about their Member of Parliament after the Union was about to be tested.

Peace negotiations had begun during the early part of 1802, but despite Britain regaining naval supremacy at the Battle of Copenhagen, the British Government chose to enter into the Treaty of Ameins, which allowed France to retain most of her new conquests. The peace would be brief, Napoleon walking away from the table having already decided to use the respite from military engagement to regroup his army.

However, on the back of the patriotic goodwill that still prevailed following Nelson's victory, and in advance of the imbroglio he presided over becoming public, Addington decided to call a General Election.

A few weeks prior to Parliament being prorogued, a private bill had been proposed by John Dent, the Member for Lancaster, calling for a ban on the sport of bull baiting. The objections that had been made to Sir William Pultney's bill two years previously were repeated. William Windham, a former Secretary of War, ridiculed the subject being even raised in the House. Martin had little or no involvement with this bill. Still finding his feet during his first year in Westminster, he had devoted most of his energies to socialising and persistently arguing to whomever would listen that he should be given a salaried post. By the time the bull-baiting bill came to the vote, Dick was back in Ireland to fight the crucial election. He must, however, have noted with interest that the motion only failed by 51 to 64 votes, at a time when many members had left the House, like himself, to electioneer. Perhaps the way to success was to sneak a bill through almost unnoticed.

There was a fair amount of damage limitation for Martin to conduct when he arrived home in Galway. He had argued forcefully three years before that a union of parliaments would quickly result in full catholic emancipation and all he could now do was to tell voters how let down he also felt. But though Martin's reputation was far from flawless, very rarely was his honesty ever questioned. Criticism on this matter was confined to the suggestion that his motive in supporting equal rights for Catholics was to obtain the franchise for people who would then support him.

His campaign received an early blow which also hurt him personally. Lord Clanricarde, whom Dick considered an old friend, not only now refused to support him but also was actively backing the opposition. Furthermore, the Marquis of Sligo, the owner of the ill-fated wolfhound whose death Dick had striven to avenge, had long since ceased his friendship. Sligo had long been concerned about the activities Martin allowed on the estate that neighboured his: he now decided to take action.

Sligo wrote to the Viceroy claiming that Martin continued to allow fugitives from the '98 Rebellion to live openly on his land, and even furthered the spirit of revolution. He urged the Lord Lieutenant to provide a garrison west of Galway 'till Dick Martin's place is filled by a better member of society than is likely to be form'd from his precept and example'. Martin's argument, when called to defend himself at Dublin Castle, was that these allegations were being made because he had supported the Union. The argument was ill-based, since Clanricarde and Sligo (influenced to a certain extent by Martin) had actually supported unification, but Dick had no idea why his old friends were now so inimical to his re-election.

Their stance, coupled with the failure of the establishment to deliver the lucrative governmental posts that had been promised, had both surprised and hurt Dick. These were however classic examples of how he failed to understand the effect of his actions on other people. What he saw as humane behaviour was regarded with disdain and bemusement by the likes of Clanricarde and Sligo. People within the mainstream establishment considered his reckless approach to his own finances dishonourable and irresponsible. There were four reasons why Martin was not being offered the sinecures he was expecting.

Firstly he was considered a maverick, partly because of the issues he took up and partly due to his ability to make rapid and complete u-turns, as he did in respect of the Union, or suddenly change his support as he had done from Grattan to Flood. Secondly he was known to operate outside the law on his own estate. Thirdly, Martin had completely forgotten the enemies he had made in political circles 25 years before when his first crusade as a novice in Parliament was publicly to attack its endemic corruption. People have long memories, and many of those whom Martin exposed all those years ago were now in positions of power. Lastly, there was growing resentment in London that this anti-establishment bankrupt had somehow managed to become a close friend of the Prince of Wales.

Dick also confused people with his mercurial personality and a style of humour that was often misread. The art of diplomacy was not one of Martin's strengths. Nor was it his style to harbour a grievance and exact recompense at a later date. Since childhood and throughout his youth, Martin throve on direct confrontation, then drawing a line under the issue and moving on without holding a grudge.

He would spend much of his life being misunderstood, but due to his energy, focus and total belief in what he was fighting for, coupled with his unnerving ability to move quickly from one crusade to another, he invariably had no comprehension of the ill feeling he left in his wake. He was always surprised when people took their revenge much later. Basically, Humanity Dick Martin had absolutely no sense of consequence.

Circumstances had contrived to place Martin on the verge of an election defeat and the very unpleasant financial implications that would follow. Suddenly, for no apparent reason, his one and only opponent, a man called Burke who was supported by Clanricarde, withdrew from the election. Martin was returned unopposed.

Further good fortune followed when Dick found a way of selling the government post he was now forced to resign, for a sum that not only cleared a very pressing debt but also left him with the not inconsiderable amount of £4000.

Political and financial good fortune was to be followed immediately by personal tragedy. St George, Dick's youngest son by Elizabeth, died at his boarding school in Bristol at the age of fourteen. Thomas, the elder son, was forced to deal with the loss of his brother at first hand without the immediate support of his father, a traumatic event that would cause manifestations of resentment for the rest of his life.

Further family grief followed when Dick's sister Mary, to whom he had always stayed emotionally close, lost her husband, Patrick D'Arcy. While Dick was helping her deal with her loss, his half-brother Anthony contributed to family problems.

Since dropping out of university, where he was studying for a career in the Church, young Anthony had returned to Dangan, enjoying a somewhat carefree life as the local squire. Dick's part in the boy's life had started as role model, and swashbuckling elder brother, and moved on surrogate father on the death of Robert. Dick was always more suited to the first role and it is fair to say he had left Anthony and his elder brother much to their own devices. Anthony, now thirty-one, had fallen in love with the seventeen-year-old daughter of Jean Pierre de L'Espinasse, the former Director General of the Dutch West Indies Company for Essequibo and Demerara. Although the Martins had historic connections with the aristocratic Dutch-French family,

Monsieur L'Espinasse would not give his blessing to his young daughter marrying the aimless Squire of Dangan. It will never be known if Anthony was acting on his older half-brother's advice when he eloped with his young love and married her in Gretna Green.

*'The Giant Factotem amusing himself'; this cartoon by Gillray shows Pitt dwarfing William Wilberforce, Henry Dundas, Henry Addington, Thomas Erskine, Richard Brinsley Sheridan, Charles Grey and Charles James Fox.*

Chapter 22

# Petulant Opposition

Even without the support of the influential landowners and the mysterious withdrawal of his opponent, Martin probably would still have won the election. On returning to Galway bereft of positive news for Catholics, he was candid about how everyone had been duped over what the Union had seemed to offer. Although out of favour with the establishment, many of whom were his frustrated creditors, Dick retained the support of the rank-and-file voter, much to the bemusement of the hierarchy of the County.

The wealthy James D'Arcy of Galway wrote to the Lord Chancellor of Ireland, bemoaning Martin's rubber-like resilience:

> So singular are his talents, so popular his manner and so fortunate his address, that without possessing an atom of public confidence, he at the very moment when he seems to have lost all public favour, and is actually without credit for a guinea, starts up to the astonishment of all with a greater command of influence than ever.

It is not impossible to understand why Dick retained popularity. His reputation for personal fearlessness carried enormous weight amid the culture of 19th-century Ireland, and indeed England. Bravery has its own charm, but it is clear that Martin's attraction went beyond that. Terms like 'popular manner' and 'fortunate address' are an attempt to define the indefinable in what must obviously have been a very charismatic personality. Charisma and good humour covered many flaws in his character. He enjoyed the best of both worlds in the eyes of Galway people, being accepted into royal circles but never really being part of the establishment, presiding as he did over his mysterious, fugitive-laden lands and smuggling empire. Moreover, and perhaps most significant in the long run, his genuine concern for the happiness of his own people was something that could not be faked.

Martin decided to remain at Ballynahinch instead of returning immediately to London. The estate was suffering from lack of management in his absence and his cash windfall needed to be spread among his many pressing financial needs. He was also now a clever enough politician to know that public opinion can move very quickly, so he strove to build on his current popularity.

In the summer of 1803 Martin heard rumours of a new rebellion, fuelled by the frustrations the Union had caused. Robert Emmet was the youngest son of an eminent Dublin physician who could name the Lord Lieutenant among his patients. The young Emmet entered Trinity College in 1793 but was expelled for political activities in April 1798. By July 1803 he was twenty-five, and had conferred with Bonaparte and Talleyrand in Paris on behalf of the United Irishmen.

He then met Thomas Russell, a former friend of Tone's who was based in the north. Russell undertook to lead an uprising in Ulster. Moving around Dublin in disguise, usually at night, Emmet managed to build up a following of men and arms, to the extent of testing an explosive rocket in the suburb of Rathfarnham. By July he was ready to go.

When Martin heard that French arms had been landed in Connemara, he sent word to Dublin that he would offer his garrison to support the quashing of any rebellion or French invasion. The Castle did not need to take up Martin's offer, since the uprising was short lived. On the evening of 23rd July 1803, Emmet and two of his officers donned green uniforms and joined a large crowd marching on the Castle. The carriage of the Lord Chief Justice, Lord Kilwarden, unfortunately rode into the rear of a column of rebels, who turned on him and piked him. The mob quickly dispersed and Emmet fled to the nearby Wicklow Mountains. No uprising occurred in the north, and he was soon captured.

Robert Emmet's place in Irish history and folk law depends chiefly on his brief act of defiance at his trial. After being sentenced to death he made an impassioned speech from the dock, ending in the famous words:

> 'Let no man write my epitaph; for no man who knows my motives dare now vindicate them, let not prejudice or ignorance asperse them. Let them and me rest in obscurity and peace, and my tomb remain uninscribed, and my memory in oblivion, until other times and other men can do justice to my character. When my country takes her place among the nations of the earth, then, and not till then, let my epitaph be written. I have done.'

Emmet was hanged in Thomas Street Dublin, on 20th September; Thomas Russell suffered the same fate in Downpatrick a month later.

Situated midway between Galway and Castlebar was the busy market town of Ballinasloe. The most important event in the town's calendar was the October Fair, which gentlemen from west of the Shannon used as an annual meeting place. Emmet's uprising and the perceived failures of the Union gave the 1803 fair an increased attendance and sense of occasion.

Martin took the opportunity of addressing the hundreds of Catholics who attended the fair. He made clear that, although he sided with Emmet's motives, he would never back an armed uprising. Political means, however slow and frustrating, were the way forward. The Catholics attending Ballinasloe decided to set up committees in each of the counties represented there, and Martin agreed to put forward a motion in the British parliament demanding full and unequivocal catholic emancipation. At the time he failed to appreciate was that it would be another year before he was in a financial position to return to Westminster.

The 1802 general election had strengthened neither Addington's position in government nor his resolve to carry on as Prime Minister. The following two years saw a bizarre situation: nobody wanted to run the country. On 26th April 1803 Addington finally found the conviction to tell the King he wanted to resign. He suggested that, as war with France was now again imminent, Pitt, with his vast experience, should be brought back to head the government. George, now recovered from his latest bout of sickness, reluctantly agreed.

But Pitt did not want the job; worse still, he thought that the leader of the opposition, Charles James Fox, should be asked to form a government. The King despised Fox, who was a cousin of Edward Fitzgerald, for many reasons, but in any event even Fox was not interested, taking great delight in the confusion that reigned. The game of political pass-the-parcel ended with Pitt, probably with a hidden smirk, agreeing to return to office in April 1804 on the clear understanding that he had a free hand to appoint ministers of his choice.

Watching British political disarray with great interest, Napoleon was now well prepared to resume hostilities. He had used the time to strengthen his troops in the Italian and Egyptian regions and, significantly, persuaded the Pope to crown him Emperor of France. The Emperor now wanted an empire, preferably the whole of Europe, the Mediterranean and beyond. The French already controlled Belgium, Holland, Switzerland and most of Germany. India was in Napoleon's sights and he had bought the American province of Louisiana from Spain. Ironically it was the British who were held responsible for breaking the treaty of Amiens, when they failed to surrender Malta as agreed. Bonaparte had already made political mileage out of the wording of the treaty, the first for centuries that did not describe the English king as being also the monarch of France.

Also enjoying the brief period of peace were the British upper classes, who were able to visit France for the first time since the Revolution. No doubt the Martins would have been amongst them if their finances had been healthier. Ten thousand British tourists were interned in France when war finally broke out a week before Emmet's ill-fated rebellion.

Instead of immediately delivering his pledge to the Catholics at Ballinasloe, Martin was obliged to spend the whole of 1804 desperately trying to obtain a salaried position within the Government, and with equal desperation attempting to shore up the economy of his estate. He travelled to Dublin to lay his grievances personally before the Lord Lieutenant, but to no avail. However, by the start of 1805 the Martins were able to return to London and Dick took up his seat at Westminster, buoyed by the news that Fox was to raise the catholic question early in this parliamentary session.

There was more immediate business for the House to consider. In the aftermath of the Emmet rebellion, Britain had suspended the writ of Habeas Corpus. Effectively, military law was in place in Ireland, and being maintained, because British intelligence was under the impression that another rebellion was being plotted by Irish revolutionaries based in Paris.

Martin took his place in the House of Commons on 8th February for the Habeas Corpus debate. Sir Evan Nepean moved for leave to bring in a bill for the further continuation of the act of the last session, suspending Habeas Corpus in Ireland. He felt it necessary by 'the existence of dissatisfaction in a considerable degree in Ireland and by the avowed intention of the enemy to invade the country.'

A number of Irish members, including Martin, questioned whether such extreme measures were required against such a great mass of loyal subjects. William Pitt, now reestablished as Prime Minister, gave his government's position on the matter. He explained that he respected the views of the Irish gentlemen present, but it should be taken into account that, 'Great Britain was at war with France, whose attention is in the first instance directed towards Ireland where its emissaries are perpetually at work.' Pitt went on to state, 'Irishmen who have fled the country for crimes have been embodied into a regiment which maintains contact with the disaffected in their own country who continue to spread the flame of revolution.'

Charles Fox, still leader of the Whig opposition, now took up the argument that Habeas Corpus should be reinstated in Ireland. He accused Pitt of putting the fate of its whole people at the discretion of the Viceroy and his agents merely because a small number of them were bad subjects. If Martin had not already done so, he must have realised that his political ambitions now had an important ally in Fox, who was coincidentally also a close friend of the Prince of Wales.

When the debate continued a week later, the argument had turned to whether or not one man, the Viceroy, should be given so much power. Martin, now fully into the swing of how Westminster debates worked, brought his own trenchant style to the occasion.

He rose to say he

never knew a Lord Lieutenant who was not represented as being a very amiable man. He had never heard of a Secretary who was not said to be possessed of the highest talents and overflowing with humanity and benevolence. But these descriptions of persons were not always to be depended upon. These panegyrics were easily obtained, but the people of Ireland would indeed be very hardly dealt with, if they had no other security for their liberties than the character of those who happen to be in power.

When four days later Sir Evan Napean moved that the Bill be given its third and final reading, Martin leapt up to interject that he intended to propose an amendment. The Speaker pointed out to him that it was normal practice for the House to allow a bill to be fully read before a member tried to amend it. When Martin was eventually allowed to put forward his amendment it was laced with irony. He pointed out that the 'wicked and disaffected persons' that this act set out to address could quite easily come to Britain and 'carry on their machinations with safety.' Accordingly the Act must be extended to protect the entirety of Great Britain. Martin's amendment was, naturally, unsuccessful.

Despite the pleas of Irish Members, Fox's powerful argument and Martin's incisive sarcasm, the Bill was carried and the protection afforded by Habeas Corpus remained suspended in Ireland.

Martin used some of this current period of residence in London to develop a loose friendship with Fox. Fox was five years older than Dick and had been in politics all his adult life. Being the illegitimate great-great-grandson of Charles II gave Fox Stuart blood, and his father's habit of siphoning a fortune from government coffers while he was Postmaster General tainted his political career, from the start, in the eyes of the establishment. A man of very loose morals, Fox had already gambled away a fortune by the time his *bête noire*, Pitt, first ascended to power. On the day that Pitt resumed the premiership, bailiffs were entering Fox's house in St James' Street.

King George despised Fox with a passion, not least because he blamed him for turning the easily influenced Prince against his father. Fox had been a thorn in the his side throughout the American War of Independence, openly supported the French Revolution, and was instrumental in pressing for regency when the King first became afflicted with the symptoms of madness in 1788. The man even had the audacity to encourage card players at his gaming club, Brookes, to rename the king of a suit as the 'lunatic'. Possibly for no other reason than than it might topple the monarch over the precipice into further madness, Fox now took up the crusade of catholic emancipation.

The moment in the session that Dick had really been waiting for came on 25th March when Fox proposed a Roman Catholic Petition with the opening statement that he 'never rose with more satisfaction in the whole course of his life.' The Petition would not be fully debated until 13th May, when it was again Fox who commenced proceedings.

The veteran agitator made an impassioned speech that could not have put the case more comprehensively. He maintained that Catholics were loyal to the Crown, especially in times of war. It was right for all people to enjoy the benefits of the law and right that Catholics and Protestants be placed on an equal footing. Referring to the old Penal Laws, Fox felt that it was not necessary to discuss why this legislation had been originally passed but 'if restrictive law is made on account of peculiar circumstances, the moment they cease, restrictions cease to be polite.' Suspicion of Catholics and repression of them was a by-product of a 'long ago civil war.' He finished by saying, 'not wishing to liken black African slaves to the people of Ireland, there were similar circumstances likely to produce general dissatisfaction.'

Dr Duigeran, the Member for Armagh took it upon himself to make the initial reply. He reminded the House of the actions of James II, a 'bigoted papist', the Irish Acts of George II and the atrocities committed by the 'Romanist' White Boys and Defenders. Individual rebellions were the very reason why no more rights should be conferred on Catholics.

Henry Grattan, preceded by the reputation gained in the Irish parliament that had carried his name, now took up the argument. He reasoned, 'As the causes have ceased, all animosity arising out of these causes should cease.' Grattan with great precision took each individual rebellion and demonstrated that repression and not religion was the cause. There were no longer 'abdicating Princes, popish plots or pretenders.' Catholics were loyal subjects.

Further counter-arguments followed. Yielding to catholic claims would be a sacrifice of the Constitution; introducing Catholics into parliament would have fatal consequences, Charles I being a good example; and the somewhat patronising point that concessions might also prove fatal to the Catholics themselves by tempting them into a struggle for ascendancy which would lose them the privileges they currently enjoyed.

The debate dragged on through the night and was becoming increasingly acrimonious when Pitt stood up in an attempt to bring it to a conclusion. He stressed that he was sympathetic to the claims and had himself supported previous repeals, but felt that 'the privileges now demanded, when weighed against the Protestant interests in Ireland could only be detrimental to the internal tranquility of that kingdom.'

Pitt failed to end the debate, which went on to 5 o'clock in the morning. After an emotional closing speech from Fox, the vote was taken with 124 Members voting for the motion and 336 against. Martin had not spoken once during the debate, and the result was no great surprise to him. Emancipation would only come with a new king.

Under the pressure of the recent disappointing events, Martin's renowned good humour gave way. He spent the remainder of his time in London expressing his increasing dissatisfaction at being continually overlooked for posts that would provide a desperately needed salary, while churlishly opposing anything the government were proposing in parliament. He visited Sir Evan Nepean, the Home Office Minister whom he had rudely interrupted in the House, asking for a sinecure. Nepean, apparently overlooking the incident, offered Martin the Weighmastership of Cork at a salary of £600 a year. Martin asked for £1000 and, when this was not forthcoming, turned the offer down.

The Martins returned to Ballynahinch after parliament broke for the summer recess, but Dick's petulance continued. He was asked by the Lord Lieutenant to support Charles Blake in a by-election due to take place in a neighbouring seat, caused by the current member Richard Trench succeeding his father as Lord Clancarty. Bowles Daly, an anti-unionist, was standing against Blake. Despite the historic animosity between the Martin and Daly families, Dick chose not to support the Viceroy's choice of candidate. Daly was duly elected and established a foothold of power that Martin would desperately regret in years to come.

*Portrait of Richard Martin*

# Chapter 23

# Royal Friend (and Outlaw)

**M**artin was quite content to remain at Ballynahinch for the remainder of 1805. He had unsuccessfully investigated all avenues of financial recompense. In addition, the parliamentary door was now firmly closed on the catholic question.

On a more positive front, Dick reflected on his interesting new acquaintances in London, especially the likes of William Pultney, Richard Sheridan, John Dent and Lord Erskine, all pioneers of the fledgling animal rights campaign. Martin used this time on his estate to formalise further his own version of animal protection, and to nurture in his mind a plan to extend such protection on a wider stage.

**M**eanwhile Britain was in crisis, and in grave need of strong leadership. Pitt was under no illusion about the threat posed by Napoleon, and his first move on regaining the highest office was to put twenty years of personal animosity aside and invite Charles James Fox to join his Cabinet as War Minister. The Prime Minister ignored the displeasure of the King, realising that however much both men disliked Fox, he was a man of great resource.

Camped near Bolougne was the largest army ever assembled to invade Britain. Only the 22 miles of sea that the French Emperor described as 'nothing but a ditch' prevented an invasion. The ditch, however, was protected by the Navy, now under the command of Admiral Lord Nelson. Without their naval support, which lay helplessly in the Atlantic west of the blockade, the French army had to content themselves, like Hitler 135 years later, by merely staring across the sea at their old enemy.

Pitt and Fox agreed to attempt to put together a new coalition with Austria and Russia, the only two countries left in Europe, with the possible exception of Spain, that could match Napoleon's forces. The talks nearly broke down over Tsar Alexander's demand for the British to hand over control of the strategically important island of Malta, and it was only Napoleon arrogantly crowning himself King of Italy that provoked both Russia and Austria to collude with Britain.

In August 1805 Napoleon suddenly decided to move the Grand Army eastward from Boulogne. He had seen writing on two walls. His navy was never going to break through Nelson's blockade, and he needed to pre-empt an attack from the newly formed coalition. With incredible speed Napoleon brought 190,000 troops across the Rhine by the end of September. The Austrian General Mack, having invaded Bavaria with 60,000 men, fell back to the River Danube where he hoped to link up with the Russians. Napoleon was too quick, and surrounded the Austrian forces at Ulm, forcing surrender and allowing the French to march on and occupy Vienna. In the meantime Russia persuaded Prussia to join the alliance and Tsar Alexander, confident that the combined forces could now defeat the French army, chose unwisely to engage them at Austerlitz on 2nd December. There, on the frozen lake, Napoleon gained one of his most decisive victories.

In the mean time Nelson, no longer obliged to defend the Channel, went after the French navy. After a transatlantic game of cat and mouse, a massive naval battle eventually took place off the Spanish headland of Trafalgar on 21st October 1805. Nelson gained the greatest naval victory in British history but paid for it with his life. Britannia now ruled the sea, but most of Europe was French.

On 23rd January the following year, William Pitt died in his small rented house facing the luxurious lodge at Richmond that the King had recently gifted to Addington. A few months previously Pitt's lifelong friend the Earl of Melville, formerly Henry Dundas, had been forced to leave office after impeachment for malversation. Pitt began drinking heavily and was finally broken by the French victories, which to him meant that his life's work was ending in failure. Just before dying he pointed to a map of Europe and asked for it to be rolled up saying, 'It will not be wanted these ten years.' His prediction was only out by one year.

King George only now realised the worth of Pitt, whose qualities he had always taken for granted. Who was to replace him? Although facing the gravest crisis of his long reign, George could not bring himself to turn to Fox, the only man in Pitt's league as a statesman. However, he had learned a painful lesson from having a sycophantic puppet running his Government in times of military emergency. Returning to Addington would be a repeat of having Lord North in charge during the American War; only the stakes were higher this time with the despotic Napoleon breathing at Britain's door.

George turned first to the competent Lord Hawkesbury, who declined the offer. There was only one other barely credible candidate, Lord William Greville, a former Home and Foreign Secretary. The problem with Greville was that he was an ally of Fox and a vocal supporter of catholic emancipation. George however recognised that needs must when the Devil drives, and made Greville First Minister a month after Pitt's death, on the condition that his cabinet be a coalition containing 'Foxites' and 'Pittites'. Georgian spin-doctors tagged the new Administration 'The Ministry of All the Talents'. It would transpire that its talent content was low.

One outcome of the enforced Cabinet reshuffle was an immediate monetary benefit for Martin. The opposition members, enjoying power for the first time, were keen to reward their supporters in the House and Martin (whose consistent voting against the Government had in fact been out of truculence rather than Whig loyalty), was now given his long overdue sinecure. From 1st May 1806 Martin was to be the Commissioner for Hearth Money Collection. Quite what the role entailed is unclear but the post did carry a generous and much needed salary. A second post as a Gauger soon followed it.

As another knock-on effect of governmental changes, Ireland was given a new Lord Lieutenant. The Duke of Bedford was appointed Viceroy that summer and, on arriving to take up his post in Dublin Castle, was immediately faced with two issues, both concerning the notorious Richard Martin. There are no better examples of the paradoxical double life that Martin led.

Requiring an introduction to the new Viceroy, Dick went to the highest-placed of his many friends and asked the Prince of Wales to effect it. He received a prompt reply from Colonel McMahon, the Prince's Private Secretary:

The Prince commands me to make you his best regards, and to assure you that he has committed to the charge of Sir John Newport on the eve of his departure from London, a confidential request to the Duke of Bedford that His Grace should extend every service and attention to you, as "one for who H.R.H. has entertained the strongest sentiments of friendship, and to whom he consider'd himself under very peculiar obligations, for the zealous, prompt, and most handsome support he had render'd the Government."

Coinciding with the royal recommendation, was a complaint to the Viceroy that Martin had used a gang of mercenaries to evict an innocent tenant off his Connemara estate. A farmer called Duane was in the process of making improvements to his farm when an army of 200 armed men from Martin's yeomanry, trumpets sounding, stormed over his land knocking down walls and using their horses to waste tended fields. Lieutenant Evans, who led the soldiers, informed the unfortunate Duane that they were acting on the express orders of Colonel Martin. Duane went on to tell the Lord Lieutenant that he now feared for his life from a Frenchman who, having been harboured by Martin since the abortive invasion of 1798, was being used to murder anyone who crossed the King of Connemara.

Bedford weighed up the evidence of this unknown farmer against the introduction from the Prince and wisely decided to take no action. Martin always listened compassionately to pleas of poverty. He welcomed numerous people made destitute after the callous actions of more stereotypical Irish landlords. However, he would take no prisoners if roused and it is likely that Duane had somehow tried to cross him. Martin's own small army indeed contained a number of criminals who relied on the authorities never venturing into the Wild West domain of their master. It may well be that there was a French cut-throat among them although, if there was someone Martin wished dead, he was more likely to have have confronted the other party himself or, as he had done for many years, turned the other cheek.

By the latter part of 1806, Martin's finances were so much improved that he did not need 30 miles of bog and mountain to protect him. Harriet delighted in spending the winter in the comparative luxury of her father-in-law's old home, Clareville. This elegant house, situated alongside the river in what is now the town of Oughterard, was within easy reach of Galway and provided the young family with a far better winter habitat than desolate Ballynahinch.

Dick's eldest half-brother, Robert, eventually married in October of that year, bringing to an end a 300-year-old feud. His bride was Mary O'Flaherty, and the couple moved into Bushy Park, a property next door to Dangan where Anthony had returned with his young bride, to live happily with Dick's stepmother, Elizabeth.

Happiness was further increased when Harriet gave birth to a second daughter, named Georgina Thomasine after the animal-loving aunt with whom Dick had spent so much of his childhood. Baby Georgy was born on 23rd November, the day before polling began in what was to become a tempestuous Galway election.

Lord Greville had struggled in the role of Prime Minister from day one. He was not a strong leader, and the charismatic Fox was exerting more and more influence over the entire cabinet by virtue of his greater intellect and political experience. But by July of 1806 Fox was seriously ill, a lifetime of excess taking its toll. He died from dropsy on 13th September, aged fifty-seven. Within eight months Britain had lost arguably both its greatest prime minister and greatest opposition leader.

Greville's only significant decision since taking office was to move into Number 10, Downing Street, which annoyed the Chancellor of the Exchequer, who considered the house an annexe to his office. Now he decided there was nothing to lose from going to the country, and on 12th October called a General Election.

In Galway, Martin was confident of winning regardless of who stood against him. His popularity was high. For the first time in many years he could properly finance a campaign and, in addition, stories of his militia trashing a miscreant's land and murderous French revolutionaries on his payroll were helpful commodities in a Galway election. He soon knew who his opponents were: Bowles Daly, whom Martin in a fit of pique the previous year had allowed to enter politics, and the dashing young Giles Eyre, sponsored by Martin's friend-turned-foe, Lord Clancarty. The three men would contest the two parliamentary seats.

Eyre was a younger version of Martin: he already enjoyed a well earned duelling reputation. Dick, however, knew and fully exploited Eyre's main weakness: he was illiterate. The swashbuckling candidate was addressing a large crowd, expounding the reasons why they should elect him, when Martin stepped onto the platform and said:

'I declare solemnly before all here assembled that I am willing this moment to retire from this contest and to allow my opponent to be returned unopposed if he will only sign this declaration which I hold in my hand.'

Nobody knew what was in the declaration, least of all the helpless Eyre, who never fully recovered his credibility during the campaign.

Martin's main problem was, as ever, physically getting his supporters into Galway to cast their votes at the only polling station. Both Daly and Eyre relied on support from voters close at hand, and with an early lead were both demanding that the poll be closed. After ten days, Dick's support began arriving in a ramshackle fleet of boats from Connemara. Chaos ruled on the Galway quayside, and Martin's greatest task was keeping his people sober long enough to cast their votes. The other two candidates claimed he was taking full advantage of the sea of unknown faces, whose owners were blatantly voting several times.

By the time Parliament reconvened on 15th December there was no sign of a return from the Constituency geographically furthest away from Westminster. But Martin had somehow managed to keep the polls open for 24 days and was now confirmed winner with a majority of 470 votes, while Daly secured the second seat. Dick celebrated by throwing a massive banquet where he made three raucous toasts. The first was to the local Lord Clanricarde, who had little time for Martin. The second was for Dick's old Cambridge friend George Ponsonby, who had recently succeeded as Lord Chancellor of Ireland, and the third was to 'religious toleration!'

Martin, his finances unwontedly healthy and his family life more settled with both the wayward half-brothers married, was optimistic about the prospects for the new session. The Prime Minister was an advocate of catholic emancipation and the King was ailing by the day. Dick had now formed a plan in respect of animal rights, while his friend Wilberforce was on the verge of achieving the abolition of slavery, an issue close to Martin's heart since his time in the West Indies and America as a youth. With a young family to transport to London, Dick had delayed taking up his seat in the Commons until the onset of spring; however, political events in the early part of 1807 were to overtake his plans.

William Wilberforce, frustrated by the delay to his anti-slavery legislation caused by the general election, wasted no time when Parliament reconvened. Within weeks his Slave Trade Act was on the statute book:

> From the 1st May the African Slave Trade, and all manner of dealing and trading in the purchase, sale, barter or transfer of slaves, or of persons intending to be sold, transferred, used or dealt with as slaves, practised or carried on in, at, to or from any part of the coast or countries of Africa, shall be utterly abolished, prohibited and declared to be unlawful.

The law, of course, only applied to the areas of Africa under British rule and in practice it would take many years for the legislation to have effect. America would need another 60 years and a civil war before she followed suit, but for Wilberforce it was the end of a seventeen-year political crusade and allowed him to turn his attention from human to animal rights.

Until his death, Pitt had kept the promise made to the King six years previously and prevented the catholic issue being seriously raised. Greville, determined to forward the matter, but recognising the monarch's stance was never going to be negotiable, hatched a plot to exploit the Kings failing health. His motive may have been defensible, but his means were dishonourable.

Another problem that now plagued George, was the onset of cataracts. His sight had been failing for years. He could not recognise faces further than a few feet away and was having great difficulty reading. His once neat handwriting degenerated into a large scrawl, which covered a page in a few lines, and he tended to continue long after the ink in his pen ran out.

Greville asked him if a minor change could be made in the law, doing away with the anomaly that Catholics were allowed to hold the rank of Colonel in the Irish army but not in Scotland or England. George grudgingly agreed, but only on the assurance from his Prime Minister that this was not a thin edge of a wedge. By the time the legislation was drafted and returned from Westminster for Royal approval the change was extended to every level in the army and navy.

George's illness did not affect his tremendous attention to detail. Trusted assistants read all his documents to him. Ministers who thought they were dealing with a senile old man 'insensible to what is passing' were to be sorely disappointed. George allowed the bill to proceed purely to flush out the treacherous members of his Government who supported it. On many occasions he had outwitted the likes of Pitt and Fox and he had no intention of letting a lesser man such as Greville out-manoevre him.

As the deceptive legislation was being finalised, George personally travelled from Windsor to Westminster to confront his Prime Minister. Greville unwisely refused to renounce his policy and the King responded, calmly, 'Then I must look about me.' The catholic question had claimed its second political victim of the new century and the

Ministry of All Talents was at an end. It could not even be remembered for its most famous piece of legislation: Wilberforce was not a member. The Whigs, who had been delighting in their first term in power after many years in the political wilderness would now have to wait a further 23 years.

George was faced with the repeat problem of finding a half-competent Prime Minister at a time of national emergency. Although now approaching seventy and in very bad health, the Duke of Portland possessed one overwhelming virtue in the Monarch's eyes: he was anti-catholic. The elderly politician accepted the King's commission on 20th March 1807.

An immediate election was called, but nobody in Galway wanted to repeat the experience of four months ago, so Martin and Daly were returned unopposed. Dick retained both his salaried posts in the administration but Lord Bedford, whom he had befriended, was replaced as Lord Lieutenant. The new Viceroy was the Duke of Richmond, who then appointed the untried Arthur Wellesley as Chief Secretary.

Martin decided to remain in Ireland for the rest of the year. Amongst other local business he was overseeing the marriage of his eldest daughter Laetitia, whom he had raised lovingly despite his suspicion that Wolfe Tone was her natural father. The following May, Laetitia married Charles Peshall, an English Army Captain whom she had met while staying in London with her parents.

Relationships were less good between Dick and Laetitia's brother Thomas. The boy had never really forgiven his father for deserting him in a remote English boarding school so soon after the death of his mother, and leaving him there to cope on his own following the death of his younger brother. Thomas was now reluctantly following in Dick's footsteps at Cambridge, but correspondence between them was limited and strained. Neither father nor son knew that Thomas's fate was on a collision course with the army of Napoleon Bonaparte.

# Chapter 24

# Little Acorns

In his relentless drive across Europe, Napoleon's next target was Prussia. Prince Frederick William's initial hopes were that his country would be offered a pivotal role in Napoleon's grand design. When the French Emperor formed the Confederation of the Rhine in July 1806 it became apparent that the Prussian leader did not figure in the plan and so he mobilised his army of 130,000, equal to that of the French. Led by aged officers still basking in the reflected glory of Frederick the Great, they were crushed within three weeks. Thirty thousand grateful Poles, freed from Prussian rule and promised independence by Napoleon, joined the French forces. Napoleon now fixed his sights on Russia.

Although unfamiliar with the conditions of northern Europe, France emerged victorious from its first encounter with the Russians at Eylau in February 1807 and followed up with another victory at Friedland the following June. Expecting a gruelling campaign stretching into another frozen winter, Napoleon was surprised when Alexander sued for peace, the Russians having lost faith in their British ally.

An alliance signed a month after Friedland carved Europe into two spheres of influence: the west to Napoleon, the east to Alexander. At face value the French had not achieved much in respect of occupied land, but for Napoleon it avoided a long-drawn-out Russian campaign and permitted the execution of a plan to bring Britain to her knees.

Knowing that, despite Nelson's death, Britain still had control of the Channel, rendering an invasion impossible, Napoleon commenced a trade war. He would 'conquer the sea by the power of the land'. Since war had broken out the British had been prevented from exporting goods through French-controlled ports. Now, with Napoleon's grip on the coastline extending from Italy to the western seaboards, to the Baltic and Russian ports, Britain was effectively shut out of Europe. Napoleon now turned the pressure up by extending his embargo to any neutral country carrying British goods.

The weak link in Napoleon's extraordinary blockade was the Iberian peninsula, or at this stage specifically Portugal, a traditional ally of Britain. The only army route to Portugal was through Spain, which under the feeble rule of King Charles IV and without the capacity to resist France was, *ipso facto*, her ally. To close the gap in his iron ring, Napoleon dispatched his brother-in-law Marshal Junot to lead an army through Spain and attack Britain's last remaining European ally.

There was, however, trouble brewing in Spain. With such a weak king, the country was in reality ruled by the Queen's favourite courtier Manuel de Godoy. The Spanish Crown Prince Ferdinand, suspecting Godoy of planning to usurp the throne, turned to Napoleon for help. The Emperor, always happy to act in the role of God, summoned Prince Ferdinand and King Charles to hear his verdict on who was to rule their country. His solution was that both Charles and Ferdinand should renounce the Spanish throne and instead his brother, Joseph Bonaparte, should rule. The Spanish Royal family was imprisoned, along with the upstart Godoy.

If there was one turning point of the Napoleonic Empire it was this nepotistic decision. Had the popular Prince Ferdinand been elevated to the throne it would have ensured the support of the Spanish people; instead, Napoleon was faced with an immediate uprising. The Spanish used their word 'guerilla', meaning 'little war' to describe their form of resistance. Within eleven days of arriving in Madrid in July 1808, Joseph was driven out of the Spanish capital. The Peninsular War, or the 'Spanish ulcer' as Napoleon called it, had begun.

By the time his elder daughter married, Martin had focussed on where his political ambitions lay. For the last few years he had concluded that catholic emancipation was impossible while George was king, but there were daily rumours of the King's death, and his overall physical condition prompted growing calls for his son to adopt the mantle of Prince Regent. Dick also had secondary objectives such as parliamentary reform and a growing interest in introducing more humanity into the criminal justice system. And, far more unusually, he had formed the notion that it was indeed possible to legislate for animal protection.

Martin's veteran colleague Henry Grattan was more optimistic about immediate success for emancipation, despite the added problem of an anti-catholic prime minister, and intended to introduce another petition at Westminster. He asked Dick and a number of others to hold meetings of local Protestants, in order to prove that they did not object to Catholics being given equal rights.

Meanwhile, numerous Catholic groups had formed in Ireland following the Ballinasloe Fair five years before, and at the top of the pyramid was the new Catholic Committee in Dublin, whose senior members included Dick's Gormanston and Barnewell cousins. This organisation was already a sufficient threat for the Lord Lieutenant to use the Convention Act, originally designed to prevent Wolfe Tone's United Irishmen holding assemblies. At one stage, four of the Barnewells were temporarily imprisoned, but an outcry from all manner of Catholics caused the Viceroy to back down. It was in this heated climate that Grattan saw fit to raise the emancipation question once more in the House.

Immediately after Laetitia's wedding, Dick travelled to London with his family, more on the principle of being seen to back Grattan than anticipating his success. His main priority was to continue with a plan he was working on with Lord Erskine.

On 25th May 1808, Grattan commenced the latest round of the catholic issue. Recalling the last acrimonious occasion in the House, he started by urging a good-tempered debate. He stated that it was not his intention to revive topics such as the Battle of the Boyne, nor 'the business of 1745'. He pointed out that 'if you go back then so will the Catholics, history versus history, men of blood versus men of blood.' He rhetorically asked, 'What do Catholics want? Not a transfer of power or the absurd establishment of a Catholic Parliament, but they do require a restoration of their legal rights.'

In order to negate the objection that these measures would incite Protestants, the old statesman went on to refer to the recent Protestant meetings in Galway, Clare,

Tipperary, Killkenny, Roscommon, Waterford, Meath and even in the north at Newry, where resolutions had been passed that the 'Exclusion of Catholics from Parliament is not only degrading, but dishonourable in the highest degree.'

Grattan followed by attacking the newly formed 'persons called Orangemen' and asking them to 'awake from their folly'. He added, 'Believe me, the best way to guard the Catholics of Ireland from foreign attachments is by discouraging religious bigotry amongst Protestants.' He closed his stirring petition with the statement, 'I move it on the grounds of natural justice and shall conclude with two wishes. Firstly, that you may long preserve your liberties. Next, that you shall never survive the loss of them.'

Grattan now sat down, expecting the normal rigorous response from the government benches. What he faced was total silence. It was an amazing show of arrogance, led by the cabinet minister and future prime minister, George Canning. The message was obvious. The petition would not survive a vote, the King did not want it to progress and it was a complete waste of parliamentary time raising it in the first place. This stance did, of course, tally with Martin's prejudged, albeit cynical conclusion.

Nevertheless, the one-sided debate continued, with speeches of support from many English members including Wilberforce. In the absence of cabinet argument, backbenchers took up the case against Grattan's petition. Eventually Martin felt compelled to speak, making little attempt to hide his frustration:

'Notwithstanding what has been said about moderation and calmness, I have never heard more inflammatory language uttered with a calm voice and a sermonic tone, than what has come from the gentlemen on the other side of the House. Nothing like it has been uttered for a century within these walls.'

He went on to warn of his fear, based on what he knew was the climate in Ireland. 'When the cry in Ireland was Union or rebellion, I was in favour of Union; but I have since learnt it is possible to have a rebellion after a union.'

By now Prime Minister Portland felt enough was enough, and tried to conclude the debate, 'considering the lateness of the night.' Catholic supporters ensured that it continued, Martin having the final word. At 6 in the morning a vote was taken and the petition failed by 128 to 281. As Martin made his way home in the early morning light he could only hope for the speedy succession of the Prince of Wales.

Apart from the inevitable socialising, most of Martin's stay in London that year was spent in the company of his new friend Lord Erskine.

Thomas Erskine was four years older than Dick. He was a Scot, born in 1750, the youngest son of the 10th Earl of Buchan, The family's title belied their financial status and young Thomas grew up in an upper apartment in a less than fashionable area of Edinburgh. Leaving St Andrews University before matriculating, and with his father unable to support him entering his chosen profession of the law, Erskine joined the Navy as a midshipman and spent four years stationed in the West Indies, where, like Martin, he witnessed the atrocities of the slave trade at first hand.

By 1772 Erskine was back in London, now married and still ambitious to join the legal profession. One day he entered a courtroom where Lord Chief Justice Mansfield was presiding. Impressed with the young man's appearance and attitude, Mansfield encouraged him to read for the Bar. Somehow managing to combine his studies with supporting his young family, Erskine qualified in July 1778. One of his first cases involved defending Thomas Baillie against a criminal libel action brought by the powerful Lord Sandwich. With a ferocious and eloquent attack on Sandwich, Erskine won the case for his client and achieved instant fame and an immediate supply of lucrative work. Never one to balk at contentious briefs, nor at taking on the establishment, Erskine successfully defended Admiral Lord Keppel from a charge of incompetence in the American War, and Lord Gordon from one of of high treason.

Erskine was intrigued by events in France leading up to the Revolution and it was in Paris during the fateful summer of 1789 that he first made the acquaintance of Richard Martin. By now Erskine was specialising in criminal conversation cases, hence his defence of Petrie against Martin's action. He was the highest paid lawyer in the country and, encouraged by his friends Fox and Sheridan, entered Parliament in 1783, although continuing to practise law. He was incensed at what he thought was the government's over-reaction to events in France, and defended many of the reformers accused of being revolutionaries. In one celebrated case he issued a writ of subpoena against William Pitt, compelling the Prime Minister to give evidence.

For some inexplicable reason Erskine could never mirror his matchless eloquence and sublime oratory in court, in his parliamentary speeches. In the House he was a wretched speaker, on one occasion breaking down completely. But he worked closely with Fox to pass legislation reforming libel law in 1792 and helped Wilberforce with his anti-slavery legislation. By 1806 his support of the Whig party was rewarded by a brief spell as Lord Chancellor. With a new government now in power, Erskine had been replaced and took his seat in the House of Lords.

It is little wonder that Martin became close friends with a man who shared much of his empathy with humanitarian causes and who had demonstrated so little trepidation in locking horns with the establishment. Erskine also shared another of Dick's passions, a love of animals and was already well known for the eccentric way he kept not only pet dogs but a goose and two leeches which he named Home and Cline, after famous surgeons of the time.

Erskine took a keen interest as Dick explained how he had, for years, administered a brand of law on his estate preventing the maltreatment of animals in any fashion. Both men agreed that measures must be taken to end the rampant abuse that occurred daily on the streets of every town in the country. Horses were systematically flogged until the last ounce of service had been given and then were often left to die in the most appalling conditions. In addition the practices prevailing in abattoirs and slaughter-houses were nothing short of barbaric. However the activity that most disgusted the two men was the abuse of animals for no other reason than gambling and entertain-ment, in the animal-baiting and cock-fighting pits that abounded.

Martin and Erskine discussed what could be done. There was a form of animal protection in the law insofar as someone perpetrating injury on an animal owned by another man could be prosecuted, but this was really a form of property protection, and people were allowed to be as cruel as they wanted to the creatures they owned.

They agreed that the first and possibly most difficult hurdle to overcome was the total lack of comprehension of the concept of rights for animals. The problem had already been encountered when their mutual friends Pultney and Dent had attempted to introduce their bills. Most members of parliament considered the matter far below the dignity of the House.

Even if Erskine and Martin were successful in achieving legislation, they knew there would then be the problem of how it could be administered amongst not only an ignorant public but also a potentially inimical judiciary. They both knew that it would be a long struggle, but the sooner it was started, the faster they would arrive at their goal. It was agreed that Erskine, who carried more weight in the House of Lords than Martin did in the Commons, would introduce a prevention of cruelty to animals Bill as early as possible in the new year.

Events contrived to delay their plans; another government was about to fall, not this time because of arrogance, incompetence or deception, but good old-fashioned financial scandal. In January 1809 Colonel Wardle, the member for Oakhampton, accused the King's second son, Frederick, Duke of York, of corruption. Despite his military limitations, which made him the butt of the children's rhyme, the Duke was Commander-in-Chief and the most loyal of the King's seven sons. Frederick was accused of allowing his mistress, Mary Anne Clarke, to sell army commissions and was himself taking a rake-off on the transactions. George, convinced his son was beyond reproach, unwisely ordered a public enquiry. The Prince of Wales delighted in assisting the resulting hue and cry and, although the mistress and not the Duke was found guilty, the process opened a can of worms implicating many high-ranking figures in the administration. The opposition clamoured for the Prime Minister's head.

The scandal prevented Erskine from raising his bill in the Lords until 15th May 1809. It had, however, allowed him and Martin to reconsider its content. When preparing the wording, Martin recalled the phrase used by Parr and Samuel, his mentors at Harrow. The Bill called for the prevention of 'wanton' cruelty to animals.

There was surprisingly little resistance from the Lords; those opposing probably felt that there was little merit in wasting their time arguing against the Bill, as they knew it stood no chance in the Commons. Erskine used the opportunity to tell his fellow lords of a recent incident in Coventry Street where he approached a man whose overladen cart was being drawn by a solitary horse that had no protection against the chain cutting through the skin on its back. Its fetlock joint was dislocated and 'upon every exertion of this wretched creature the bone was visible to the eye.' Erskine recounted how he had offered the man a guinea to part with the horse but the owner replied, 'Why? I can work this horse three weeks longer and after that I can sell him to the slaughterhouse and thereby make four or five pounds.'

By June 2nd the Bill had been read the requisite three times and passed through a committee stage. Commenting on its successful passage Lord Eldon, who had succeeded Erskine as Lord Chancellor, approved of the principle of the Bill but felt that the 'application of it would be attended with some difficulty.'

Sir Charles Bunbury, another supporter of the cause and senior to Martin, was chosen to propose the Bill in the Commons. William Windham, who had been the main objector to the previous Bills proposed by Pultney and Dent, again took the floor to argue the case against. Instead of merely dismissing the subject, this time Windham relied on a train of logic. If the Bill was designed to prevent the actions of the drivers of horses it unfairly penalised this lower order of society. Surely the Bill should be extended to prevent the upper classes indulging in the sports of hunting and fishing?

Windham was being very clever in his attempt to scupper the Bill. Erskine and Martin had reasoned to themselves that the only way to succeed was to bring in a restricted law at this early stage aimed at specific, that is to say wanton, cruelty to working animals. Anything above and beyond was this was going to fail. Windham, by widening the argument, and at the same time taking the moral high ground, exposed the Bill too early to issues that were never going to be addressed within current society.

The vote was lost but only by 37 votes to 27. Being realistic men, and Dick having had painful experience of the long haul to catholic emancipation, he and Erskine were not too disheartened. The Bill had attracted support from a number of influential members such as William Wilberforce and Sir Samuel Romilly. There was, however, much more work to be done.

Martin reasoned that there if was one thing that most influenced politicians it was public opinion. By the summer of 1809 the Government, already on the ropes and reeling from the corruption punches, began in-fighting. Portland, realising that poor health was undermining him, built his cabinet around strong men, including three future prime ministers. Egos were clashing, and two of the most influential members, Canning and Castlereagh, attempted to settle their differences in a duel. Portland's health eventually gave out. He suffered a seizure on 6th September and was forced to resign. Three months later he was dead.

The poisoned chalice was passed on to Spencer Percival, whose place in history would be achieved by virtue of his tragic fate (he was the only British Prime Minister to date, to be assassinated). A competent man, Percival had already served as Chancellor of the Exchequer. Being an ardent Anglican, his strong anti-catholic views meant that he passed the King's mandatory qualification for Prime Minister. It was a daunting task he took on: Britain was by now noticeably suffering from Napoleon's trade war.

Back in Ireland, Martin faced two personal problems: the spectre of bankruptcy had returned, and his disaffected eldest son was now home. Dick's two salaries, when added to the revenue generated from the estate, did not come near to covering the cost of supporting his family, a private army, a large staff of servants, the refurbishment of Ballynahinch that Harriet had undertaken with such zest, running three other houses and servicing his substantial debts.

Thomas, now twenty-three, had returned from Cambridge before taking his degree. A good looking, well built man with the charisma enjoyed by many of the Martin family, he had quickly fallen in love with a local Galway girl, the daughter of a wealthy chandler. He was also clear-sighted enough to realise that many of the financial problems on the estate were caused by his father's intermittent and erratic involvement in its running.

He suggested to his father that he take over the practical care of the estate; he also wanted to marry the chandler's daughter, whose family, after the custom of the time, were prepared to a put up a dowry large enough to clear most of Martin's debts. Dick readily agreed to Thomas taking over as manager but, despite all his compassionate, liberal and indeed forward-thinking attitudes, he could not bring himself to allow his eldest son to enter a 'stepdown' marriage, with the further indignity of a tradesman salvaging his finances.

Thomas was livid; a furious row ensued. His father would not back down and a heartbroken Thomas departed bitterly from Ballynahinch. He took a commission in his brother-in-law's regiment, and embarked to fight in the Peninsular War.

*Ballynahinch Castle*

# Chapter 25
## The Prince's Humanity

The year 1810 was not a good one for Martin. His obstinacy and pride had driven his son to fight in a particularly vicious war, instead of taking up a vital family role. To add to his problems, the recent government reshuffles would deprive him of the salaried posts he so much needed in order to stay financially afloat.

Dick had in fact listened to Thomas's advice during the brief time he was at Ballynahinch. His management of the estate over the years had been sadly wanting, due in part to his prolonged absences. There was no choice now but to put his political ambitions to one side and apply himself to turning around the only resource he had left. This meant maximising rents, without compromising his humanitarian standards, and looking for additional income apart from the dubious smuggling commissions. All the mining activities had been disasters, as were the few abortive attempts at land reclamation.

Martin turned his attention to the kelp industry. The plant abounded along his coastline. Combining the many small one-man operations, and pooling resources, might improve margins for all concerned. An upside of the lengthy European war was that demand was driving up the price of the processed seaweed.

Harriet's plans for Ballynahinch were nearly completed and the house, for many years spartan and ramshackle, now more appropriately resembled its title of 'Castle'. A hard year, both emotionally and physically, ended happily when the Martins' third daughter, Mary Jane, was born on 10th December 1810.

In London the new Prime Minister, Spencer Percival, must have been daunted by the dimensions of the problems that confronted him. The Peninsular War was going badly wrong. Britain had suffered defeat at Antwerp, and America had entered the trade war on Napoleon's side. Perceval was also without the two most competent ministers from the previous cabinet. Canning and Castlereagh were on the political sidelines, in disgrace after their duel, at which Canning had been wounded. From their falling out, a twist of fate forced Perceval to appoint as Foreign Secretary the Marquis of Wellesley, who would advocate a greater role for his younger brother Arthur in the military campaign.

By the beginning of 1811 the King could no longer play any practical role as Monarch. His spells of insanity far eclipsed the times he was lucid. He was now almost totally blind and completely exhausted. When Perceval met him on 29th January the King indicated that he would no longer oppose a regency. The previous year had seen something almost resembling reconciliation with the Prince of Wales, who was now a man approaching fifty, his hedonism and desire for power beginning to fade. Father and son had discussed how a Regency would work, the Prince agreeing not to sanction anything his father opposed.

Parliament moved quickly and on 6th February the heir to the throne was made Regent. By ensuring the powers conferred were to lapse after one year, the King had put his son on trial. Rumour mills went into full motion as people speculated which of the Prince's cronies would be given power. The Prince surprised everyone, quickly making it known that he did not intend making any changes to the government, thereby dashing Whig hopes. He further allied himself with his father's undoubted concerns by reappointing his disgraced brother Frederick as Commander-in-Chief.

Martin, forced to observe his friend's action from remote Connemara, was in two minds. The Prince might indeed be acting very sensibly in not granting Catholics emancipation while his father was still alive; on the other hand he might be a typical Prince of Wales, who became more and more like his father on accession to the throne. Dick must have been frustrated that circumstances prevented him being in London where he could find out his friend's real intentions at first hand.

In any event, the Prince completed his trial period without doing anything outrageous and the King raised no objection a year later when the Regency was extended indefinitely. The old monarch had made a brief recovery and appeared on horseback in Windsor Park the previous May, then retired to the Castle, never to be seen outside the walls again.

Frustrated being out of the front line at Westminster, Martin began taking an active interest in happenings in Ireland. The Catholic Committee had originally been formed in a Dublin public house in 1760 with the aim of coordinating catholic opinion and lobbying the Irish Parliament. By 1793 Wolfe Tone was Secretary and had urged a more militant strategy, resulting in the breakaway United Irishmen, which half of the Catholic Committee left to join. The moderate half not surprisingly kept a low profile during and after the '98 rebellion. Now run by an influential group of catholic nobility, including Martin's cousins, and strengthened by the structure of county groups, instigated in part by Martin at Ballinasloe eight years before, the Catholic Committee was becoming increasingly powerful.

As a Protestant, Martin was naturally not a member, but he was encouraged that the Catholic Committee were taking a firm line of exerting political pressure and not resorting to armed uprising. He felt that to increase this pressure there should be unity and support from the protestant side of the fence. Dick became involved with the Friends of Toleration, a Protestant movement which practised what the name implied. He was guest of honour at one of their dinners, where he praised Catholics in Galway for their example of 'affectionate and conciliatory conduct to their Protestant neighbours'.

Martin increasingly acted as ambassador between the catholic and protestant organisations, and was received well by them all. A large dinner in Dublin toasted 'Richard Martin and the Freeholders of Galway'. His activity culminated in April 1812 when he addressed a meeting of the Galway Protestants. He asked them to withhold support for any parliamentary candidate who did not swear the oath he was about to take, which read:

> I do most solemnly declare, upon my honour, that until the Catholics are admitted to ALL the privileges of the British Constitution, by granting the prayer of their Petition, I will neither solicit nor accept any office, title or employment, nor will I solicit the same for any other; and it is in consequence of this solemn declaration,

made as an Irishman to the Irish people, that I solicit the support of the Irish Constituents for my return to the Imperial Parliament.


Whether Martin would have relinquished the government salaries that had already been taken away from him is impossible to say, but eight years later he was to break his own pledge. Now, having worked hard to repair his finances, he was in a position to return to London and take up his seat in Westminster. He was looking forward to assessing the Prince Regent at first hand and also renewing his friendship with Lord Erskine, but the most pressing reason to be in London was to be on hand for news of Thomas. There had been no direct contact with his son since he joined the army, but Dick knew from Laetitia, whose husband was in the same regiment, that they were about to engage the French in Spain.

Arthur Wellesley, whose military ambitions had not been fulfilled behind a desk in Dublin, was by now in charge of the British troops in Portugal, dispatched to meet the French where it was perceived they were at their weakest. The armies met at Vimiero, Wellesley emerging the victor. The French were let off lightly, being allowed to return by sea to France. It was this agreement, the Convention of Cintra, that had led to the cabinet feud between Canning and Castlereagh. The British public wanted French blood, not the sight of 26,000 Frenchmen and their commander being transported by British ships back home to be allowed to fight another day. Three British commanders were brought before a military court of enquiry. They were exonerated, but only Wellesley was allowed to see action again.

Napoleon, unused to the taste of defeat, acted quickly and angrily. He dispatched a quarter of a million of his best troops to Spain, firstly to destroy the native guerilla movement and then to confront the British. The British forces, now led by Sir John Moore, were already in north-west Spain, confident they could proceed and cut the French off from their own country. They were past the point of no return when Moore realised the French had already crushed the Spanish, and their only hope was to retreat to the coast and await a naval rescue. He desperately marched his troops through the winter snow with the French in pursuit, arriving at the port of Corunna only to hear that the British fleet were still at sea, hampered by the appalling weather. The French now arrived, far outnumbering the British. Moore was among the dead in the brutal defeat that followed.

Viscount Wellesley persuaded his cabinet colleagues to give the command of what remained of the British army to his younger brother, who against the odds secured an immediate victory at the Battle of Talavera. General Wellesley's reward was the title of Viscount Wellington, which five years later would be elevated to Duke.

After Wellington had secured Lisbon, with its impregnable fortification, the French finally retreated and Britain regained Portugal. Wellington resisted urgings from London to press on into Spain, deciding instead to spend a year rebuilding his mauled and demoralised army. Content with two minor victories at Fuentes d'Onoro and Albuera, his patience was paying off as Napoleon's army became stretched from Spain to Russia.

At the beginning of 1812, Napoleon's *annus horribilis*, Wellington decided to make his move. He needed to seize the vitally important border citadel at Badajoz, overlooking the southern route between Spain and Portugal. The British had twice failed to wrest this fortress from the French and Wellington knew his army would incur heavy casualties during this attempt. Among the regiments chosen for the assault was the 88th Regiment of Foot, the Connaught Rangers, which included Charles Peshall and Thomas Martin.

A siege began on 16th March but by 6th April Wellington concluded there was no alternative but to storm the massive fortifications. For two days, and through forty attacks, a volcanic combination of gunpowder and musket shot fell on the heads of wave after wave of British troops. A shower of logs, barrels and rocks met those who got their breaching ladders as far as the 150-foot walls of the fort. Lines of muskets, bayonets and pikes cut down the men who succeeded in reaching the top.

The Connaught Rangers had lost nineteen officers and over 400 men when their commander, General Picton, called for one last assault, led by Lieutenant Mackie. Mackie succeeded in getting a ladder against the rampart and screamed for his men to follow up. Immediately behind him was Private Martin, who was hit in the shoulder by a French bullet. Badly wounded Thomas continued to climb until he was hit again in the head.

The walls were breached and the British troops now swarmed into the fortress, forcing the French General Phillipon to surrender later in the day. As Wellington surveyed the carnage, he knew that the tide of the Peninsular War had turned in his favour

When Dick arrived in London, the only news from Badajoz was that there had been a British victory but with heavy casualties. He anxiously tapped his contacts in the Government for details of both his son and son-in-law. Laetitia, who was now living in London, shared Dick's fear of the worst. When more details arrived they were encouraging. Laetitia's husband was slightly wounded and Thomas was alive although badly hurt. The next raft of news answered their prayers. Thomas had survived the worst and was now to be sent home to Galway.

Martin wrote to Harriet, asking her to travel to London, as he had decided to remain there until Parliament was prorogued for the summer. Leaving baby Mary in the safe hands of the O'Flaherty family, she looked forward to introducing the older daughters Hatty and Georgy to the delights of London.

Spencer Perceval was keen to make the acquaintance of the former 'Hair-Trigger' Dick, and passed a message to him asking where they could meet. Martin's tongue-in-cheek reply that it should be 'within pistol shot of the treasury' was tragically prophetic. On 11th May, John Bellingham, a bankrupt businessman who blamed the government for a botched deal in Russia, entered the lobby of the House of Commons with a pistol concealed in his coat. On sight of Perceval he walked up and shot him at point-blank range. Britain had lost a potentially great Prime Minister.

Unlike many of his predecessors, Perceval had been in full control of his Cabinet. He had quietly and efficiently put the Regency in place, successfully quashed riots in the north of England and seen the Napoleonic war change in Britain's favour during his watch. Eyes turned to see if the Prince Regent would now make one of the Whigs Prime Minister. Instead, the handover of power was without contention. Robert Banks Jenkinson, Lord Liverpool, who was making a good job of War Minister when Perceval was assassinated, was the fairly obvious choice. He remained at the helm for the next fifteen years.

Martin hastened to put himself in as much contact as he could with the Prince Regent. This meant a whirl of socialising for the Martins, but Dick had a serious motive; he wanted to find out the Prince's true stance regarding Catholics. It did not bode well that he appeared perfectly happy for Liverpool, who was openly anti-catholic, to become his Prime Minister.

Dick was also active in the House, making speeches at every opportunity in respect of Catholic emancipation, supporting a motion of no confidence in the Government, and finding time to involve himself in prison reform. He was becoming well known for his style of speaking, never making long speeches but using incisive, usually humorous, soundbites. He often found the opportunity to quote from the Latin classics and once from *Romeo and Juliet* in the context of a debate on pension law.

During the summer Martin and Erskine picked up the animal rights cudgels, but there was no time to instigate anything in either House before Parliament was dissolved. Liverpool had called a General Election, but this time Martin did not immediately rush back to Ireland. His problem was that he knew he could not afford to fight a contested election and needed the likes of Lord Clancarty at least to agree not to put up candidates against him. Clancarty still held a grudge, because it was Martin who had persuaded him to support the Union. Dick felt that the best way to ensure this influential support in Galway was to pull as many strings as he could before he left London.

Dick asked the former Prime Minister Henry Addington, now Viscount Sidmouth, to write in his favour to Clancarty. He also approached Lord Liverpool, and Robert Peel, the new Irish Chief Secretary, to do likewise. When Martin left London he knew that he faced a fight in Galway, but must have felt he would retain his seat and be making regular visits to the capital, because the Martins were confident enough to leave their two eldest daughters at a boarding school in Kent.

He was, however, none the wiser about what plans the Prince Regent entertained. They had met socially a number of times that summer; on the most recent occasion the Prince had asked Martin who was going to win the forthcoming election in Galway. Martin famously replied, 'The Survivor, Sir!' The Prince had given nothing away about his longer-term stance on religion. He had, however, given Martin a new nickname. As he became increasingly aware of how he ran his mysterious Connemara estate, and of his animal rights plans with Erskine, George, always a wag at parties, had taken to calling his friend 'Humanity Dick'.

# Chapter 26

## Lost Years

By the time Martin arrived back in Galway, Thomas had already been repatriated. The worst of his injuries proved to be the wound to his shoulder, which left him with a slight stoop for the rest of his life. Galway had already welcomed its home-coming heroes with a banquet in honour of Thomas and his cousin's husband William Poppleton, who also had served valiantly in the Peninsula. It is unlikely that Thomas's reunion with Dick conformed to any clichéd scenario, destined as they were for a strained relationship throughout their lives, but both must have at least privately realised they had made rash mistakes. Thomas moved back into Ballynahinch, with Dick more than happy for him to act as its manager, as planned prior to the bitter falling-out.

On the election front there was nothing but bad news for Dick. Sidmouth, Liverpool and Peel had been good as their word and had put pressure on Clancarty to assist Dick's re-election, but to no avail. The influential local peer was putting up candidates for the two seats, both of them Dalys. Giles Eyre, the unfortunate butt of Martin's humour during the last campaign, was also standing.

It is difficult to understand why the Prime Minister, one of his predecessors and the current Irish Chief Secretary were happy to try to elicit support for the maverick member for Galway. They were all staunchly anti-catholic, Martin had been a thorn in the Government's side and Peel was a passionate devotee of hunting. The only viable assumption is that leverage was exerted by the Prince Regent.

More bad news followed. Other, less powerful but significantly influential members of the Galway establishment, all of whom controlled voters, were against him. The worst of Dick's problems, however, was that a technicality was used to exclude over 2000 of his freeholders, on the grounds that their voting registration was received too late.

There was one last chance. Bowes Daly had previously promised Martin that he would not stand against him at this election. There may have been an arrangement entered into when they both stood unopposed at the previous contest. Daly admitted the promise but refused to abide by it. Martin took the course of action that any Member for Galway worth his salt would have done: he challenged Daly to a duel.

Dick had not wanted to fight for 28 years, but was prepared to come out of retirement for Daly. Reputations such as Martin's do not diminish over time; in fact they grow to mythic proportions. Daly on the other hand does not appear ever to have blazed, and was prone to nervous mannerisms even without this kind of pressure. His response was to go the authorities and have Dick arrested. Martin was released after being bound over to keep the peace, an undertaking which included not shooting his opponent.

Even to a man with Dick's sometimes illogical optimism, the odds were overwhelmingly stacked against him. What little money he could access would be wasted fighting a pointless campaign; he withdrew from the contest, deciding instead to support Eyre and at least try to prevent a Daly monopoly.

Thomas, in an attempt to stop the Dalys increasing their stranglehold over the Galway Corporation, decided to stand for the Town seat, and would have done so had Valentine Blake not stood. The Blakes from Menlo Castle were old friends of the Martins. Despite these efforts, Eyre was unsuccessful and Dick's worst-case situation, of both Dalys being elected, materialised.

Immediately after the election, for the first time in his life Dick fell seriously ill. He collapsed with a fever and for weeks lay close to death at Clareville. Harriet stayed at his bedside throughout and nursed him through the winter as he slowly regained his health. By the following spring he had recovered enough to move back to Ballynahinch.

The war of attrition against the French, and Napoleon's trade stranglehold, were combining to create social problems serious enough to provoke widespread riots in the north of England. As if Britain did not have enough problems, America now declared war on her former motherland. This was triggered by the Royal Navy seizing American ships that were obeying Napoleon's embargo, thus giving America an excuse to react to the annoying British presence in Canada. Lord Liverpool's government moved quickly to negotiate a peace but, by the time the message crossed the Atlantic, impatient military men on both sides had already commenced hostilities.

Events were panning out better in Europe. Napoleon had decided to attack Russia, although his army was already stretched as far as Spain. In a strange way he both won and lost the 1812 Russian campaign. When he entered Moscow, he found a burning city. The cruel Russian winter was already beginning to close in, his army of 100,000 men had no food and they were a long way from home. For a month the Emperor tried to negotiate with the Tsar, now 300 miles away in well stocked St Petersburg, but eventually the French army had no alternative but a long retreat. When its remnants arrived in Warsaw, 70,000 had died from a combination of hypothermia, starvation and being picked off by gangs of peasants and Cossacks. Napoleon had already deserted his men, setting out from Moscow on a sleigh bound for Paris.

By the spring of 1813, Martin was recovering. Thomas was enthusiastically throwing himself into running the estate and Dick was happy that his son adhered to the established code of benevolence. Although he was used to staring bankruptcy in the face, this time even his philosophy of optimism was tested to its limit. Losing the protection of parliamentary membership meant that once again he was forced to rely on the remoteness of Ballynahinch, and the protection of his men, to prevent ignominy. For many years Martin's most loyal servant was a native of Connemara called Ned Bodkin. Years after this dismal period of Dick's life, Bodkin described to Jonah Barrington his role on the estate and how his master was protected:

> 'Tis me that tans the brogues for the Colonel's yeomen, besides I'm bum bailiff of the town lands and make out the election registries; and keep the Squire's accounts, and by my sowl, that same is no aisy matter, plas your honour, til one's

used to it. But God bless him up and down, wherever he goes, here or hereafter, he's nothing but a good master to us all.

Why if the prossy-sarver [a bailiff serving papers] is cotched in the territories of Ballynahinch, by my sowl if the Squire's not in it he'll either eat his own parchment or go down into the owld coal hole sure enough, whichever is the most agreeable to the said prossy-sarver . . . The varmit generally gulps it down mighty glib; and by the same token, he is seldom obstreperous enough to go down into the said coal hole . . . We always give the prossy-sarver, poor crethur, plenty to moisten his said food with and wash it down well anyhow; and he goes back to the 'Sizes as merry as a water-dog, and swears, God forgive him, that he was a kilt at Connemara by people unknown, becaize if he didn't do that he knows well enough he'd soon be kilt dead by people he did know, and that's the truth.

Little wonder that the establishment were loath to back Martin in elections when court bailiffs returned from the depths of his estate, blind drunk from the poteen with which they were forced to wash down unsuccessfully served bankruptcy petitions. Little surprise that most creditors wrote off the debts.

The Martin family was incomplete at Ballynahinch, with Harriet's two eldest daughters still at the English boarding school. The Postal route was laborious to and from the house but Harriet managed to write, one letter describing her relief that their father did not go through with his duel with the cowardly Boyes Daly, whose 'petty conduct has made him ridiculous among men . . . but I know I rejoice at his cowardice since it saved us from a dreadful shock.' Dick's duelling days, of course, had finished by the time he met Harriet.

Young Richard, now sixteen, was studying at Ballynahinch in preparation to enter Trinity College, while Thomas had fallen in love again, this time with someone more than acceptable. This was Julia Kirwan, the niece of a close friend of Harriet's and distantly related by virtue of numerous marriages over the years between the Martin and Kirwan families. Dick was a proud father when the couple married on Valentine's Day 1814, and moved into Ballynahinch. Within a year Thomas and Julia were the parents of Mary Martin, the future 'Princess of Connemara', fated to be the last surviving member of the family at the estate.

There was one family tragedy for Martin during this period: his beloved sister Mary died. Since she was already widowed, and childless, Dick had administered her small estate, the bulk of which would have been left to him as her next of kin.

Despite the previous disastrous attempts at mining, Martin was once again attempting to extract financial deliverance from the rough Connemara terrain. For centuries locals had laboriously polished pieces of stone until they assumed stunning shades of green. Martin knew that the potential supply at his feet could compete with the very best marble in the world. Father and son started earnestly quarrying at a major source of the stone they had discovered in the Twelve Ben Mountains, close to Ballynahinch.

Although it would take a couple of years building the production facilities and setting up distribution channels, the potential of the business, compounded with Martin's natural optimism, must have temporarily satisfied many of his creditors and might even have allowed him to establish new lines of credit. After assiduous work on the estate as a whole, during the longest adult period of his life he had spent in Connemara, Martin was now in a position to venture back into civilization and address two pressing legal matters.

The bumptious Bowles Daly would not let Dick's challenge rest. Society had moved on a long way since Dick's wild youth and duelling, although still taking place, was now frowned upon by the authorities. Martin was found guilty of threatening behaviour but escaped serious punishment by binding himself over once again to keep the peace. He did, however, fully exploit the proceedings, making Daly a figure of ridicule and dishonour.

The other case was of Martin's making. His solicitor, Edward Burke, by forging documents and committing perjury, cheated Martin out of £420; Dick pressed charges and was in a position to take the matter to court, but the offence of forgery carried an almost mandatory sentence of death and, although he had killed men over matters of honour, he decided this was not an equitable outcome and dropped the forgery charge. After dispensing with his lawyer, McNally, he continued to pursue the lesser charge of perjury, causing disruption in the court as he represented himself, the matter getting out of hand and resulting in the judge having to call the militia to restore order.

Afterwards Dick resolved that, when he returned to Parliament, he would make greater exertions to reform a criminal justice system still rife with medieval punishments. To the end of his life, when circumstances forced Martin to the sidelines, getting back into politics was never a question of if, only of when.

Wellington had won the Peninsular War by the spring of 1814. Napoleon, his army and reputation both in tatters, found his allies deserting him, and he abdicated. Twenty-one years after executing Louis XVI, the French people invited his brother to be their King and by the Treaty of Fontainebleau, Britain and her allies signed a peace agreement with France that reduced her borders to where they had been in 1792. Napoleon was given his own kingdom: the small Mediterranean island of Elba; but Europe had not seen the last of the little Emperor.

Louis XVIII immediately set out to restore the French aristocracy to their pre-revolution status. The people were having none of this and, when word reached Napoleon that he retained the loyalty of the army, he set sail from his island domain, landing in the south of France on 26th February 1815. Three weeks later he was in Paris, the Bourbon king having fled. By 16th June Napoleon's army faced Wellington's near the Belgian town of Waterloo in a final showdown.

Remarkably, the two Generals had never previously faced each other across a battlefield. The French outnumbered their adversaries by 74,000 to 67,000, but were decisively defeated. Napoleon retreated to Paris and from there attempted to abdicate once more. Incredibly, when the British caught him in Rochefort on the French Atlantic coast he was planning an invasion of South America. They confined him on the remote south Atlantic island of St Helena, where he remained up to his death nine years later.

Castlereagh, now back in favour with the Government, was tasked with overseeing the peace negotiations. Wisely deciding that making them too humiliating to the French would only prime a timebomb, Britain settled for a small gain in territories, compensation of 700 million francs and leaving Wellington in charge of an occupation army for a period of three years. Castlereagh felt the treaty would ensure peace between the European powers for seven years. In fact it lasted nearly sixty.

The American sideshow was also settled. The British had attacked the American President's official residence, scorching the outside walls so badly that they had to be painted white, but then suffered a heavy defeat at the hands of Commander Andrew Jackson in New Orleans. Both sides called it a draw and the American War of 1813 was over. With peace on all fronts, Lord Liverpool, his position secured, called a General Election in 1818.

It was Martin's opportunity to re-enter the political arena. This time Ned Bodkin made sure all Martin's freeholders were on the electoral register, but he still faced candidates put up by his political enemies and had limited funds for the campaign. There was never any question of Dick not standing, and when the preliminary posturing was over he faced his old foes, the Daly cousins, Bowes and James.

Martin now enjoyed a stroke of luck. For many years he had been friendly with Martin Joseph Blake, a wealthy landowner from Tuam in the east of Galway County. Blake was strongly in favour of catholic emancipation and he bought into Dick's confidence that the Prince Regent would ensure it once the King was dead. Martin convinced Blake that it was important for him to be in Parliament when this happened, and Blake agreed to bankroll Martin's campaign.

Dick wrote to the Prince asking him to help secure support in the election. The only contact he had had with George over the last six years was when he previously wrote asking if he would find Richard, who by now had obtained a degree at Trinity, a suitable army commission. The Prince had obliged and young Richard was placed in the 3rd Dragoon Guards. The new request was less successful. Whether the Prince made the decision himself or whether it was made for him by his Secretary is uncertain, but it was indicated that Martin was not a person who should be seen to have Royal approval. Robert Peel, however, gave his open support to Martin from Dublin Castle.

The contest followed the customary lines. Martin wrote to his sponsor in blackly humourous style: 'I beg you will send me a case of pistols to remain with me until the election is over.' Bowles Daly wrote that he 'was tired of the rascality of elections . . . no person with any ounce of principle can contest an Irish town or county.' Someone in the Daly camp was insufficiently principled to attempt to kill a man called Reddington, one of Dick's team, while he was enjoying a day's racing at the Curragh. Earlier, Reddington had been responsible for starting a riot at a Daly rally.

As usual, the Galway-based candidates sprinted into an early lead until the hordes of Martin's supporters arrived from the depths of Connemara, amid the usual chaos and allegations of skullduggery. When the dust settled, Martin and Bowes Daly were the elected Members for the County of Galway.

Dick's six years of frustration were over and he could return to Westminster. Moreover, if reports were correct, the King would not survive much longer to obstruct his hopes and plans.

Dick and his Constituents or humanity extended!

# Chapter 27

# Abuse of Parliament

Humanity Dick was now sixty-five years old, a senior politician by modern standards and an old man according to 19th-century mortality rates. It was 43 years since he had entered Parliament as a young man focussed on one political objective, total emancipation for Catholics. The goal was only partly achieved, and for Martin this partial success had to be weighed against the price of Union. Nevertheless, he was as keen as ever to re-enter the fray.

During his period out of office, Martin had reflected on a strategy for achieving animal rights legislation. His own law in Connemara was now well refined. All forms of animal baiting were outlawed and the boundaries of acceptable chastisement for working animals were clearly known to all tenants and freeholders in Martin's ancient barony.

He and Harriet decided to live in London for this parliamentary term, only taking the occasional trip back to Ireland. Thomas was now running the estate and developing the marble business. His reputation as a host was already established. Ballynahinch, despite its remoteness, was renowned for hospitality, fine food and the best French wines, the latter being commission in kind from the local illicit import and export trade. Thomas had blamed his father for taking too much out of the family finances for years; now Dick was beginning to complain to his son that he was doing the same. This exchange of views continued until Dick's death.

The Martins took a house in Manchester Buildings, near to Westminster: not as grand as their previous London home but perfectly adequate. Mary, their youngest daughter, came to London with her parents this time. There was an emotional reunion with the older girls, Hatty, now a young woman of eighteen and Georgy, twelve. Hatty was looking forward to life in the capital as the debutante daughter of well known Irish socialites.

Martin wasted no time in taking his seat in Parliament. On 8th February 1819, during a debate to sanction a Government appointee to the powerful Bank of England Committee, he set out his stall to show how he would take action in the House.

Lord Liverpool, who was to become one of Britain's longest-serving Prime Ministers, had assembled a strong Cabinet which included the Duke of Wellington, the future Prime Minister George Canning, and, memories of the inter-Cabinet duel being long forgotten, Lord Castlereagh, who had persuaded Martin to support the Union. Castlereagh proposed the appointment of a Mr Broughton to the Bank of England. It should have been just a formality, and a number of backbenchers had already made speeches singing the appointee's praises.

Dick now spoke in the style he had made his own: a dry, trenchant delivery, loaded with irony and drawing on tangential analogies and personal anecdotes. He made the point that there were many gentlemen at the Bar, 'learned lawyers, that his Majesty would be ill advised to appoint to the judiciary.' He could conceive of a man, 'highly skilled in divinity, yet the ministers of his Majesty would not be advised to make him a Bishop.' He finished by saying he was 'not ashamed to say that Government could not have induced him to vote for that appointment.' In his wry way Martin was saying that this was a Cabinet fix-up and certain MPs had been bribed and cajoled into supporting it. Opposition members jumped on to Martin's bandwagon. When the time came to vote on the matter, there was a majority of 42 against the appointment.

Martin brought another old grudge with him to Westminster and, two weeks after his interference in governmental cronyism, he aired it. The way that the trial had been conducted four years earlier, when he brought a charge of perjury against his former solicitor, still rankled with him. He now wanted the judge, Baron McClelland, who had thrown him out of court under military guard, brought to justice.

On February 12th Martin rose to move that the Judge's actions were unacceptable, most notably he did not take Dick's word that his primary witness was too ill to attend court. Even after hearing medical evidence to that effect, the Judge would still not adjourn the trial. Martin continued, 'Every man in Ireland, capable of pronouncing an opinion on the subject, with whom he had spoken, agreed in stating that a more outrageous determination than the one in question never had been come to.'

Castlereagh spoke in defence of the judge, saying he knew him personally and he was of the highest character and one of the most respected judges not only in Ireland but in both kingdoms. He urged the Member for Galway to withdraw his motion, which was not backed up with any documentary evidence and in any event the matter could not be heard without a representative from the Irish Administration present. Martin would not withdraw, but the Speaker forced him to postpone his motion to a later date, no doubt hoping that someone would persuade him to let the matter drop.

Two months later Martin was back on the floor of the House, even more determined to be heard, and now annoyed that Parliament had cast the same slur on his character as Judge McClelland, by not accepting his version of events. This time the friends of McClelland were prepared. After Dick had again outlined the catalogue of judicial mistakes, Hill, the Member for Londonderry, stood up. The first point he made was that this matter should not be before Parliament, as it was not an accusation of partiality or corruption but of an alleged error of judgment. However, as the Honourable Member had seen fit to raise the question then it needed to be addressed. He had spoken at length to Baron McClelland and it would appear that Martin's version of events was not accurate. Certain affidavits referred to were never produced in court and the absence of witnesses was not a reason to postpone the trial, the prosecution having not used due diligence to ensure their attendance.

Hill stated that Martin had acted inappropriately at the trial by first dispensing with the services of his counsel, and then, after making a lengthy opening statement, reflecting with great severity on the conduct and character of the accused, refusing to be cross-examined. Judge McClelland was faced with no choice but to take the action he had taken. Hill claimed it had also transpired that Martin had subsequently harangued the Judge when they met by chance in Dublin Castle, not only about the case against Burke but also for the Judge's handling of a previous matter when the Member for Galway was before him on a charge of challenging a Mr Bowes Daly to a duel. More speakers rose in support of the Judge and made their feelings clear that

Martin should not be using the House for this purpose. The Commons was not a court of appeal and should only hear matters regarding judges in a case of corruption.

Dick finally responded. He said the members who had imputed he was not alleging corrupt motives to the learned gentleman were wrong. The conduct of Baron McClelland *was* corrupt. The Judge had acted on 'the seat of justice from motives of personal resentment.' That is why he, Martin, was charging McClelland with corruption and wanted him dismissed and censured. The charge against the Judge could not be one of mere ignorance. It was criminal conduct.

Dick could not then resist the opportunity of pouring scorn on his old foe, Bowes Daly. Quite what he said was not recorded but Hansard, the official record of parliamentary debates, noted that the Honourable Gentleman described Mr Daly in 'so theatrical a manner as to keep the House in a continued roar of laughter.' Martin's motion was 'negatived without a division', parliamentary terminology for when the House is so overwhelmingly against something that there is no need to take a formal vote. This only made Dick even angrier, and two months later he returned to the attack.

On 2nd June he brought a charge against Baron McClelland for Breach of Judicial Duty. He started by saying he was fully aware of the difficult task he was undertaking and the House should deal in the 'severest manner with any man who should be daring or wicked enough to bring forward any unfounded charge or calumny against a judge.' It had now become necessary for him to prove his 'own truth and integrity in making these charges.' Using his famed ability to draw analogy, Martin went on to compare himself with a military officer whose charges against a superior were unfounded and who now faced his own court-martial.

Now in full flow, Martin went on to ask: 'What would be the House's opinion of him, himself, for he would not shrink from saying so, should he adduce false charges and groundless calumnies against a learned judge?' He immediately answered his own question. 'They ought to expel him from their own assembly; but what would they say when he told them that he had seven or eight witnesses, who were ready not merely to substantiate his averments, but to prove them to be altogether true?'

Dick outlined events from four years ago in the Galway courtroom. Apart from the Judge's mistake in not adjourning the matter, and his obstinacy in not allowing Dick to represent himself, there was also the issue that Baron McClellad had overreacted in summoning the army to clear the courtroom of everybody except one Honourable Member (Valentine Blake) who 'by some stratagem or other, had the good fortune to hide himself under one of the benches.' 'Was this', Martin asked, 'conduct to be tolerated in a judge whose bounden duty it was to administer justice with impartiality?'

He was now in danger of making a complete fool of himself by so doggedly pursuing an issue so trivial and inappropriate for Parliament. Castlereagh attempted once more to put the nut out of the range of Martin's sledgehammer. He pointed out that although it was not customary in this country to introduce soldiers into a court to retain order, in Ireland the practice was frequent. Knowing Martin as he did, Castlereagh realised that face had to be saved. He praised Dick's great ability in the House and saw no reason why the Member for Galway would not be capable of presenting his own case in a court of law. He assured Martin that if the objective of this current motion was to: 'exculpate himself in some measure, he could assure him, and in saying so he was sure he spoke the sentiments of the House, that, as far as he was concerned, there was not the slightest occasion for the proceeding.'

Martin performed an immediate u-turn and the charge against Judge McClelland was withdrawn. The whole episode was typical of him. He would pursue something he felt passionately about (and nothing angered him more than injustice), with total disregard for the system he was working within.

Throughout 1819 Martin was omnipresent in the debates. Nobody raised the Catholic issue, because its advocates knew it was pointless until the Price Regent became king. Martin contented himself with getting involved in a myriad of issues, many of which could not have been more than passing interests. These included increasing the Duke of York's Civil List allowance, the repeal of window tax, libel laws, and even the Barnstable Bridge Bill. His one impassioned speech was reserved to call for humanity for the victims of 'Peterloo', the demonstration in Manchester at which the army had turned on the crowd, leaving twelve dead and hundreds injured.

Martin's parliamentary style was now fully developed. He would interject, usually late in a debate, with astute points of logic, probably opposing the direction which the arguments were taking. He throve on intellectual gymnastics, akin to a dinner party guest who argues the contrary for the sake of devilment.

Renewing his friendship with Erskine, he found there was now an additional member in the small group of animal rights pioneers. Dr John Lawrence was a farmer from East Anglia; it is possible Martin had first made his acquaintance many years before when he was studying at the home of Joseph Gunning.

Lawrence was also a writer, whose work frequently dealt with the philosophical issues of whether animals could and should suffer pain. In one essay he reasoned that a beast whose body is nourished by the same food and hurt by the same injuries as Man, is entitled to the same justice. He condemned injuring and killing animals in the name of sport, though he did not object to hunting a predator such as a fox. He felt that the balance of nature called for man to kill animals, but not to torture them. He especially criticised overworking sick or tired beasts of burden. In Martin he found a pragmatist who could mould these ideals into workable practices.

Over the last six years Martin and Erskine had concluded that to achieve animal protection in law their strategy should be gradually to make members of both parliamentary houses perceive the need for it. Persuading Parliament to sanction complete protection immediately was never going to work. There must be a foot inserted in the door, which could then be gradually pushed open.

On 29th January 1820, King George III died. He had reigned for 60 years. Shops closed, the whole nation went into mourning and 30,000 people travelled to Windsor for the funeral. He had been loved by the British people. His perseverance in moral standards had restored faith in the monarchy. For Catholics, on the other hand, he had been an immovable obstruction to emancipation.

The time had come for Martin to see if his friend King George IV would fulfill his long-held hopes.

# Chapter 28

# Royal Disapproval

Catholic emancipation was not at the forefront of the new King's mind. He was more concerned over what to do with his wayward wife, who was now Queen of England.

In his youth, George's dissolute ways came to a temporary halt in 1784 when he fell in love with Maria Fitzherbert, a woman six years older than himself, a commoner and, to the horror of both Prime Minister Pitt and the King, a Catholic. Worse still for the Prince, Maria was extremely moral and would not content herself with being a royal mistress. She wanted marriage or nothing and, after her half-hearted attempt at suicide, the Prince gave in to her demands on 21st December 1785, when the couple were wed in a modest ceremony at a private house in London.

To avoid a constitutional crisis, George III and his government had two options. Using the Act of Settlement, the Prince and his possible children could be excluded from the throne. Alternatively the marriage could be declared illegal under the Royal Marriages Act. The latter choice was adopted. Within a few years the Prince was bored with his love and returned to his circle of cronies and mistresses. Either from compassion, or from foresight in ensuring her silence, the King arranged for Maria to receive an annuity of £6,000 a year.

Ten years later the Prince, in dire financial straits and trying to ingratiate himself with his father, agreed to an arranged marriage with Caroline of Brunswick, his own niece. A perfect royal bride on paper, Caroline turned out to be far ideal for either Prince or country. She was fat and ugly, and she smelt. Her demeanour was crass, and over the years would become increasingly indiscreet. The Prince described her as 'the vilest wretch this world was ever cursed with' and went on a 24-hour drinking binge prior to the wedding. Within a year, after somehow managing to produce a daughter, they were openly living apart.

In 1806 the Cabinet mounted the 'Delicate Investigation' to look into rumours that the Princess had given birth to an illegitimate child. The investigation concluded that she had not, although her life was promiscuous in the extreme. The Prince wanted a divorce, but Liverpool and his cabinet considered this an even worse option. A subsequent enquiry mounted by spies working for the Prince showed that Caroline, now living on the continent, was having an affair with Bartolomeo Pergami, a former member of the Royal household.

For years the British public had been exposed to a Prince of Wales and his errant, estranged wife fighting for public adoration. The Princess, despite her flighty ways, was more adept at working the media, and public affection was now firmly on her side. Her husband was deemed to be the wrongdoer.

When the old king died, the stakes were automatically raised. Six months into her husband's reign Caroline arrived at Dover to claim her place as queen. George, confident that he had sufficient proof, insisted his government put his wife on trial for adultery, which for a queen was a treasonable offence and therefore carried the death penalty.

The trial in Parliament commenced, amid a frenzy of public interest, in July 1820. Caroline's lawyers wanted to bring witnesses from abroad to give evidence, but this was blocked by the government's use of the Aliens Bill, which prevented them from entering the country. Martin, who had maintained a friendship with both parties, now chose to get involved, not quietly and discreetly on behalf of the Queen, or loudly in favour of the King, as many royal friends were doing, but on the floor of the House of Commons.

Martin was happy to claim, 'as the Queen's friend, if he may be so bold,' that she would not get a fair trial without the freedom to call whatever witnesses she wanted. Like a bull who was unsatisfied by the amount of china already broken, Martin turned on those ministers supporting the King, saying that with these witnesses the Queen's acquittal would be certain and then 'the trials of the corrupt Ministers would begin with a certainty of their conviction and punishment.' He could not resist the inevitable anecdote, drawn from his time in pre-revolution Paris. There, he recalled, a hackney coachman, 'nothing like the caricature we see, he was a plump, round, well-fed citizen,' asked of Martin what he felt about the French King and Queen. Dick told the House his reply was that he 'did not think any gentleman would consent to be their king,' but he, Martin, would consider proposing himself.

So in a brief speech Martin had managed to upset his old friend, now the King, accuse senior members of the House of corruption, and insult the French royal family. The following day he was back on the floor of the House complaining about the reporting of his speech in the *Morning Herald*. The paper claimed Martin had compared ministers to a 'big bellied hackney coachman' and that after insulting the King of France the Member for Galway claimed he would make a better king. Martin said that he had confronted the reporter but was not prepared to put the matter to a trial by battle, preferring instead to bring the publisher before the Bar of the House. It appears that the issue was resolved when the paper agreed not to report Martin's speeches in future.

By now, the Queen had been allowed to call foreign witnesses, and Liverpool and his Cabinet realised that the spectre of losing the trial was looming. Ministers to-ed and fro-ed between the royal protagonists to broker an agreement whereby the King did not have to retract his charges but, conversely, the Queen did not admit them. This was not enough for Caroline, who now demanded she be included in the church liturgy, the official prayer for the royal family, which George had excluded her from. Martin argued in Parliament that now she had been accused it was essential she be allowed to clear her name. He did, however, make the sensible suggestion that it might be diplomatic if Caroline remained living abroad.

The royal scandal had eclipsed everything else, including a brief uprising in Ireland. Economic conditions throughout Britain were bad following the financially crippling wars with France, but in Ireland the safety net above starvation was much thinner, compounded by the greed and lack of compassion demonstrated by many landlords. For years there had been many secret societies amongst the catholic peasantry. One society, the Ribbonmen, rose to arms and took especially violent retribution against landlords in the west of the country. As they put it, 'human nature could no longer bear the slavery they are in and it is better to be shot than die of hunger.'

The Ribbonmen did not target the Martins, but many other Galway landowners, such as the Dalys, now feared for their lives. In the middle of the preamble to the Queen's trial, Martin's local adversary James Daly proposed a bill calling for greater powers to crush the insurrection, effectively reverting to the old penal laws. Not surprisingly, Martin did not agree. He told the House that Daly was overreacting and denied there was a rebellion in the County of Galway. 'In the baronies where his property was situated, everything was tranquil.' He recommended that his honourable colleague withdraw his motion.

Martin also took the opportunity to stress the plight of the Irish peasant. While not condoning the criminal actions of the Ribbonmen, he asked rhetorically, what were their objectives? His answer was, not to have to pay more than a reasonable rent, which to English landlords might appear low but to an Irish peasant was all the land would support. Castlereagh backed his old friend's argument, saying because of Martin's 'great knowledge and experience he might be considered competent to form a correct judgment.' Daly's motion was rejected.

Thomas was struggling to produce enough revenue to support his father in London, but once again Dick faced an embarrassing cash flow predicament. To solve the problem he chose to break his impassioned pledge sworn eight years earlier to the mass meeting in Galway. He asked for and was given the salaried post of Commissioner of Fisheries. With problems mounting back home, Martin returned to Ballynahinch in advance of the start of Queen Caroline's trial.

One immediate problem he faced was an outraged patron. Martin Joseph Blake was fuming that Martin had so blatantly reneged on his pledge made in support of Catholics and was also frustrated at the lack of parliamentary progress made by Martin towards emancipation. Blake's financial support was secured on the Martin estate and he now demanded his money back. Martin could not oblige, and again it was only the protection afforded to Members of Parliament that kept him out of prison.

Thomas had worked hard on the estate but deeply resented the drain his father's lifestyle was causing. Dick on the other hand felt that his son wanted too much for himself too soon. More copper, this time within reach of the coast, had been discovered on the Martin-owned High Island. Dick wrote to his solicitor that from this Thomas 'looks to immediate wealth.'

The marble business was producing high quality material, but sales were not ensuing, owing partly to the financial climate of the time and partly to a market prejudiced against Irish goods, although Dick knew from first-hand experience of some of the grandest houses in Europe, that his Connemara marble was as good, if not better than any competitor's.

By the time Dick and Harriet returned to London at the start of 1821, the case against Queen Caroline was on the verge of collapse. Government witnesses were proving unreliable, and Martin wasted no time in rejoining the ranks pressing for the case to be dismissed and the Queen's name be reinstated in the royal prayer. Not for the first time, Dick incurred the wrath of the Speaker, who called one of his

*How to get Un-married, cartoon by J.L. Marks, George IV is assisted by Lord Castlereagh.*

interruptions out of order. Martin replied that it would be quicker for the House to hear his point than to try and stop him making it.

Lord Liverpool finally threw in the towel by moving that the case be adjourned for six months. Everyone knew this was merely face-saving, and a victory for the Queen. Earl Grey, the leader of the Whig opposition, declared her innocent of adultery and her thousands of supporters celebrated by illuminating their houses and stoning the windows of government ministers. The King was beside himself with rage, threatening briefly to sack his entire administration and retire to Hanover. Anybody who had remotely sided with the Queen was expelled from the his circle. This included his old friend, Humanity Dick Martin.

Martin shrugged off the royal snub and set about his other aims for the session. Plans were falling into place for statutory protection for animals but, in the mean time, he turned his attention to the two other issues he had become increasingly passionate about.

On 27th February 1821, Martin set the wheels in motion to overturn a cornerstone of the British judicial system. A person accused of an offence, other than treason, that carried the sentence of execution was not entitled to have a counsel act for his or her defence. Instead the presiding judge served as the accuser's advocate. Martin's Capital Crimes Defence Bill called for this anomaly to be overturned. He stated that the argument for the Bill was self-evident and the reverse was 'utterly inconsistent with the benignity of our criminal code.'

Two members opposed the Bill, but Martin was given leave to propose it, which he did on 30th March, citing the recent trial of John Bellingham, the man recently found guilty and hanged for assassinating Spencer Perceval, as a classic case of a defendant much in need of a lawyer. The Judge at Bellingham's trial had refused to adjourn in order for a medical affidavit, claiming Bellingham to be insane, to be admitted.

Sir Robert Gifford and Sir Samuel Shepherd, Solicitor General and Attorney General respectively, were now prepared to put a counter case. They both reasoned that they had no cause to doubt that courts served defendants fairly. Any change to the system was unnecessary and would waste time. Martin's friend Sir James Mackintosh spoke in favour of the Bill and Sir Joseph Yorke opposed, building on the argument about time-wasting when he said that if the court had to hear two advocates then 'Counsellor Bore'em and Counsellor Bother'em' would each speak for two hours, so that with the number of cases currently before the judiciary this added up to 12,000 hours of lawyer-speak annually.

Yorke's terrifying scenario carried the day and the Bill was negatived. Martin had, however, set a chain of events in motion that would soon overturn this archaic injustice.

Two months later, perhaps realising that he did not have the credibility to propose such weighty legal issues, Martin's other judicial crusade, that of abolishing the death penalty for forgery, was put forward by Sir James Mackintosh. Dick spoke in favour, outlining his own experience of wanting to prosecute his former solicitor but having to withdraw the indictment because of the sentence it carried. This, he reasoned, meant that many guilty forgers were not brought to justice, who would be if the offence carried a more equitable punishment. This Bill also failed, but again it would only be only a matter of time before more humane attitudes prevailed in British justice.

Since returning to London after his six years on the sidelines, Dick had been working with Lord Erskine and Dr Lawrence to achieve animal rights, while learning from previous failures. On 17th May, Martin started by selling the House of Commons a dummy. He claimed he had been handed a petition by a group of stagecoach owners, influential tradesmen in London, who were complaining they had no redress against reckless employees who damaged their valuable horses. In fact the law did protect them, as an owner of a horse could take legal action against anyone injuring his property, but nobody in the House spotted this and Martin was given leave to introduce a bill that would provide the requested protection.

Erskine, drawing on his experience as a former Lord Chancellor, helped Dick word the Bill, which stated that, if anyone should 'wantonly and cruelly beat, abuse or ill-treat' a horse, then that party could be brought before a court and charged. There was no reference to who actually owned the animal and the bill was deliberately restricted to horses.

It was paid scant attention on its first reading and progressed to committee stage on 1st June. Here it was broadened to define the animals protected as 'mares, geldings, mules, asses, cows, heifers, steers, oxen, sheep, and other cattle'. It was named the 'Ill Treatment of Cattle Bill', and a sparsely attended Commons briefly debated it before passing it to the next stage by three votes. Like a cat burglar, Martin was tiptoeing quietly through Parliament.

The Bill almost fell at the next hurdle, its second reading, when one member suggested it would only be a matter of time before someone tried to protect dogs, and even cats. The vote was returned 26 For and the same number Against, leaving the Speaker with no choice but to side with convention and cast his vote in favour of progression.

Dick now pressed one of his primed public relations buttons. He arrested two men in Giltspur Street, London, for acts of cruelty to a horse; no mean feat for a man of sixty-seven, but Dick had always been totally oblivious to the prospect of harm besetting him. He brought them before magistrates at the Guildhall on 16th June 1821, knowing the court was powerless in law to do anything. The problem faced by the Judge was duly reported by a contact of Martin's at *The Times* under the heading 'Cruelty to Animals'.

Dick recounted the incident when he spoke at the Bill's third reading on 29th June. He had anticipated getting this far, and his efforts from a few months before now produced their results. William Wilberforce, Sir James Graham, Sir W. de Crespigny and Charles Grant, the Chief Secretary for Ireland, all produced petitions from their constituencies supporting the Bill. Knowing the majority of members attending were in his favour, Dick did not rock the boat by instigating any debate and the Bill was carried with a majority of 24.

Martin had successfully paved the way for his law to be carried by the Commons. However, Erskine's efforts fell short in the upper chamber. There it met rigorous opposition from the powerful Earl of Lauderdale, who rehashed the old chestnut of the subject not being fit for legislation. The Lords rejected the Bill, and Martin's game of snakes and ladders left him back at square one.

If he was minded immediately to try again, then the decision was taken away from him. Parliament was prorogued by the King, who, having postponed his Coronation until his wife was disposed of, could wait no longer to be crowned, and intended to follow the ceremony with a royal trip to Ireland. The event almost cost Dick his life.

# Chapter 29

# Home and Dry

The final act of the melodrama of George and Caroline was played out on the steps of Westminster Abbey. She arrived for her husband's coronation only to have the door slammed in her face as she cried, 'Let me pass; I am your Queen!'

Two weeks after being crowned in a splendour befitting England's most narcissistic King, George set out from Portsmouth for a state visit to Ireland. The royal yacht, accompanied by a naval squadron, sailed around the south and west coasts of England and Wales bound for Holyhead. From there they intended to cross the Irish Sea to Dublin.

On 7th August Queen Caroline died from uncertain causes in London. The royal fleet was still at sea, but news of his wife's death awaited the King when he arrived on the island of Anglesey, off the coast of North Wales, the following day. The difficult question whether to delay the planned trip in order to be seen to have a period of mourning was decided for him when a tremendous storm hit the North Wales coast hours after his arrival. It lasted for four days, which George spent at Plas Newydd, on the small Holy Island adjacent to Anglesey. He ordered that the usual salute of guns to mark a royal death should not be sounded.

On the same day, Richard Martin arrived in the nearby port of Liverpool, along with several other dignitaries from London travelling to Dublin for the King's visit on the new steam packet ship, the *Earl of Moira*. Packets were an advance in travel which occurred during Dick's lifetime. Though smaller than the old sailing boats, they had the obvious advantage of not being dependent on prevailing winds and could guarantee to cross the Irish Sea in a day. The lower class of passenger travelled on deck, the gentry below in an ornate state room, where they entertained themselves by drinking and playing cards.

The *Earl of Moira* was due to leave Liverpool's Pier Head at 5 o'clock in the afternoon. Passengers attributed the 90-minute delay in sailing to the weather, which was worsening by the hour. The actual reason was that the captain and his senior officers were finishing a drinking session in the town and at half past six, against advice, they set sail with 100 deck passengers and 30 in the cabin.

An hour later and 5 miles out of port, the ship, with her captain now so drunk he could not stand, struck Burbo Bank off the Cheshire coast. Passengers and crew worked together and managed to free the vessel, calling for a return to Liverpool. The Captain, still drinking, would not entertain this caution and ordered the ship to continue westwards. His crew obeyed the order but, an hour later, *Earl of Moira* struck another sandbank, this time a mile and a half from shore. She was now badly damaged, and the only option was to batten the hatches and wait for morning and high tide.

As dawn broke there were screams from the hold as water broke through into the state room. Pumps were immediately manned but could not cope with the flooding and within an hour everything below deck was under water. Panic followed as the storm showed no sign of abating, meaning there was little prospect of a passing ship coming to the rescue. Two valuable horses were thrown overboard in an attempt to keep the ship afloat. Mountainous waves crashed over the deck, each one sweeping more terrified passengers overboard to their deaths. By 7 o'clock the deck gave way, beginning at the stern and breaking up to the main hatch, the railings coming away piece by piece, casting the small lifeboat adrift. All that remained afloat was the part of the deck near to the mast, where remaining survivors desperately held on to what shrouds or ropes they could find. Waves continued to pound the ship, one alone carrying off fifteen helpless souls, another taking the Captain and First Mate.

A small boat, crewed by two men, appeared close by but, despite the cries from the *Earl of Moira* they were only interested in salvaging the many pieces of luggage that floated alongside. By now, although the storm was beginning to pass, many of the exhausted passengers still grimly hanging on to anything they could find must have given up all hope of rescue, when the Hoylake Lifeboat appeared. Its crew managed to attach grapples to what was left of the stricken packet but the small boat could only provide salvation for a few women and children and turned back towards Liverpool leaving people still clinging to the top of the mast, now the only part of the *Earl of Moira* still above water. Many gave up at this stage; weary with their effort they released their grip and floated out to sea.

Soon other boats, alerted to the shipwreck, appeared on the horizon. The crew of the first two to arrive alongside demanded money to take people aboard. Some were fortunate to be able to pay there and then, securing their passage to safety. Eventually a boat with a more Samaritan-like captain appeared and the remaining survivors were taken on board. Fewer than twenty people survived from *Earl of Moira*. Some time later a poem was penned, recalling the tragic event:

### Loss of the *Earl of Moira*

You landsmen and you seamen,
Come listen to me
A dreadful story I'll relate
As you shall plainly see.
For the loss of the *Earl of Moira*
I'm sorry to say,
With one hundred souls on board
For Dublin sailed away.

From Liverpool in the afternoon
At six o'clock did sail
On the eighth day of August
With a sweet and pleasant gale
In eighteen hundred and twenty-two
As you will understand,
On Burbo bank our vessel struck
Close to the Cheshire land.

After great toil and slavery
Our Packet we got clear,
And running for the Cheshire shore
We sought safety there.
But when putting her about
She happened to miss stay,
On the wharf back our vessel struck
As all on board did see.

On the seventh about ten o'clock
Our hearts filled with fear.
At half past two with water filled
We could not keep her clear.
At half past five in the morning
It made us sigh full sore
The sea was running mountains high
Along the Cheshire shore.

Our vessel on her broadside
In dreadful state she lay,
The long boat and the luggage
Were washed entire away.
Then all that were able
Got up into the shrouds
The cries of men and women
Might reach up into the clouds.

The dying groans of young and old
In agony and pain,
The boats soon came alongside
But it was in vain.
Because we had no money
There and then to pay,
Those that could they took on board
And with them sailed away.

The fatal *Earl of Moira*
That Packet of great fame
For many years she had sailed
All on the raging main
Fifty passengers perished
I dare to say or more,
On our gallant ship for she was lost
All on the Cheshire shore.

Note: the second verse wrongly refers to 1822 (source: Lloyds' List, Tuesday 14th August 1821)

The King received the news during his enforced stay in North Wales. He would have been made aware that his former friend Humanity Dick was one of the unfortunate passengers and amongst the many presumed drowned.

After four days, George was anxious to not to delay his journey any longer but, although the storm had passed, the wind direction still frustrated his sail-driven fleet. Despite the fate of the *Earl of Moira*, he chose the less salubrious alternative of another packet ship, the *Lightening*, and proceeded to Ireland.

There he found Dublin in a high state of excitement and expectation, awaiting the greatest social event in the city's history. A new arch in Sackville Street had been built to commemorate the royal visit and any run-down house near to St Stephen's Green demolished. George went straight to the Viceroy's lodge in Phoenix Park, and supporters of catholic emancipation took great encouragement from his agreeing to meet a delegation from the Catholic Church, a likely sign that he harboured none of the bigotry of his father.

On 22nd August, the grandest levée ever to take place in Dublin Castle was held for the King, who arrived in a state coach accompanied by Viscount Sidmouth and Castlereagh, now the Marquis of Londonderry. Through the throng of 2000 people, all anxious to be introduced to him, George saw one man whose hand he wished to shake more than any other. Humanity Dick had somehow survived the wreck, and George was more than willing to forget the stance his old friend had taken during the Queen's trial. Soon afterwards a pair of Arab stallions arrived at Ballynahinch, a reconciliation gift from the King. Dick reciprocated with a fireplace fashioned from his own marble.

Martin, eternally grateful that Harriet and their daughters had not accompanied him on this particular trip, was reunited with them on the estate, where they stayed for the rest of the year. It was now the turn of the couple's eldest son Richard to take a bride: Emily Kirwan, the fourth daughter of John Kirwan, a King's Counsel in Dublin. The only problem was that Richard, now twenty-four, had yet to find a career. After he finished university the intention was for him to enter the Church and Dick had already approached Wellington's brother, Marquis Wellesley, recently appointed Lord Lieutenant, to see if a living could be secured.

Richard's own plans, however, were for a military life, and after making an approach to Lord Downshire he was offered a commission in the Royal Downshire Regiment. A traditional Martin-Kirwan wedding took place on 7th November and the couple moved to the regiment's headquarters in England.

After spending Christmas with Thomas in Ballynahinch, the Martins returned to London shortly after the new year of 1822, Dick determined to succeed this time in his fight for animal protection.

Together with Erskine, Lawrence and a handful of close friends and supporters of the fledgling animal rights movement, a network of clergymen had been contacted with a view to them lobbying their respective MP's to vote for Martin's forthcoming bill. One clergyman, the Reverend Henry Crowe, vicar of Buckingham, had published a book, *Zoophilus*, which chronicled several instances of extreme cruelty, including the practice of making dogs turn spits by running around an enclosed wheel next to a roaring fire, horses being kept without food for weeks before slaughter, and baited bulls having their horns and ears cut off and pepper blown in their noses in order to provide better sport. Crowe went further than Lawrence in condemning all forms of field sports and hunting.

When Martin introduced another Ill Treatment of Cattle Bill, its terms were little changed from his unsuccessful attempt the previous year. He decided Parliament needed to be softened up in advance of debate and, although it was not strictly relevant, he accompanied the first reading with a petition from the south London borough of Camberwell, which called for an end to all forms of animal baiting.

Within walking distance of the Houses of Parliament there stood the notorious Westminster Pit, the leading venue for the sport. Although a haunt for street thieves and petty villains, it was also frequented by the nobility and gentry, many of them MPs, who were attracted by the opportunities the carnage presented for gaming. Colossal bets were wagered on the outcome of each fight, and on how long a baited animal would survive the onslaught.

*The Westminster Pit*

Martin gave the House a graphic account of a recent event, starting with the notice advertising it, which read:

Jacco Maccacco, the celebrated monkey, will this day fight Tom Cribb's white bitch, Puss. Jacco has fought many battles with some of the first dogs of the day and has beat them all, and he hereby offers to fight any dog in England of double his own weight.

To the astonishment of the members, Martin went on to describe the fight in all its gory horror, stopping at various points for dramatic effect. After half an hour of fighting, Puss had managed to tear away all of Jacco's underjaw. The monkey, no doubt in extreme agony, had responded by lacerating Puss's windpipe. Both animals died a most painful death. Ignoring shouts to desist from such detail, Dick went on to describe a visit he had made to the Pit where a bear and at least fifty badgers were kept in appalling conditions in the interest of entertainment. By now the House was stunned into silence and the Bill passed its first reading without debate.

Dick timed the second reading for midnight on 24th May. The lateness of the hour and the fact that it was preceded by a tedious debate on military pensions, ensured a low attendance. However, this time Sir Samuel Shepherd, the Attorney General, was lying in wait and moved that the Bill 'be read a second time this day six months', a procedural manoeuvre intended to scupper the proposed legislation. Martin responded that he was surprised that the learned gentleman 'placed himself in opposition to the common sense of the whole nation.' He claimed his bill was supported by local magistrates and 'there was not a pulpit in London' that had not spoken in support of it. A vote was taken, and 29 members, against 18, voted for the Bill to proceed.

On June 2nd Martin returned for the third and final reading. Again he chose a time that would ensure an almost empty house. Three members, Monck, Scarlett and surprisingly Thomas Buxton, who was part of Martin's inner circle and whose support Dick thought he could rely on, spoke in opposition. Buxton argued that the Bill should be withdrawn at this stage in order to make certain amendments in time for the next session of Parliament. Dick was having none of it, saying he was 'satisfied of the propriety and justice of the measure; and, as he thought the majority of the House was with him, he should press it.'

The Bill was duly read for a third time and, without a vote, was passed. It was now up to Erskine to produce the goods in the Upper House.

The network of clergymen who had so effectively influenced the Commons, had also been working on their superiors, the Bishops, all of whom sat in the Lords. Martin had been promised backing from Lords Downside and Ormonde. This time Erskine was better prepared, overcoming the inevitable objections that the Bill was below the dignity of Parliament and unworkable in practice. By 18th July it had been read in that House the requisite three times, and passed.

The final procedure for any proposed statute is for it to receive royal assent. Had Martin's Bill reached this stage the previous year, it was likely that the King, out of spite, would have rejected it. Now he was only too pleased to grant Martin his burning ambition. The 'Ill Treatment of Cattle Act', or 'Martin's Law', as it became known, received royal assent on 22nd July 1822. All animal rights law in the world stems from that auspicious day.

# Chapter 30

# Law in Force

The day after his Bill received Royal Assent, Dick made the first arrest. He knew that 'Martin's Law' was only the start of a very long road, with steep learning curves for the public, the constabulary and the judiciary. Undaunted as ever, Dick saw no reason not to propel everybody around those curves at breakneck pace.

On 23rd July 1822, Martin strode unaccompanied into Smithfield Horse Market, not a place for the faint-hearted at the best of times, and arrested two drovers who were maltreating horses in their charge.

Smithfield Market resembled hell on earth. Charles Dickens later described it in *Oliver Twist* as a place where 'countrymen, butchers, drovers, hawkers, boys, thieves, idlers and vagabonds of every low grade were mingled together in a dense mass'. The largest animal market in the world, it was surrounded by a variety of knackers' yards, tripe dressers, cat's meat boilers, paunch-cookers and catgut spinners, all contributing to the overwhelming stench and brutality of backyard butchery.

The horse traders were not the kind of individuals that most sane people go out of their way to cross, and what the two toughened men made of the elderly gentlemen who believed he had the right to arrest them is open to conjecture, but three weeks later Samuel Clarke and David Hyde found themselves before the bench of Alderman Waithman. The prosecuting advocate was none other than Humanity Dick Martin himself.

*Smithfield Market*

The Magistrate was as bemused as the prisoners accused under this unheard-of law, but Martin quickly enlightened the court with a lesson about his new statute. He went on to declare that he had observed Clarke 'beating a horse in so cruel and violent a manner with a large whip that the poor animal was completely wealed from its shoulder to its tail. The beast could have done nothing to merit such treatment, as he was standing quietly tied to a rail. The barbarity of the prisoner was therefore most wanton and unprovoked.' The concluding statement neatly echoed the wording of his law.

Clarke's defence was that the horse was 'sleepy and dull'.

Turning to the other defendant, Martin claimed that he had seen him beat a horse over the head with the butt-end of his whip and on further inspection found that the horse's neck was fixed by a rope to ensure the head was carried in a manner that would achieve the highest sale price. Hyde pleaded that he had only beaten the horse to make it stop kicking; adding that although he was selling horses he was in fact a butcher by trade. Martin jumped to his feet shouting, 'Yes, I perceive that – a horse butcher!"

Alderman Waithman had no choice but to find the accused guilty, and fined them 20 shillings each. They were the first people in the world to be found guilty, under the law, of cruelty to animals. Martin could enjoy some degree of satisfaction, and no doubt he did. He had been lawmaker, arresting officer, prosecutor and chief witness. Of course these roles came naturally to Dick: he had been performing them in Connemara for nearly 30 years.

A few days later Martin was in court again, this time prosecuting Bill Burn, a costermonger he had arrested for maltreating his donkey. Here Martin, after giving the magistrate a briefing on the new state of affairs, went a stage further in presenting the case. He proceeded to bring the unfortunate donkey into the building to show his injuries. To this day, Martin remains the only man ever to produce a donkey as a witness in a British court. The occasion prompted a popular song:

'If I Had a Donkey'

If I had a donkey wot wouldn't go,
D'ye think I'd wollop him? No, no, no!
But gentle means I'd try, d'ye see,
Because I hate all cruelty.
If all had been like me, in fact,
There ha' been no occasion for Martin's Act
Dumb animals to prevent getting crackt

Wot makes me mention this this morn,
I seed that cruel chap, Bill Burn-
Whilst he was out a-crying his greens-
His donkey wolloped with all his means.
He hit him o'er his head and thighs,
He brought the tears up in my eyes,
At last my blood began to rise;

'As Bill and I did break the peace,
To us came up the new Police,
And hiked us off, as sure as fate,
Afore the sitting magistrate.
I told his worship all the spree,
And for to prove the veracity,
I wish'd he would the animal see.

Bill's donkey was ordered into court,
In which he caused a deal of sport;
He cock'd his ears, and ope'd his jaws,
As if he wished to plead his cause.
I prov'd I'd been uncommonly kind,
The ass got a verdict – Bill got fined;
For his worship and I were of one mind.

Bill said: "Your worship, its very hard,
But 'tisn't the fine that I regard;
But times are come to a pretty pass
When you mustn't beat a stubborn ass."
His Worship said nothing, but shut his book;
So Billy off his donkey took,
The same time giving me such look.

The introduction of the donkey was, of course, a well conceived publicity stunt. Doing something so outrageously eccentric that it would inspire a popular song was about the quickest way for Martin to get a message to the masses.

*The appearance of the donkey before the judge is apochryphal. He was in the lobby*

Next up was a coachman who brought his employer along as a character witness. The owner of the coach said his servant was a good-tempered man. Martin was fully prepared, having added the role of private detective to his many guises. 'Why, man alive,' said Martin, 'your wife told me a very different story when I called upon her. She said he was a very ill-tempered fellow!' He even went as far as drawing on the received science of the day. Pointing to the dock, he appealed to the judge to observe that the defendant must have a bad temper: 'Anyone who knows anything about physiognomy can see that in a moment.'

On one occasion in court, Dick found himself before his friend Sir Richard Birnie, who pointed out that the man standing beside Martin was the famous comic actor Joseph Munden. 'Oh my God, so it is!' said Dick

'Pray, Mr. Martin,' interrupted the Judge, 'Do you not know that you are subject to a fine for swearing in front of a magistrate?'

'By Gad Birnie, you're right!' replied Martin, dropping a crown into the poor box.

Throughout the summer and autumn of that year Martin was omnipresent in the streets and courtrooms of London, using every opportunity to maximize publicity and therefore awareness of his Act. He was not always successful. One judge, Mr Minshull, was having difficulty understanding the use of the words 'wanton' and 'cruelty'. After several attempts at clarification Martin lost his patience, paraphrasing *Macbeth* to the Bench.

'Time has been when the brains were out the man would die,' said Martin.

'My brains may be out now, but I am still alive', replied Judge Minshull, discharging the case.

Not surprisingly, since they were encouraged by Martin creating his own publicity, the press were beginning to take an interest in the elderly Irishman policing the streets of London with a statute of his own making. His breezy and eccentric manner while conducting cases in court was eminently newsworthy. The *Courier* reported the next case before magistrates at the Guildhall. Dick had arrested a young coachman in Cheapside for being over-zealous in the use of his whip. After presenting the case for the prosecution and giving evidence, Martin heard the young man try to defend his actions on the grounds that he was new to the job. Dick now added another role to his one-man show; he became the lawyer for the defence, submitting to the magistrate that the charge should be dropped if the young man agreed to have a lesson in how to admonish a horse leniently.

Martin had become very experienced in judging public reaction. He knew it would be counter-productive if claims were voiced that his Act was protecting animals but punishing innocent families. Thomas Worster was a greengrocer whom Martin had arrested in Fleet Street for beating a donkey with a buckled leather strap. Martin told the court that the accused 'is one of those class of drivers who, though human in form, have no other signs or emblems of the human nature in their composition.' When the Judge fined Worster ten shillings, his wife approached the Bench saying they were too poor to pay the fine. Martin promptly agreed to pay it himself, providing Worster swore never to mistreat his or any other animal again.

When another miscreant was about to be fined, he ran out of the court, only to be captured in the street and brought back before the judge. By now the man was bellowing uncontrollably. Martin at first showed him little pity. 'Hold your tongue Sir; it is the poor horse and not you that should cry.' When it became apparent that the man was petrified of being unable to pay the eighteen-shilling fine, or leaving his family destitute by being sent to prison, Martin intervened and paid up for him.

These highly original methods of redress fuelled his new law with the oxygen of publicity. John Stevens, a man accused of maltreating his horse in Covent Garden, was advised to whisper in the animal's ear, 'You are a good horse and I am a bad man.' When Stevens tried to defend his actions on the grounds that he had been ordered by his master to beat the animal, Martin subsequently arrested the master as well. While prosecuting a coalman employed by the merchants Goudge and Thrupp, he even went as far as offering his services for a day delivering coal, in order to teach other employees how horses could be handled humanely.

Whatever people thought of Martin (and opinions ranged from crusading saint to certifiable lunatic), he had certainly made an impact. He was the talk of markets and coffee houses. Newspapers were filled with his activities and cartoonists had been provided with a new butt for their humour. Within a few short months the whole country, although without the benefit of today's mass communication, was aware that the law now protected animals.

In the midst of this hectic activity, Martin received the sad news that Castlereagh had died, cutting his own throat in the bedroom of his country home in Kent. There were rumours that he was being blackmailed, and King George had only recently warned Lord Liverpool of the Foreign Secretary's depression. Dick had known Castlereagh for nearly 30 years and, despite regular political differences, the men had grown to be close friends. Both had been proved wrong in their aspirations for the Union. Dick had respected Castlereagh for sorting out his differences with Canning on the duelling field. Castlereagh, in his memoirs, wrote that Martin was one of the wittiest speakers in parliamentary history.

Martin was forced to suspend his one-man war against perpetrators of animal cruelty by the beginning of winter, when problems in Ireland, and particularly at Ballynahinch, recalled him home. The dire economic climate in the south of Ireland had been intensified by a succession of bad harvests. Many parts of the country were in a state of famine. The west coast was badly hit, with desperate peasants forced to survive on tree bark. Even on the Martin estate bodies lay in the fields and the awful fever caused by famine was already rife. Throughout the winter Dick and Thomas worked as best they could to help their people.

Marginal cheer was provided for the family when Richard, after deciding that a military life was not for him, returned with his wife Emmy to Ireland. The young man had been granted a good living, at the parish of Dunboye, County Meath.

By the spring of 1823, Dick realised that he was no further use at Ballynahinch, and was anxious to return to Westminster, not only to continue his crusade for animals, but also to encourage those fighting for catholic emancipation into concrete action. The cause had lost its leader two years before when Henry Grattan died, and events in Ireland, Dick felt, necessitated speedy measures. He could smell revolution in the air.

While the Catholic south was starving, the Protestant north was relatively prosperous. The Orange Order, founded nearly 30 years beforehand, was becoming increasingly confrontational. It had become customary to celebrate the anniversary of the victory over King James at the Battle of the Boyne, to the increasing annoyance of Catholics, who were already embittered by not getting their fair share of commerce in the north. The previous year, Lord Lieutenant Wellesley had banned the protestant ceremony of decorating King William's statue in Dublin, in order to prevent bloodshed. This resulted in his being pelted by broken bottles when he attended the theatre, while the audience were handed leaflets proclaiming 'No Popery!' In the rural areas to the south a group of Protestants were causing even more resentment by preaching that the catholic religion itself was the cause of their poverty.

Martin stated in the press that, in contrast to the provocation taking place in the north, in Galway, where Catholics outnumbered their Protestant neighbours by fifty to one, no demonstrations were ever held that would cause offence.

By now the Catholic Association was headed by Daniel O'Connell, a farmer's son from Kerry who had studied in France and returned to Dublin to practise law. By the early 1820s he was one of the wealthiest lawyers in the country. The Catholic Association formed strong links with the Church, giving it a fast track to mass membership. Martin was concerned that, without immediate emancipation, the organistaion would go down the same revolutionary path as Wolfe Tone's United Irishmen.

Martin arrived in Dublin in the last week of March, en route to London. He was booked as a passenger on *Alert*, a steam packet sailing that Tuesday night for Liverpool. By the following morning the ship was in sight of the Welsh coast. In fair weather, and for no apparent reason, she struck the West Mouse rock, breaking up and sinking within half an hour. Over 100 passengers were lost; only 17 survived. Days later all the London papers carried the notice of the death of Richard Martin, Esq. MP for Galway. Tributes from his parliamentary colleagues were generous.

Dick had in fact been struck down by a bilious attack in Dublin and had been forced to miss his ship. The incident only served to add to his larger-than-life reputation for indestructibility.

# Chapter 31

# Birth of a Movement

No doubt amused by his premature obituaries, Martin, now in his seventieth year, arrived in London as energetic as ever. He had three objectives: first to resurrect the issue of catholic emancipation, second to continue his increasing involvement in criminal law reform and third to develop and enforce his animal rights legislation.

Martin aimed to extend his Law, so that more animals would be given the protection that had been given to 'cattle'. He wanted to ban the sport of animal baiting and improve the conditions that prevailed in abattoirs. This was not going to be easy; objectors were already asking where it would stop, lampooning Martin's Law as eventually giving protection to rats and fleas.

He decided to test the parliamentary waters on 21st May 1823 with a bill to ban animal baiting. Immediately he was criticised for attacking a sport frequented by the lower classes but avoiding a ban on similar cruelties perpetrated by the upper classes when they went hunting. Dick knew that there was no chance of Parliament banning field sports and that is why his bill was restricted to baiting. His counter-argument was as clever and lateral as ever, drawing on his recent experience of being shipwrecked. If there were hundreds of people stranded on a rock, he reasoned, but your boat was not big enough to save them all, would you not still attempt to save a few? Despite amending his proposal to protect only those dogs which were being subjected to organised fighting (giving an example of the owner of a defeated dog who cut the animal's paws off and buried it alive), he saw his bill defeated by 29 votes to 18.

He continued to police the streets of London, his favourite haunts being Whitehall, Charing Cross and Smithfield Market, where his reputation was now established. Martin knew that each case brought before a court, if properly reported in the press, would make the constabulary, judges and the general public more aware of how his law worked. He also realised that there was a limit to what he could achieve himself and, despite his parlous financial position, employed an Inspector to assist his policing activities. Furthermore, he was laying plans to set up a formal organisation to carry on his work.

The combination of the hiatus created by the Regency, the notoriety of the Queen's trial, and the period while the new king found his feet, meant that the Catholic Question found itself placed on a political backburner. Although Martin and others remained hopeful that the King would not show the same resistance as his father, it was not for the Monarch to raise the issue in Parliament. The Cabinet itself was undecided. George Canning was a strong advocate, but support was limited, especially without a general threat to national security to focus minds on the problems in Ireland. With Irish MP's taking up only 100 of the 658 seats at Westminster, catholic freedoms were in danger of becoming a non-issue.

When the matter was eventually raised in the House, opponents from both government and opposition agreed that, unless there was unity in the Cabinet, the matter should rest. Martin drew the analogy that this was akin to a man who, when challenged to a duel, shot himself in case he might lose. On a more serious note, he warned that Catholics, and supporters of their emancipation, were not prepared to let the cause become a party issue. The motion to progress the matter was defeated by 313 votes to 111.

On the third front, Martin, who had personally campaigned in the past for rights to be conferred on prisoners accused of capital crimes, and for the death sentence for forgery to be removed, was becoming increasingly keen that general reform should be attempted throughout the criminal justice system. There were still barbaric punishments available to over-zealous judges. Women could still be burned at the stake, while condemned men continued to be hung, drawn and quartered. Conditions in many prisons remained no better than in the middle ages. Across the legal board, punishments failed to fit the crimes.

The problem Martin faced was that his reputation as an eccentric maverick spoiled his credibility when putting forward legislative measures. He supported a bill proposed by Sir James Mackintosh, but it was defeated at the third reading on 23rd June 1823. By now Robert Peel was Home Secretary. On the face of it, Martin and Peel had little in common. Peel was anti-catholic, a keen huntsman and, worst of all to Dick, a close friend of the Dalys, who played host to Peel on his frequent hunting trips in the west of Ireland. Peel and Martin did, however, have a mutual respect for each other, bordering on friendship. Martin concluded that his best bet in the field of criminal justice was to work with Peel.

When Martin returned to Ireland at the end of 1823, he found that O'Connell's Catholic Association had grown at a phenomenal rate. Its success was owing to O'Connell astutely cajoling the Catholic Church into providing an instant infrastructure, collecting membership subscriptions that were affordable by even the poorest Catholic. A penny a month was being given across the country, by thousands of people. When added together, the collections gave O'Connell a significant war chest to meet his aims, which were: firstly, to give Catholics equal rights, and secondly to give governmental rule back to the Irish. The message was not, of course, new but the method was, and O'Connell was preaching to an already converted and increasingly frustrated audience.

One cause of famine in Ireland was that, although naturally rich in lush farmland, the country was not self-sufficient under its current agricultural system. With little security of tenure, catholic farmers had low incentive to improve their land. If they did, rents would be increased or their land seized. In contrast, protestant farmers in the north, who did not labour under the same difficulty, were prospering.

Catholics had lost patience with their politicians and, however unfair it might have been for O'Connell to single out Martin for criticism, when speaking at a rally in Galway he accused the local Member of Parliament of being a worse enemy of their cause than the Protestants. Martin arrived home to the accusation that he was more interested in the plight of London cattle than in his starving constituents.

Dick was in Galway to celebrate the coming of age of the young Earl of Clanricarde. Since connections between the families went back centuries, Dick was confident that the Earl would be equally concerned about the stranglehold the Daly family now enjoyed within the City Corporation. In fact, Clanricarde was to be the most notable signatory to Martin's political death warrant.

Martin's stay in the city allowed him to augment his old reputation. Staying as usual at Black's Hotel in Merrick Square, he was angered when his watch was stolen. Entering the lounge Martin saw the stolen article hanging from a chain on a man's waistcoat. 'Hairtrigger Dick' approached the suspect and, without a word being exchanged, drew his sword and deftly used the tip to remove the watch from the thief's person. No resistance was offered.

Dick and Harriet spent the winter at Ballynahinch, where financial matters were dire. The copper mines were still not producing; the marble business was only providing a limited return, and the kelp market remained nailed to the floor. On the other hand, Thomas's inheritance of the Martin gene for extravagant living was now flagrantly obvious, so that father and son once again blamed each other for being an excessive drain on the family's cash flow.

By early spring 1824, Dick was back in Westminster, fired up to attack Parliament on several fronts. His first assault was to bring in a motion to amend his existing Act, to provide protection for 'dogs, cats, monkeys' and, as an exercise in parliamentary kite flying, 'all other animals'. Martin expected the last phrase to be rejected, but hoped to be left with a compromise which granted protection to the animals named. A second amendment asked that the offence be classed as a 'misdemeanor'; meaning that magistrates would be given powers to imprison offenders.

Dick redeployed his arguments with the shock tactics that had been so successful two years before. He made fellow members squirm in their seats as he cited examples that had been brought to his attention. He spoke of a dog having scalding water poured over it before being pushed into the street to die and another dog rubbed all over with sulphuric acid as punishment. Fowell Buxton, the Member for the deceased King's old seaside haunt of Weymouth, spoke to testify that since Martin's Law was introduced cruelty to animals had halved. Martin's energies were rewarded, and by early April the Commons had passed his amendments and the Bill was with the House of Lords.

Still not content, Dick again asked Parliament to allow him to introduce a new bill to prevent animal-baiting sports. Here he met stronger resistance, with Robert Peel taking the lead by offering the well tried argument designed to force Martin to have to amend his bill to include hunting and field sports, which of course would result in immediate failure. Peel, somewhat hypocritically, given the amount of field sport he personally took part in, asked why Martin was not including fishing, 'A cruel fraud practised on innocent and defenceless animals.' Peel used the logic that if it became an offence to allow antagonism between two animals in a baiting pit, then it should also apply to hounds and foxes. He finished patronisingly, by asking that perhaps Parliament should consider banning all forms of animal confinement.

Martin countered expertly by suggesting that, since Peel enjoyed shooting, then he might wish to indulge in a spot of bear baiting, and invited the Home Secretary to accompany him to the notorious Westminster Pit. He was illustrating the point that there was a distinct difference between hunting to kill and baiting to torture. Never missing an opportunity to paint an analogy, Martin asked his colleagues, would they not try to save a quarter of their men in battle, even if it was impossible to save them all? Judging the mood, he realised that on this occasion he would get no further. He withdrew his motion with the Parthian shot that there were certain Gentlemen in the House who, he felt, would not want their names printed in the papers as being part of the majority he feared were against his measures.

Undeterred, Dick was soon back in the House, proposing his 'Slaughtering of Horses Bill', designed to put an end to the barbarism that prevailed in abattoirs. He recounted that he had personally inspected many such establishments in the city and was happy to provide the House, and the reporting press, with details. These included one case in Whitechapel where Martin witnessed ten horses, some with their eyes knocked out, others with a leg damaged to prevent their escape. When he had offered the owner money to feed the hapless animals, the man preferred to spend it on drink for himself.

In fact, Martin had already taken revenge against this particular owner by bombarding the knacker's yard with 200 letters, all under different pseudonyms, dispatching the man to various far-flung parts of London to collect fictitious horses.

The Bill proposed that all slaughterhouses be licensed, and compelled to submit to regular inspections and keep detailed records that must be sworn on oath. It got as far as the Report stage, where it was defeated on the grounds that many abattoir owners would not comply, and enforcement of the measures would be too onerous.

Wednesday 16th June 1824 should have been a landmark day in the history of animal rights. The bill to widen protection to all animals, which the Commons had passed, was to be heard in the Lords. The problem was that Martin's old friend, Lord Erskine, was no longer there to assist its passage.

Erskine had been forced out of public life in disgrace. After thirteen years of loneliness following the death of his wife, the former Lord Chancellor fell in love with his young housekeeper. With her now expecting their child, Erskine announced his intention of marriage. This did not go down well with his two elder sons who, realising their inheritance was in jeopardy, attempted to prevent their father remarrying by having him committed to a lunatic asylum. Erskine disguised himself as a woman and fled with his fiancée to his native Scotland, frantically pursued by the aggrieved sons. The couple did eventually marry, but the scandal had by then ruined Erskine's reputation. He had played no further part in the House of Lords until his death the previous year. With no influential supporter to force the Bill through the upper house, it met with the usual objections, and was rejected.

Public opinion was, however, noticeably moving in Martin's favour. His publicity campaign was working, although he found it very difficult to hail a Hackney cab, since his reputation preceded him. Apart from the prosecutions instigated by Martin, others were taking place. One coach firm's owner had one of his own drivers prosecuted, and the driver of a famous opera singer had been arrested. One way Dick could judge the effectiveness of his law was by the number of death threats he received. Never one to miss a publicity trick, when the *Sporting Magazine* reported an anonymous letter threatening Martin with a 'dog's death' he took the magazine to task for encouraging such actions.

For some years there had been talk among Martin's inner circle of friends that a formal organisation should be set up to coordinate the struggle. A loose association of like-minded people were already calling themselves the 'Friends of the Bill for the Prevention of Cruelty to Animals', but their activities were mostly confined to open correspondence in publications friendly to the cause. On the same day that his latest bill failed in the Lords, Dick attended a momentous meeting at a coffee house ironically named Old Slaughter's, in St Martin's Lane.

The meeting had been arranged by the Reverend Arthur Broome, the vicar of nearby St Mary's, Bromley-by-Bow. Ten men attended, including Martin's fellow MPs Sir James Mackintosh and the champion of slaves, William Wilberforce. Mr. Foxwell Buxton chaired the meeting. Also in attendance was a reporter from *The Times*. As ever, Martin's strong character dominated the meeting. Prompted by the disappointing news just received from the Lords, concerns were raised that Parliament would go no further. Humanity Dick, falling into his best Irish brogue for effect said. 'By Jasus, I'll make them do it!' *The Times* reporter had no doubt that he would, describing Martin as a 'short, thick set man, with evidence in look and manner, even in step and action, of indomitable resolution.'

A new organisation was inaugurated and its founders passed a series of resolutions, instigating the regular circulation of publicity material in favour of animal rights, the introduction into schools of books 'calculated to impress on youth the duty of humanity to inferior animals,' and the employment of their own constables to patrol streets and markets. Martin, no doubt grateful that his activities were going to be assisted, did however make a crucially important point to the embryonic organisation: that they should not be seen solely as a 'prosecuting society'.

The group gave themselves a name: the Society for the Prevention of Cruelty to Animals, or the SPCA.

The new Society met on five more occasions that summer and, by the time that Martin was preparing to return to Ireland, they had received considerable and favourable publicity. Although unsuccessful in Parliament that year, Dick must have felt the momentum building in his favour.

His other passion, catholic emancipation, was about to receive its greatest blow since he entered politics. Worse still, it came from the very source to which he had for years pinned his hopes.

News was leaked about an exchange of correspondence between Robert Peel, in his capacity as Home Secretary, and the King about a request from the Irish Lord Lieutenant that 'letters of precedence' be given to a catholic barrister, a previously unheard-of favour. The message Peel received from the Palace rejected the request, adding that 'The King desires Mr. Peel to remember this, as it may be a guide for his future conduct relative to the Catholic question.'

Martin was devastated; his old friend had come down off the fence on the same side as his father. He also feared for the reaction to this news in Ireland and the response from the increasingly militant Catholic Association.

# Chapter 32

## A Shotgun Attack

Dick was to have no further contact with King George, although the Monarch did eventually offer his old friend an olive branch in the form of a peerage. He refused it.

His immediate concern was how the Catholic Association would react to knowing that there was, after all, royal resistance to their immediate goal. He feared that rebellion was increasingly likely, and calculated that the end result would be the same as it was in 1798. Dick sought an urgent meeting in Dublin with Daniel O'Connell.

The Association had grown astonishingly over the previous year. There were now 960,000 members, ranging across the social spectrum from the aristocracy, such as Dick's Gormanston cousins, to the poorest peasantry. The threat posed was becoming increasingly obvious to the authorities, who had already tried unsuccessfully to prosecute O'Connell. The problem the Association presented to the Lord Lieutenant was that it was big, rich, well organised and doing nothing illegal.

When Martin and O'Connell met they managed to patch up their differences. Although O'Connell was a firebrand speaker, much more imposing on a platform than Tone had ever been, he remained a firm believer in the continuance of political pressure, in spite of the King's stance now being known. But within the heterogeneous Association there was a growing element that favoured reaching for the gun and pikestaff. O'Connell asked Martin to address the hierarchy at their headquarters in Capel Street, Dublin on 25th September 1824. Of the hundreds of speeches Martin made during his long life, this was probably the most important.

Martin stood before the meeting better qualified than any other man to say what he had in mind. His family's Jacobite heritage, his own personal treatment of Catholics in Connemara, his persistent, 50-year political fight for emancipation, his first-hand experiences of the '98 rebellion and its aftermath, all combined to give him a unique pedigree. Martin was now the senior statesman in Irish politics, the only serving Member of Parliament who had supported Grattan and Flood in the 25 years preceding Union.

Dick began by reminding the audience that it was he who had suggested such an organisation as theirs, at the Ballinasloe Fair in 1803. He took credit for the idea of having a modest subscription collected. Drawing on his experience and knowledge of feelings across the Irish sea, both inside and outside of Parliament, he knew that the injustices befalling Catholics were becoming increasingly difficult for a growing number of people to tolerate. He praised the Catholic Association for achieving such a massive membership, which it was impossible to ignore. It was on the very verge of success, success that could only be won by maintaining the peaceful pressure it had so shrewdly exerted to date. He warned them of the perils of rebellion and recognised there were people before him who were considering such means. But he urged that the surest way to avoid failure was 'to bridle their feelings and not let them escape through their mouths with impetuosity or lack of control'. It was excellent to have a giant's strength, but tyrannous to use it as a giant. He finished by promising to do everything within his power to assist their cause in Parliament and beyond.

When he left the meeting, Martin could not know whether he had succeeded in steering the Catholic Association, standing as they were at such a dangerous crossroads, down the correct road. Looking back on the event, he must have considered himself successful, and with hindsight his speech was hugely influential, but at the time the press labelled it a cynical attempt to woo catholic voters in the General Election that was due within the next eighteen months.

While in Ireland, Dick also had an unforeseen problem to address. Until now he had been relaxed about the outcome of the election, because he felt he could rely on the crucial support of the wealthy young Earl of Clanricarde, who was to marry the daughter of Martin's friend George Canning. The Foreign Secretary was in Dublin when Martin addressed the Catholic Association and Dick took the opportunity of dining with him at Dublin Castle. Here Canning dropped a bombshell. His future son-in-law was intending to put up his own candidate to fight against both Martin and James Daly for the Galway County seat. Canning felt that, with the financial resources Clanricarde intended to put behind this candidate, his election appeared a safe bet.

Martin hurried back to Galway to assess the situation. He met James Daly, who, although perturbed to hear this news, felt confident that, since there were two County seats, his would be safe. He did, however, offer Martin a deal. He suggested they combine to support each other and attempt to isolate Clanricarde's candidate. In return, Daly required Martin to cease his relentless opposition to his family's increasing monopoly of the Galway Corporation. He would even support Thomas Martin for the City seat, providing he in turn also agreed to back the Daly family.

Martin rejected Daly's proposal out of hand, but instead of remaining in his constituency preparing the ground for what was bound to be a brutal campaign, he returned to London, not only to take up where he had left off in respect of animal welfare, but also to honour his promise to the Catholic Association.

When George IV made his opening speech to Parliament at the beginning of the 1826 session, with his position on Catholics now in the open, he made a scathing attack on O'Connell's organisation, which he felt was 'irreconcilable with the constitution and calculated to endanger the peace of society and to retard the course of national improvement.' His government had also addressed the problem that the Catholic Association was not illegal. There would be a bill before the House to declare it precisely that.

Martin spoke at length during the debate. A speech two months beforehand by O'Connell had been taken out of context and it was claimed that the Association's leader was calling for an armed uprising. Martin attempted to put the record straight, drawing on his first-hand knowledge of the organisation.

He told the House that the Association 'possessed the entire confidence of the Roman Catholic population' but reassured his colleagues that they were committed to peaceful means to achieve measures that were in any event long overdue. He warned, however, that although the Association was strong enough to pacify elements within, they could equally 'awake the storm by the same means.' He continued 'As they converted the storm into a calm, they could turn the calm into a whirlpool.'

The result of the debate was of course a foregone conclusion, and the bill to outlaw the Catholic Association was duly passed with a large majority. Martin had done what he could and could only pray that the reaction in Ireland would be measured.

His energies now returned to animal rights. Logically, given his advancing years, he should have been slowing down, satisfied that he had opened the floodgates and that others were taking over his work. Instead, he went into overdrive. During the winter months, assisted now by the fledgling SPCA, he had collected more instances of cruelty, along with written support from magistrates and clergy throughout the country. His strategy during this session of Parliament was akin to political carpet-bombing.

There was another form of cruelty that had attracted his attention: vivisection. On 24th February 1825, he proposed a Bill to ban 'Bear baiting and other cruel practices.' As a sort of legislative sleight of hand, he hoped that, though focussing on bears, the wording could be used for a variety of purposes, including the banning of certain types of vivisection.

His speech accompanying the presentation of the Bill made it clear that it had widespread support. Martin claimed he had 'conversed with almost every Alderman of the City of London, with almost every police magistrate in the metropolis and with many magistrates in different parts of the country.' In his findings Dick had fastened on a previously untried argument. All these people of authority agreed that these cruel practices should be banned, but not only to protect animals. The places where animal baiting took place lured the lower orders into gambling and 'educated them as thieves and gradually trained them up for bloodshed and murder.'

After Martin had quoted details of a recent fight between two dogs, two 'fresh badgers' and a bear, he turned to his latest concern. This had nothing to do with baiting; it involved a Frenchman called Dr Majendie, a surgeon who was conducting public experiments, most recently in London, in the so-called interests of science. If the House of Commons had become inured to Martin's blood-curdling instances of cruelty on the streets and in the baiting pits, they were certainly not prepared for what he now had to share.

His preamble warned the audience that the actions of Majendie were 'so atrocious as almost to shock belief'. He was right. Apparently Majendie had paid ten guineas for a greyhound to use for a recent demonstration. The doctor started by nailing the dog's front and back paws to a table, using 'the bluntest spikes he could find'. He then doubled back its long ears and also nailed them to the table.

By now some members were shouting 'shame', others calling for Martin to stop. He continued, describing how Majendie had next made a gash down the middle of the dog's face and proceeded to dissect the nerves on one side of it, asking spectators to observe that 'when I pass my scalpel over these nerves the dog will shut its eyes.' He then proceeded to do likewise with nerves responsible for the dog's senses of taste and smell. Finally, Dr Majendie told his audience that he would continue his experiments tomorrow but, as the dog had cost so much money, he would use the same animal again. He expected the dog to live through the night and hoped to be able to cut him up alive tomorrow to show the 'peristaltic motion of the heart and viscera'.

By now Martin's audience, who were obviously more squeamish than the Frenchman, cried out for him to stop. They had little stomach left to resist Martin, and his Bill continued its passage, but not before his friend Fowell Buxton told the House that to date 71 prosecutions, resulting in 69 convictions, had resulted from Martin's previous bill.

Its next reading was less successful and the Bill was defeated. By then, friends of Dr Majendie had come out in his defence, in both the press and the House. These included Sir James Mackintosh, one of the co-founders of the SPCA, whom Majendie had treated when he was taken ill in Paris. He had found the Doctor to be 'caring and tender'. Mackintosh was convinced that if Majendie's work inflicted pain on animals, then it must be in the ardent pursuit of science.

Martin was coming under fire for making false claims in Parliament, where his speech was privileged and accordingly denied the accused Doctor the redress of suing for slander. On hearing that Majendie was in London, at nearby St Bartholomew's Hospital, Dick immediately went down there, stood on the main steps, repeated his parliamentary speech and invited Majendie to challenge him to a duel or sue. The Frenchman did neither, although he did put the record straight that he had in fact conducted his experiment on a spaniel and not a greyhound. St Bartholomew's banned such experiments, and the equally respected Guy's Hospital followed suit soon after.

Undaunted by his most recent defeat, Dick bounced back immediately and on 11th March was in Westminster with a new 'Cruelty to Animals' bill. This time his opponents had done some homework. Thomas Heathcote, the Member for Hampshire, stood up. He had paid a visit to the infamous Westminster Pit in Duck Lane where he observed the bear his Honourable Friend had previously been so concerned about. This animal had been baited for six years and 'No finer animal of the kind, or a more prosperous and hopeful set of cubs, he had seen.'

Robert Peel used the old chestnut that Martin was being unfair singling out monkeys, badgers and bears for protection. This created a 'privileged class of animals'. If Martin wanted to repress all cruelty to animals, 'then let him include in his Bill, hunting, shooting and fishing.' The Home Secretary, himself a keen huntsman, went on to recount in detail how cruel the sport of stag hunting was, in depriving the animal of its horns, 'its only means of defence'.

Martin jumped up and called Peel's bluff. As Home Secretary, Peel was a principal adviser to the Monarch. Would he therefore 'begin the salutary reformation by recommending to the King that he was to put down the Royal stag-hounds?' Peel did not rise to the bait, and when the vote was eventually taken Martin was defeated once again by 50 votes to 32.

Thirteen days later Martin was back, this time with an 'Ill Treatment of Animals Bill', calling once again for offences under the existing law to be elevated to misdemeanors. Despite a particularly gory tale about a man who had tied his horse's tongue to a gate and proceeded to beat the animal until it was torn out, but had still only been fined £5, the Bill failed.

Next before the House was Martin's 'Cattle Ill Treatment Bill', which despite it's cunning change of title also failed. By now Peel was begging Martin to bring in one law to cover everything he wanted to provide, thereby preventing the Statute Book being increased to a very 'inconvenient bulk'. Martin was fully aware that he was beating his head against a closed door, but he was no fool. Each time he brought the matter up in

Parliament it attracted publicity in the press: some supportive, some derisory, but publicity all the same.

His main support was from the *Courier*, which wrote of the eccentric Irishman:

Mr. Martin is indefatigable . . . He is the man to carry a good cause through a host of opposing prejudices. He has that quality of steady, unflinching perseverance, which turns neither to the right, nor to the left, but moves, however slowly, straight onward to his point, satisfied that, so long as he does not stand still, nor retrograde, he must get to the object at last.

*The Times*, not usually a publication to shower Martin with praise, had to admit that he now enjoyed the support of the majority of butchers and drovers in Smithfield Market. On the other hand, one reporter working for his fiercest critic, the *Morning Chronicle*, wrote:

That Irish jackass Martin throws an air of ridicule over the whole matter by his insufferable idiotism. I hope to see his skull, thick as it is, cracked one of these days; for that vulgar and angry gabble with which he weekly infests the Police Offices of the Metropolis, is a greater outrage to humanity, than any fifty blows ever inflicted on the snout of a pig or the buttocks of beeve, blows which, in one and the same breath, the blustering and blundering blockhead would fain prosecute, punish and pardon

In addition to the wave of publicity Martin created by his parliamentary frenzy, he continued to police the streets, the press now reporting his every move. One day he was walking in Regent Street when he saw a youth mercilessly beating his horse with a large stick. Dick stepped up and chastised the youth, who in return let out a torrent of abuse and continued to assault the animal. Martin forced the stick out of the his hand and a fight ensued, the youngster coming off worse in the affray.

When the case came up before the magistrates, the *Morning Chronicle* brought Martin's evidence into question. This, coupled with a campaign the paper had run which, Martin claimed, encouraged an attempt on his life, was the final straw. He sued for libel. When this case came to court Martin proceeded to lose his temper with the newspaper's counsel, who disputed Martin's affidavit. Martin always shrugged off insults to his state of mental health and his 'ridiculous' Irish brogue, but questioning his honour was off limits, even in a court of law. He thundered across the courtroom, 'How dare you, you scoundrel, doubt my affidavit!' The Judge, fearing a fight, cleared the court.

The SPCA continued to grow. A number of eminent people lent their names to it, and several committees were formed, with separate responsibilities in developing the aims agreed at the Society's inauguration. It was now housed in its own premises, where the Reverend Arthur Broome and Secretary Lewis Gompertz, another founder, worked full-time.

This growth was not without problems and the fledging Society had run into financial straits, Broome at one stage spending a brief time in prison, since he was held responsible for the debts. Martin, with considerable experience of insolvency, was amongst those whose efforts ensured the Society persevered through the problems and continued its work.

Martin took a keen interest in a bill that came before Parliament in the May of 1825; and presented him with a particularly difficult conflict of interest. Despite banning the Catholic Association, and possibly due to Martin's influence, the Government had been working behind the scenes with Daniel O'Connell. Liverpool and his Cabinet, especially Canning, realised that something had to be done in spite of the King's position on the matter.

A bill was drafted that would at last allow Catholics to become Members of Parliament. As ever, something needed to be offered to the Protestant hard core in return. It was agreed that the bill would contain a clause that disenfranchised the 40-shilling freeholders, the vast majority of whom were Catholics, from being able to vote in elections. On balance it was a big step forward for the cause, but to Dick, who relied heavily on these small freeholders in his constituency, it meant that his forthcoming re-election would be impossible. Martin did not think twice about his decision, he voted for the bill, as he felt it would 'advance the great question of Catholic emancipation.'

However, he could not resist the opportunity during the discussion to attack his old enemy, James Daly. The 40-shilling freeholders had been given a quantity of stick during the debate, no doubt to justify why they were being excluded from the electoral process. Referring to Daly's actions at a previous election, Martin raised the query that, if his opponent was willing to cast such a stigma on these people, why then did he confine them like slaves in the hold of a boat bound for the election booths in Galway, using them 'like bees, to smother them in the hive, after obtaining the honey'?

Although the Commons passed the bill on its first reading, Catholics were once again to have their hopes dashed, and Martin was given political salvation he had not asked for, when the King prevented the bill's further passage.

Faced with an election that it would still take a supreme effort to win, Martin chose to remain in London through the winter and into the new year of 1826. He made two more unsuccessful attempts to extend his law: a bear baiting bill, where he described an animal which had its tongue torn out to use as a collection plate, and a bill to prevent cruelty to dogs, this time using as his shock tactic the story of a dog that had been skinned alive and thrown into a river.

In the middle of this self-created maelstrom of activity, Martin also found time to progress his work on criminal reform. He possessed an endearing ability to put fire-doors between issues in which he was involved. A difference of opinion over one issue did not have to cloud another. Robert Peel also had this quality. Despite their frequent skirmishes in parliament and their fundamental disagreement over catholic eman-cipation, Martin shared his ideas with the Home Secretary, who included them in his pioneering Criminal Justice Bill, to be presented during the next parliament.

A general election having now been called, Martin returned to Galway to fight his last and most controversial campaign.

# Chapter 33

# A Very Dirty Election

Martin's arrival at Ballynahinch was an opportunity for the largest family reunion for years. Hatty, Georgy and Mary-Jane, now 24, 19 and 15, respectively, accompanied Dick and Harriet. Richard and Emily joined Thomas, Julia and their ten-year-old daughter Mary, with their two small sons, Richard and John. Sadly their first child, a daughter christened Anne Thérèse, had died in infancy. Dick's half-brothers, Robert with his twelve-year-old son and Anthony, with five of his eventual ten children, travelled over from Bushy Park and Dangan. The only member of the family missing was Dick's eldest daughter Laetitia, now living in America where her husband Charles was British Consul for North Carolina.

Dick and Thomas soon got down to the sorry subject of business. Prevailing hard times meant that rental income was low. The price of kelp had halved again in the last year. The copper mines were long since written off. Even the smuggling trade was suffering from the lack of a good war. The only hope rested with the marble business, which although producing high quality stone, some of it appearing in European aristocratic homes as an Italian marque, desperately needed capital investment to make manufacture more efficient. Lines of credit to the Martin family were now practically non-existent, although Dick brought news from England of a possible investor, a Yorkshireman called Beaumont.

The grim reality for Dick was that age and access to Ballynahinch were no longer in his favour; if he failed to be re-elected to Parliament, and no longer enjoyed the legal protection that the office afforded, he would be faced with imprisonment. Stakes were higher than ever in this election.

Galway was bracing itself for a fierce fight. Clanricarde had indeed put up a candidate, James Lambert. Worse still for Martin, it appeared that a deal had been done with James Daly, along the very same lines that Clanricarde had proposed to Dick the previous year. Technically the nobility were not allowed to meddle in elections, but the area remained grey, and all manner of support was overlooked, providing cash was not openly put up for a candidate's expenses. The *Galway Advertiser*, a paper loyal to Martin, fired a sarcastic shot across Lambert's election bows:

Now we know very well that a peer ought not to interfere in elections. It is unconstitutional – nay it is enough to vitiate an election, if a member of the Upper House should by chance appear at the Hustings. This is the theory of the Constitution. But as everybody knows they do interfere, that the House of Commons is in truth returned by the House of Lords, we certainly feel gratified, when we see a young nobleman take a part so credible, as Lord Clanricarde did after the refusal of Mr. Daly to surrender his power over the Corporation.

The paper was unaware that Clanricarde had put up another candidate in the City who would support the Daly monopoly, thereby freeing Daly from fighting the election on two fronts. In return Daly and Lambert would tacitly support each other, focussing their attacks on Martin.

Dick's first action was to appeal to Canning to intervene and stop Clanricarde's puppeteering. Canning promptly washed his hands of the matter, writing to Martin that he hated 'all local politics.' He had in fact already lined up his son-in-law for an influential government post as his Under Secretary at the Foreign Office and the young lord wasted no time in using this power to further his candidate's election.

Valentine Blake, a lifelong friend of Martin's, who had grown up in Menlo Castle, on Lough Corrib, had been promised a ministerial post in return for his support of Lambert. Dick's cousin John D'Arcy's two sons were both offered lucrative posts in return for his freeholder's votes. Martin Ffrench was offered the sinecure post of Distributor of Stamps but turned it down, preferring to remain loyal to Martin.

Dick called foul, again writing to Canning, who replied: 'I hardly can think for two reasons that Lord Clanricarde made the promises you refer to. First, I never gave him any authority of the kind and secondly Lord Clanricarde assures me he never made any such.'

When Martin weighed up his chances, he must have feared the worst. However the money and power lined up against him were counterbalanced by three factors. Dick was a veteran of many dirty Galway elections, and had learnt a few tricks over the years. It also helped that the current Sheriff of Galway, who would have to maintain order during the campaign, was James Martin, Dick's cousin. Most importantly, O'Connell's Catholic Association had decided to throw their weight behind him.

O'Connell, probably the most gifted lawyer in Ireland, had spotted a loophole in the legislation intended to outlaw his organisation. Charitable bodies were not covered and therefore the New Catholic Association rose phoenix-like out of the legal ashes. The penny subscriptions continued to be collected for the purported function of helping distressed Catholics. The Association had been busy in the meantime, identifying a candidate in each constituency who was sympathetic to their cause and in return would be supported by the catholic vote and the organisation's funds. Martin was an easy choice in Galway and he realised that with this support, coupled with his experience, he at least had a chance, although all the local bookmakers were making him the outsider of three.

The war of words soon began. Martin knew that Daly was a certainty, so it was Lambert he must beat for the second seat. A meeting was called on 25th May 1826 at Kilroy's Hotel, but moved to the new Tholsel in order to accommodate the number of people who turned up. The Committee of Independence, a body whose sole aim was to oust control of Galway from the Dalys, arranged the meeting. It was also a well set trap for James Lambert, who had been told that he should attend and at least be seen to offer his backing.

Martin made a passionate speech, praising Counsellor Lynch, a well respected member of the Committee who had recently died. He then reminded the packed audience how much effort he had put into the anti-Daly cause, both in Ireland and Westminster, since the Committee's inception thirteen years beforehand. His speech received loud cheers. Dick now motioned to the totally unprepared Lambert to follow him on the platform. Lambert was lost for words, having had very little to do with the organisation. His response was to say meekly that he 'would not trespass on the meeting'.

Now on the platform, in full view of the vociferous crowd, the knife could be turned in the unfortunate Lambert's back. Thomas, arriving late to create greater effect, rose from the audience and made public the details of Lord Clanricarde's proposal to his father and the subsequent offer to him to stand and support the Dalys. Amid loud noises of disgust, he told the collected throng of Clanricarde's most recent arrangement with James Daly to put up a friendly candidate for the City. As Dick and his press contacts had already made it well known that Lambert was Clanricarde's candidate for the County seat, the poor man must have been praying for the platform to collapse and put an end to his misery. It was not a good start to his campaign.

At the public meeting to confirm the candidates officially, Martin and Lambert clashed again, this time with Lambert managing at least to land a verbal punch. Martin lambasted his opponent for not signing his petition many years ago supporting the Catholic cause. In full flow he turned to Lambert, accusing him of being in Clanricarde's pocket, goading him with the suggestion that if by chance he succeeded in getting into Parliament, he would not know how to vote unless his master was in town. Lambert's response went straight to Dick's rawest nerve, accusing him of obtaining his election expenses by robbing creditors of their rights.

At the many hustings throughout the County, Martin's theme was consistent. He had worked tirelessly over 50 years for this constituency. His opponent had done nothing, but worse still Lambert was in Clanricarde's pocket, so the young Lord was nothing better than a common criminal, flagrantly breaking the law by bribing voters and illegally bankrolling his candidate's campaign.

By the time the election booths opened, the contest was heated to boiling point. A mob of Valentine Blake's tenants made the short journey to Dangan and broke Anthony Martin's gates down. Anthony's response was publicly to horsewhip Blake. After an altercation with John D'Arcy, Dick was bound over to keep the peace by their mutual cousin, the Sheriff. Lambert's brother was imprisoned for shooting one of Martin's agents.

Galway elections always witnessed many public skirmishes between rival factions. The 1826 contest saw anarchy bordering on civil war. Martin's supporters blockaded the roads into Galway from Connemara and the west, preventing anyone known to be voting unfavourably from entering the city. A group of Dick's followers fled for their lives when the building where they were meeting was firebombed.

When the first count of votes was made public, Daly had a strong lead, Lambert was second, Martin a dismal third. This was the normal pattern, since almost all Dick's voters arrived late into elections by sea from Connemara. Feelings were running high when the ragged flotilla of small boats finally moored alongside the Galway quay; the usual party atmosphere replaced this time by a sombre fife and drum. Lambert, too, was relying on votes coming in from far-flung corners of the constituency and inevitably, with both sets of supporters housed in the same part of town, riots broke out. Martin's men outnumbered Lambert's but the Sheriff was reluctant to intervene, despite Lambert's claims of intimidation.

On the Saturday before the polls closed the voting to date was announced, with Daly home and dry but the gap between Lambert and Martin closing fast. That night the house on the green near to the dock where many of Lambert's voters were lodged was burned to the ground.

The count on the following Monday, only three days before voting ended, showed Daly with 6,023 votes, Lambert 3,635 and Martin 3,450. A common accusation directed at Martin during elections was that his vote was rigged by many of his supporters: faces unknown to the voting clerks, taking full advantage of the chaos and voting a number of times. Martin's daughter Hatty, many years afterwards, in her book *Canvassing*, described the scene:

> The whole town was alive at the dawn of day; crowds of partisans of all ages and ranks gathering around the Committee rooms of the opposing candidates; electioneering agents oratorising, explaining, or mystifying, as suited their purpose; looking over certificates, and making Pat Conny sensible he was only to be Pat Conny for the first time he voted, but not Dennis Sleevan the second time, in regard of poor Dennis not being convenient just then, because he was buried last week. And reminding Martin Donovan he mustn't forget to slip a flea inside his lease, that he might swear with a safe conscience, that the life in it was still in existence, and other trifling, though necessary, arrangements for the proper carrying on of their employers' interests. And voters were eating, drinking, shouting and whirling their ferrals to give the "the raal fighting touch".

James Lambert did not receive a single vote more, following the fire attack. The final result read:

| Mr. James Daly Esq | 6,206 Votes |
| Colonel Richard Martin | 3,719 Votes |
| Mr. James Lambert Esq. | 3,635 Votes |

There was the usual outcry from the losers. Lambert claimed his voters had been intimidated and the election rigged by Martin engineering multiple voting. Normally the dust settled quickly after an election. The abuse and violence was put into the context of unavoidability and afterwards people buried their hatchets and got on with life. Galway elections were not dissimilar to rugby matches where players enjoy a drink together within an hour of attempting to gouge each other's eyes out. 1826 was different. The wounds were much deeper and Lambert, or more importantly Clanricarde, was not going to let his defeat rest.

For Martin it was his finest electoral victory, achieved against overwhelming odds. He remained legally immune from his creditors and was keener than ever to return to Westminster. The general election had been a triumph for O'Connell and his Association. Their strategy of supporting candidates who were openly for emancipation, coupled with faultless organisation, resulted in anti-catholic MPs being ousted in four counties: Waterford, Westmeath, Louth and Monaghan. Opponents who narrowly hung on to their seats realised that unless they rethought their position on the Catholic Question they would not be so fortunate next time around.

 

Rumours abounded that the Prime Minister, Lord Liverpool, was in poor health and about to step aside and be replaced by George Canning. Martin would have no problem in forgetting the personal differences created between them by Clanricarde, as, to his credit, Canning had always been a staunch supporter of emancipation.

Dick was also excited by reports from the SPCA of how public opinion was mounting in favour of greater legal protection for more animals. He felt confident that during this term his new measures would succeed, especially as, since he had worked so closely with Peel on the criminal justice reforms, he was expecting him to drop his sometimes petty resistance.

Dick stayed in Ireland for the winter, setting off for London in the New Year totally unprepared for what lay in wait for him.

# Chapter 34

# Exile

To the outside world, Dick and Thomas enjoyed a strong relationship. Thomas had actively supported his father's campaign and the two men put up a united front when they attended the Galway Catholic Meeting, held on 30th July 1826. The *Galway Advertiser* reported that 'Mr. Martin, the Member for the County and Mr. Thomas Martin of Ballynahinch Castle, his son, entered and were received with the most deafening and enthusiastic cheering,' which must have been to the consternation of James Daly, who was in the audience.

However, behind the doors of Ballynahinch the relationship was strained to the limit. Thomas resented that his father, still protected against the debts crippling the estate, was about to embark for Westminster, where his attention was always trained on anything but the family business. Worse still, Dick expected the family finances to continue supporting a generous standard of living in London. On the other hand, Dick felt that Thomas was not pulling his weight in respect of the marble enterprise and in turn thought his son was living far too extravagantly.

*Thomas Martin*

Recently, more quality marble had been discovered at Barnanoran, near to Ballynahinch. The Martin marble was indeed excellent, and 'sincere' in that it did not need excessive waxing to produce a beautiful finish. Dick wrote to Richard saying that their 'coloured marble and the best verd-antique very far exceeds any marble to be found in Italy. Our marble must command in every part of Europe a superior price.' Turning to the situation with Richard's half-brother and his wife, he was less upbeat, writing, 'I see, short as I may live, that I may have plenty of money, but peace with such tempers as Thomas's and Julia's is not to be expected.'

When Martin arrived at Westminster in February 1827, James Lambert had carried out his threat. He had delivered a petition to the House asking for Martin's election to be declared invalid on two grounds. Firstly, Martin and his campaigners had incited rioting, frightening away much of Lambert's support. Secondly, they had voted more than once for Martin, using different names.

Martin had cause for concern. Normally the claims and counter-claims resulting from a Galway election would have subsided by now. Westminster's view of the far-off, lawless constituency was that everyone involved was as bad as another. This time Lambert, no doubt backed again by Clanricarde, had assembled a formidable legal team who were going to take the issue to its conclusion. Witnesses were being subpoenaed to appear before the Committee appointed by Parliament to hear the claims.

Fearing that many these accusations would be proved, Martin decided that attack was the best form of defence and soon found an opportunity to get his blow in first. The Committee was due to convene at the end of March, but a month beforehand the House of Commons was debating the general issue of bribery at elections in boroughs, as opposed to counties, which were felt, with an obvious exception on the west coast of Ireland, to be free from corruption.

Martin rose to his feet and, after making a comment relevant to Grampound, the borough under discussion, turned his speech into a full frontal assault on Lord Clanricarde. He contended that, although there might be problems in the boroughs, 'More flagrant, more abominable, more stinking corruption' actually occurred in the counties. Having grabbed the attention of the House, he continued. 'I know of a County into which a Secretary of State, or rather an Under Secretary of State, went three days before an election took place, and opened a bank to defray the entire expenses – of whom? Of his nominee, I repeat, his nominee.' Martin was now in full flow. 'So help me God, I am able to bring positive proof of what I state. I can prove that the Under Secretary, out of his own money, paid the whole expenses of his candidate – that he promised places – that he gave bribes: nay more, I will prove that he actually promised a Peerage.'

It is the convention in both Houses to veil accusations against fellow members by desisting from naming them in person. Everyone knew whom Martin was referring to, but that did not stop him from taking one final step over the line of what was considered acceptable. 'The person whom I have alluded to is the Marquis of Clanricarde, Under Secretary of State for Foreign Affairs. Yes. I denounce him as the man, and I ought to have denounced him earlier.'

There was uproar. The House had grown used to Martin's wry humour, his theatricality, his constant disregard of the Speaker, his admonishment of a French surgeon by name and the shocking examples of cruelty to animals; but this time he had overstepped the mark. He had not only made open accusations against a named member of the Lords, but had also chosen to attack a man whose father-in-law was on the verge of becoming Prime Minister. Ominously it was the Chancellor of the Exchequer who rose to reply, saying that matters in Galway were subject to a petition that 'charges the Honourable Member for Galway with almost every offence of which it is possible for a candidate to be guilty.' The ranks were quickly closing against Martin.

Parliament was by now in limbo. Lord Liverpool had suffered a stroke and Canning was poised to take over as first minister. His son-in-law aside, Martin welcomed Canning's appointment, since he felt it could only bring catholic emancipation closer. On 5th March the Commons debated Roman Catholic claims. It was Martin's last speech prior to his fate being decided. In reflective mood, he looked back on the cause in whose service he had grown grey, and to which he had 'given his vote for forty years.' He contended that catholic emancipation was a debt due from the government to the people of Ireland. Martin finished what he clearly knew could well be his last parliamentary speech by addressing the one event that continued to hurt him most. Looking back 28 years, he reminded his fellow members that Lord Cornwallis, when Lord Lieutenant of Ireland, had assured him that emancipation was immediately to follow the Union of the two countries.

By the last week of March, MPs must have felt that half of Galway was in their midst. Martin Ffrench and James Lambert nearly came to blows in the lobby, Lambert offering his hand to Ffrench, who said he 'would not contaminate himself by shaking hands with such a rascal.' Lambert, fearing for his own safety, hastily delivered another petition before the Bar of the House which resulted in Ffrench agreeing not to breach the peace again. Everybody concerned with the forthcoming hearing was reminded that the Palace of Westminster would extend its protection to 'all persons whom it might call before it as witnesses'.

The committee began its hearing. Within days it became apparent to all, including Martin, that the evidence was overwhelmingly backing Lambert's claims. Each vote was being scrutinised, and one by one the count for Martin was being reduced. By 11th April Lord Forbes, the chairman, was able to make the findings public. The committee called the attention of the House to an organised system of rioting and disorder that had taken place in Galway. Specifically, houses had been set on fire, lives lost and many people on both sides maimed and bruised. The authorities were severely criticised for their reluctance to give protection to many voters despite the adequate civil and military resources in the city at the time. The committee recommended that steps be taken to prevent the recurrence of such outrages in future. No blame, however, was attributed to either candidate and so the first part of Lambert's petition had failed.

Turning to Lambert's claim that votes had been cast illegally for Martin, the committee found this to be true. Evidence had shown that many people had voted twice and several three or four times. The committee was shocked to have to state that these voters had, on each occasion, sworn that they had not voted before at that election and some remedy must be 'applied to such a mass of depravity.' The outcome of the enquiry was that Mr Lambert should be returned duly elected.

Martin played his last card. He asked the committee to suspend its recommendations and adjourn until the following Thursday, thereby allowing him to produce evidence of such corrupt practices on the part of Mr Lambert as would disqualify him from a seat in the House. Martin told the committee that he had sent a message to the House of Lords requesting the attendance of four of its members to give evidence which would prove that an unconstitutional interference had taken place in the late election. The committee agreed to the adjournment.

The *Galway Advertiser* reported the outcome to its readers back in Ireland, eagerly awaiting news from Westminster:

> The Speaker sent a message to the House of Lords on the application of the Chairman of this Committee to request the attendance of the Marquises of Sligo, Clanricarde, Mounteagle and Summerhill to give evidence on behalf of Mr. Martin. The Lord Chancellor informed the messenger that the Lords would return an answer by a messenger of their own but the noble Lords forgot to return an answer in consequence of which Mr. Martin was compelled to close his case without the benefit of testimony.

The committee was not obliged to draw any conclusion from the Lords' apparent collective loss of memory, so without contrary evidence, it stood by its original recommendations. Lambert was to be returned as the second member for Galway County, and Martin expelled from Parliament forthwith. With the publicity the enquiry had engendered, Dick knew that his many creditors, frustrated for years by the protection he had enjoyed, would quickly have him imprisoned. He wasted no time and within days was out of their reach in France.

Although seventy-three years old, Dick saw recent events as no more than a temporary setback. He fully expected the marble business to deliver shortly, and planned to return to Britain as soon as possible in order to take up where he had left off. He made his expectations known to Thomas and sent for Harriet and the girls to join him in Boulogne, the port that was home to a small enclave of Britons suffering similar financial pressures. The family took up residence in a fashionable area of the town, at 6 rue de l'Ecu. From here Martin kept in close touch with events across the narrow strait of sea.

Lord Liverpool had not recovered his health and, within days of Martin leaving Parliament, the King commissioned Canning to form a government, knowing that royal resistance to catholic emancipation was becoming increasingly futile. The most recent Commons vote had resulted in a government majority of only four. However, Canning's exertions in achieving the height of his political ambition had already taken their toll and he died of exhaustion 100 days after succeeding to the office he had so much coveted.

His successor, Viscount Goderich, only served a few weeks longer. Without Canning's political ability he quickly lost the confidence of his cabinet and the King. Next up for the job was Arthur Wellesley, the first Duke of Wellington. Still a national hero for finally frustrating Napoleon's ambitions at Waterloo, Wellington was unlike most prime ministers in that he had little experience of the Commons, took no joy in the rough-and-tumble of debate and was a poor public speaker. Coming from a traditional Irish Protestant family, he had never been remotely supportive of catholic rights but he recognised the mood in Parliament and began his term of office with a loose notion of allowing Catholics to serve as MPs, providing the government had power of veto over the appointment of catholic bishops. Events early in his premiership were to overtake his plans.

Wellington appointed Vesey Fitzgerald, a wealthy Irish landowner and MP for County Clare, as the President of the Board of Trade. It was a rule that, on obtaining ministerial office, an MP must put himself up for re-election by his constituency, and a by-election was called. Although Fitzgerald, who had represented the constituency for ten years and been a reasonable landlord, was personally supportive of emancipation, the government he had joined was not, and so Daniel O'Connell stood as his opponent. The well tested electioneering machinery of the Catholic Association created disciplined groups of voters who were marched by local priests to the booth. O'Connell was elected by a landslide but, being a Catholic himself, could not take up his seat. Wellington and his government were faced with a constitutional crisis and the always uncertain situation in Ireland had entered waters hitherto uncharted.

Although he was politically inexperienced, much of Wellington's military genius had lain in recognising when defeat stared him in the face and retreat was the preferable option. Robert Peel, the most influential member of the Cabinet, who until then had always resisted any move towards emancipation, agreed that the time had come to concede. The following year the Catholic Emancipation Bill was passed by both Houses and given Royal Assent by a king who had insufficient influence over his government and by now was too ill to resist any further. Unlike previous small concessions, this act allowed Catholics to be MPs, cabinet ministers, judges, generals and admirals.

From his place of exile, 30 miles across the English Channel, Martin finally saw the victory of the cause he had been groomed to pursue over 60 years ago. Robert Martin had been right: emancipation had been accomplished, not by armed rebellion but by the power of organised public opinion. O'Connell quite rightly could take full credit for this triumph but he would be the first to acknowledge the debt owed to Martin for his crucial influence towards the avoidence of violence.

By now it was widely known that the King's health was failing fast. For Martin, the crucial consequence of the King's death was that a General Election would be called. Dick saw this as the opportunity he was waiting for to re-enter public life, reclaim his seat and resume his parliamentary fight for animal protection. He put more and more pressure on Thomas to produce the funds necessary to permit him to set foot in Britain safely. George died in June 1830 and an election was set for the following month. But the marble still had not produced the results hoped for and Dick, despite rumours to the contrary in the Galway press, was forced to remain in France. Even he, a lifelong optimist, now in his late seventies, must have felt that his last opportunity to return to Parliament was gone.

Despite the sidelining of their parliamentary champion and driving force, the Society for the Prevention of Cruelty to Animals was flourishing. Martin was in frequent communication with his old colleagues, advising from a distance. The committee had been extended to 26 members, who must have shared Dick's optimism that he would shortly return to Britain, since he was frequently proposed and selected for reappointment. The Duke of Gloucester had become Patron of the Society, which, deprived of the energy of Martin in Parliament, was concentrating its efforts on establishing a network of inspectors on the streets and in the markets.

In 1832, in a letter to Lewis Gompertz, Martin gave detailed instructions on how the MP Mr Mackinnon was to attempt to have his original law expanded to cover bulls and therefore prevent bull baiting. The strategy was to use a legal technicality to have bulls treated as cattle, instead of amending the legislation. As Martin put it, 'To alter is not always to improve.'

The final rift between Thomas and his father happened in 1833. Changes to inheritance law allowed an eldest son to break the automatic entail of an estate. Thomas made it known that his will left the Martin estate to Mary, his only daughter, meaning Richard could lose any inheritance he might have been entitled to, especially if Mary subsequently married. Dick wrote to Thomas imploring him not to take this step, but to no avail. Thomas had never completely forgiven his father for the traumas of his childhood. He also remembered the instance when Dick had prevented him marrying, forcing him to leave home and almost lose his life in the Peninsular War. The last fifteen years had been taken up with Dick making unreasonable demands, seemingly oblivious to the financial problems he had landed upon his son. They were never to make their peace.

By now Martin accepted that he was to spend the rest of his days in exile. He took to walking the streets of Boulogne doing what he could to ensure the wellbeing of local animals. There were moves within the French government to bring in a version of Martin's Law, and the old man willingly lent his name in support.

His duelling reputation was not easily forgotten, and Martin contrived to reaffirm it one last time. When chastising a young Frenchman for beating a horse, he was challenged to apologise or defend his honour. Martin immediately elected to fight and offered the astonished young man his card. Realising the elderly gentleman he was facing was the legendary 'Hairtrigger Dick', the challenger immediately withdrew.

Humanity Dick never returned to Connemara. At 4 o'clock in the afternoon of 6th January 1834, four weeks before his eightieth birthday, he died peacefully, attended by his devoted wife and three daughters.

# Chapter 35

# Epilogue

Dick Martin was buried in a part of Boulogne's Eastern Cemetery that suffered extensive bomb damage during the Second World War. In 1981 the RSPCA was approached and asked whether they would pay for the remains of one of their founders to be exhumed and reburied in another part of the cemetery along with a new memorial stone to mark his achievements. The Society approved the work, so that Martin's remains now rest in the Ossuary and a marble plaque in both English and French reads:

RICHARD MARTIN

1754 – 1834

BORN IN DUBLIN, DIED IN BOULOGNE. ONE OF THE FOUNDERS OF THE ROYAL SOCIETY FOR THE PREVENTION OF CRUELTY TO ANIMALS, WHICH HELD ITS FIRST MEETING IN LONDON IN 1824. A MEMBER OF THE BRITISH PARLIAMENT, HE PILOTED THROUGH THE HOUSE OF COMMONS IN 1822 THE FIRST ACT TO PROTECT ANIMALS

After his father's death, Thomas struggled on with the estate. He entered Parliament and remained the member for Galway County up until his death on 23rd April 1847, although there is no record that he ever spoke in the House of Commons. The marble mines never produced the hoped-for remuneration, but Thomas is as lovingly remembered as his father in Connemara for being staunchly humane. He died, during the Great Hunger, of a fever contracted while visiting tenants in the workhouse at Clifden. His last words were: 'My God, what will become of my people?'

Julia, Thomas's wife, lived until 1858 but, in accordance with the will that had so upset his father, Thomas left the Martin estate to his only daughter, Mary. The 'Queen of Connemara', as she became known, was the last of the Martin line to own the vast region. Classically educated and knowledgeable in French, Latin, Greek and Hebrew, she regally took over when her father died and continued to do all she could for the starving tenants. Her inheritance crippled by the debts of the previous two generations, she was finally evicted by creditors and forced to flee, like her grandfather, to the Continent. By then she was married to Arthur Gonne Bell, who chose to take the name of Martin; the couple stayed briefly in Belgium before departing for America. Within days of arriving in New York, Mary died giving birth to her only child at the Union Place Hotel. The baby did not survive and her husband went to England; he was killed in a train accident in 1883.

Thomas's half-brother, Richard, on learning that he was to be denied the inheritance, emigrated to Canada a year before his father died. He settled with his wife Emily in County Haldimand, Ontario, where the couple had seven children, six of them boys. The dynasty created survives to this day and the Martin Association actively encourages the preservation of the family's history.

Laetitia, Dick's eldest daughter, remained with her husband in America until she died in 1858. Dick's half-brother Robert died in 1840, and Anthony in 1846. Robert remained a Captain in the British Army and his grand-daughter, Violet Martin of Ross, became a famous authoress, writing and co-writing many works based on family tales, the best known being the *Irish RM* series. Anthony had emigrated with his large family to France before the famine.

Harriet, freed of debt when her husband died, immediately moved back to Dublin with her three daughters. She and her second daughter, Georgy, both died in 1840. The other two daughters, Hatty and Mary-Jane, both became writers, living together as spinsters in Dublin until they died, Hatty in 1891, Mary-Jane in 1893. They are buried together. Hatty mentioned her father several times in her writing, identifying his main quality as 'Fatherliness.'

Towards the end of the famine, the London Law Life Assurance Company and another creditor, a Yorkshireman named Beaumont, finally put the 200,000-acre Martin estate into a form of receivership. When the company was unable to find a buyer for the whole property, many tenants were evicted and it was finally disposed of piecemeal. Birchall burned down in 1830. Dangan became a workhouse during the famine and fell into ruin soon after. The old Martin town house in the middle of Galway is now Neachtain's Pub, and preserved in a manner very close to its original appearance.

*Neachtain's*

Ballynahinch, too, fell into disrepair after Mary Martin left. It was eventually bought by the Berridge family, who restored the old house and enlarged it to its present-day structure The Berridges enjoyed a reputation the Martin family would have approved, for good treatment of the tenants, many of whom had continued to endure hardships well into the 20th century. In 1924 Ballynahinch was bought by His Highness the Maharajah Jam Sahib of Nawanagar, an Indian noble and world famous cricketer. 'Ranji' was a fabulously wealthy man who fell in love with Ballynahinch and the surrounding countryside. He landscaped the gardens and woods and covered the long drive with polished marble chips. When he arrived at Galway for his annual visit he would purchase five motorcars to make the onward trip, always giving them to locals at the end of his stay. After the Maharajah's death the Irish Tourist Board acquired the property. Now back in private ownership, Ballynahinch well deserves its reputation as one of the finest hotels in Ireland.

The fledgling society co-founded by Humanity Dick in a London coffee house in 1824 attracted patronage from Queen Victoria, and became the Royal Society for the Prevention of Cruelty to Animals. Now emulated in 132 countries, with millions of members, it and similar organisations are aided throughout the world by legislation derived from Martin's original Act. This fact is recognised by the Society on a plaque outside their San Francisco office that reads: 'Richard Martin, known as 'Humanity Martin', author of the first law to protect animals in England – 1822'.

Without Martin there to berate Parliament, legislation was slow to change, although a year after his death his Act was amended to include domestic animals. Further amendments occurred in 1849 and 1854. In 1911 the RSPCA were responsible for an all-encompassing Protection of Animals Act. Hunting and a number of field sports remain legal in Great Britain.

A few days after Martin died, *The Times* reported the death of the 'Eccentric Member for Galway', a convenient pigeon-hole name, especially as at the time the whole concept of conferring rights on animals was deemed eccentric, but a description that hardly does justice to the many facets of his life.

History best remembers Richard Martin for putting in place the cornerstone of worldwide legal protection for animals. He is also known as one of the founders of the SPCA movement, although probably not given the full credit he deserves. There were other founders who, it can rightly be claimed, were pivotal to the Society's development, but one must doubt whether the organisation would have come about and grown from its modest beginnings at that time without Martin's Law already in place, and without the publicity attracted by his antics. There can be no doubt that were it not for Martin's ingenuity and persistence within Parliament, this legislation would have taken many years more to effect.

Look more closely into the background of the groundbreaking 1822 'Ill Treatment of Cattle Act', and it becomes apparent that Martin had for many years fought a non-stop campaign to change the prevailing brutal culture. Persuading his fellow politicians was one battle, but Martin then took his crusade on to the streets, as he had years before in his own fields of Connemara, seemingly oblivious to personal danger. His efforts did not stop there. He manipulated media interest in a way that was far ahead of his time, happy to play up the eccentric image while it helped him achieve his aim. As he once said, 'I do not consider myself a ridiculous man for fighting against these atrocities.'

His friend, the poet Tom Moore, wrote:

> O place me where Dick Martin rules
> The houseless wilds of Connemara.

It is there that he is still remembered as 'Humanity Dick', the King of the largest estate in the then three kingdoms of Britain, always benevolent towards his people, regardless of his own finances. Again, his actions have to be placed in the context of the time, when the norm was to strip poor people of all dignity because of their class. Martin provided refuge for both Catholics and Protestants, alleviating suffering across the religious divide. While fighting throughout his life for catholic emancipation, he constantly encouraged people of both persuasions to live together, without a hint of religious bigotry.

Ireland tends to remember him as 'Hairtrigger Dick', the most fearless duellist in a romantic era of high living and desperado personalities. Legends grow with the telling and Martin was happy for his reputation to precede him as he used it well to further his humanitarian causes.

Though one of the longest serving politicians in parliamentary history, Martin tends to be overlooked by historians. But when one digs deeper a greater importance to his political career is unearthed. Castlereagh acknowledged him as one of the best speakers of a generation that displayed a wealth of oratorical riches. Martin has not received the recognition he deserves for being instrumental in the reformation of an archaic criminal justice system, a movement more usually credited to the more highly profiled Robert Peel.

Although Martin strove tirelessly, and not always cleverly, in the fight for catholic emancipation, he again is rarely credited for its realisation. What is beyond question is that in 1824 Martin publicly advised the Catholic Association to proceed down a route of political activism and not rebellion. This was at a time when pressure within the organisation was clamouring for a call to arms. History shows that the Catholic Association achieved emancipation by political means. Conjecture may speculate how another rebellion would have fared.

Richard Martin was, of course, an eccentric, who lived life to the full, throwing himself into his passions without any sense of consequence, and an extravagant man, even by the standards of a time when extravagance had scaled the heights. His life was played out against a backdrop of one the most turbulent periods in British history and he always seemed to secure his seat in the front row.

Martin was a man of great personal contradictions, whose life is a series of paradoxes. He was a Protestant who fought all his adult years for the emancipation of Catholics; a humanitarian who was prepared to kill, often for what we would consider trivial reasons; an establishment figure who moved in the highest circles of society while openly living off the proceeds of lawlessness; a wronged husband who was prepared to have the details of his wife's infidelity made public only to throw away the resulting financial reward; a man of honour who lived his whole life in spectacular insolvency, using a variety of means to evade his creditors; a complex and mercurial personality, much misunderstood by his peers and capable of huge errors of judgment; a conscientious and loving father who prevented his son marrying on a point of class principle. He supported the Union of Parliaments, making a public pledge not to take money from a Government that did not support civil rights and then broke it to suit his purpose.

He was a fun-loving, likeable, gregarious person, whose life was marred with personal tragedy and heartache: the loss of two young children; the suspicion that another man fathered his first child; having his beloved wife leave him so publicly for a rival; being forced to kill his closest friend in a duel; living the last years of his life as a fugitive in ignominious exile; dying without ever healing the rift with his eldest son.

Yet ultimately Richard Martin was an effective blend of courage, feeling and good sense. On one level he was an eccentric, on another a well balanced man. A barrister friend wrote:

> He holds them by the very test and characteristic of the human race, laughter; and while their sides shake, their opposition is shaken and falls down at the same instant. There is a beautiful symmetry, a perfect keeping, as it were, in the whole man of Richard Martin, Esq. Every limb of his body, and every feature of his face is round and solid. He lets drive at the House like a bullet and the flag of truce is instantly hung out upon both sides.

He will be remembered as one of the most exciting and remarkable of Irishmen, but above all as the man whose legacy now protects countless millions of animals throughout the world.

# Bibliography


*Alumni Cantabrigiensis*, anon.

Barrington, *Sir Jonah, Personal Sketches of his Own Times*, Colburn & Bentley, London 1827-32

Bryant, P.H.M., *Harrow*, Blackie & Son, London & Glasgow, 1936

J.M.W. Callwell, *Old Irish Life*, Blackwood & Sons, Edinburgh & London, 1912

Clarke, John, *The Life and Times of George III*, Weidenfeld and Nicholson, 1972

Cobbetts *Parliamentary Debates*, Feb-May 1805, May-June 1809, London

Craig, M., *Dublin 1660-1860*, Allen Figgis & Co., Dublin

Fairholme, E.G. and Pain, W., *A Century of Work for Animals*, John Murray, London 1934

*Galway Advertiser, The*, June, August 1826, March, April 1827, Galway

*Galway Reader, The*, Winter 1954, Galway

Greenwood, Sir George, *Animal World*, July 1925

Edwards, Bryan, *The History, Civic and Commercial, of the British Colonies in the West Indies*

Froude, J.A., *The English in Ireland in the Eighteenth Century*, London 1881

Hansard, Feb-June 1819, June 1824, Feb-May 1825, London

Hardiman, J., *The History of the town and county of Galway*, W. Folds, Dublin 1820

*Harrow Calender with the History of Harrow School to 1853*, anon.

Hibbert, C., *George III, a Personal History*, Viking, London 1998

Joyce, Martin, 'The Battle of Aughrim', www.geocities.com/clontuskert

Mannix, D.P., *The Hellfire Club, ibooks, inc. 1961*

Ketchum, R.M., *The World of George Washington*, American Heritage, New York 1974

Lally, D., *History of Ballynahinch Castle*

Lee, C., *This Sceptred Isle*, Penguin, London 1998

*Liverpool Advertiser*, August 1821, Liverpool

Lloyds' List, 14th August 1821, 21st March 1823

Lynam, Shevawn, *Humanity Dick Martin 'King of Connemara' 1754-1834*, Hamish Hamilton, London 1975

MacCarthy, Mary Josepha, *Fighting Fitzgerald and Other Papers*, Longmans, Green &Co., London 1937

Martin, Archer E.S., 'Genealogy of the family of Martin of Ballynahinch Castle in the county of Galway, Ireland', Stovel, Winnepeg 1890'

Martyn, Adrian J., *The Tribes of Galway*, Galway 2001 www.galwayonline.ie/history/martyn, 'The Martin Tribe of Galway'

Murray, V., *High Society in the Regency Period 1788-1820*, Penguin, London 1999

McGuire, D., *History of Ireland*, Hamlyn, Twickenham 1987

Moody, T.W. & Martin, F.X., *The Course of Irish History*, Mercier, Cork 1994

RSPCA Archive File, 7th October 1997

Rudé, G., *Revolutionary Europe*, Collins, London 1967

Scott, Thomas Colville, *Connemara After the Famine, journal of a survey of the Martin estate*, ed. & intoduced by Tim Robinson 1935, Lilliput Press, Dublin 1935

Somerville-Large, P., *Irish Eccentrics*, Hamish Hamilton, London 1975

*Tales from a Connaught Circuit*, anon.

*Times, The*, 15th & 25th Dec. 1791, 31st March 1823

Van Thal, H., *The Prime Ministers*, Vol. I, Allen & Unwin, London 1934

Wallace, Martin, *100 Irish Lives*, David & Charles, Newton Abbot 1983

Winstanley, D.A., *Unreformed Cambridge*, Cambridge University Press 1935

# Index